Beyond Five Points

Beyond Five Points

By
Ernest C. Reisinger and D. Matthew Allen

Published by:
Founders Press
Committed to historic Southern Baptist principles
P.O. Box 150931 Cape Coral, FL 33915
Phone: (941) 772-1400 Fax (941) 772-1140
Email: editor@founders.org or http://www.founders.org

Printed in the United States of America

ISBN 0-9713361-0-5

Distributed by:

Founders Press
and
Christian Gospel Book Service
521 Wildwood Parkway
Cape Coral, FL 33904
Phone: (941) 549-3021 Fax (941) 540-7884
Email: DonReis@aol.com

Cover Photo:
This picture of tulips is from the Netherlands through the courtesy of Willemien Meltzer-Rossi, Aquamarijnstratt 21, 2332 HE Leiden, The Netherlands.

Contents

Preface

Recently, a classroom discussion illustrated to me just how much difference two decades can make in the theological complexion of a seminary community. The reading for the night had been fifty pages of large-page, double-column, small-type Jonathan Edwards material. A section of his "Miscellaneous Observations" unveiled some of his cogent remarks concerning divine revelation. After showing the need for a revelation and giving evidence that the Bible constituted just the revelation that we need, Edwards put a clincher on his argument. He stated that no additional content could possibly be wanted in a revelation; nor could any more impressive and convincing proofs possibly be forthcoming than those that accompanied and verified the biblical revelation.

Fascinated by this idea, but desiring to test its validity, one student proposed a possible way in which the evidence for the revelatory and inspired character of the Bible might be more convincing. I responded with a few brief remarks. Another student, Vic, contemplating seriously the implications of speculations concerning the kind of evidence that might be more convincing than what God has actually given, suggested that in reality trying to answer that question assumed an Arminian view of human nature and conversion. Such speculations were certainly not valid for "us," for "we" know that only an internal and effectual working of God's Spirit will suffice. The heart must be changed first, the eyes opened, and then a person will believe.

My first response to this suggestion indicated something about the relationship between evidence, biblical credibility, and human sin and rationality. But then I realized that something startling had happened. The student had suggested that "we" do not hold an Arminian view of sin, the new birth, and faith. Not one of the sixty students even flinched. All of them seemed to acquiesce in Vic's assessment of the situation and his representation that "we" held a historically Calvinistic view of conversion. I stopped the discussion and noted that twenty years ago confusion, protest, and querulous visages would have met such a remark. This does not mean that the entire class embraced that viewpoint. All, however, did seem to understand the nature and importance of the comment.

What has happened to make this difference? The last two decades have seen a multiplicity of factors come together to give a distinct ambience to contemporary doctrinal discussions. The seminary classroom offers opportunity for more intense investigation, but the doctrines of a forgotten orthodoxy appear more frequently, and with a growing fondness, in the broader Baptist world. Several factors have generated an increasing interest in theology in general and the doctrines of grace in particular.

First, and perhaps most important, students and teachers alike have a higher sensitivity to issues of biblical authority. This highlights the revelatory nature of Christian doctrine and the need for submission to the plain teaching of Scripture. The doctrine of inerrancy has been more than a *shibboleth*; it has provided a foundation for serious Bible study and a recommitment to have one's conscience captive to the word of God.

Conscientious biblical exposition from the original languages combined with dedication to believe what Scripture says, normally yields a love for coherent statements of biblical truth. The discipline of biblical interpretation forces a persons to develop some understanding of predestination (Romans 8:29; Acts 4:28; Ephesians 1:5, 11), election (Psalm 33:12; John 6:65; Romans 8:31-33; 9:11; 1 Corinthians 1:26-31; Ephesians 1:4; Colossians 3:12; 1 Thessalonians 1:4; 2 Thessalonians 2:13; 1 Timothy 5:21; 2 Timothy 2:10; 1 Peter 1:1-2; 2:7-10; 2 Peter 1:10), the pervasiveness and perversity of human sin (Genesis 6:5; 8:21; Psalm 51:5; Jeremiah 5:1-9; 11:6-8; Romans 1:18-32; 3:9-20; 5:12-21; 8:5-8; 1 Corinthians 2:14; 5:9, 10; Ephesians 2:1-3; Titus 3:3-5), the bondage (sinful predisposition) of the human will (John 5:39-47; 8:42-47; Romans 6:15-20; Romans 8:7-8; Ephesians 2:1-3; Philippians 3:18, 19; Colossians 3:5-10; 2 Timothy 3:1-8; Titus 3:30), the necessity and sovereignty of the new birth (Jeremiah 31:33-34; John 3:3; 6:44, 45; 1 Corinthians 1:24; Ephesians 1:19; 2:4-6; James 1:18), the substitutionary and efficacious nature of the atonement (Romans 4:23-25; 5:12-21; 8:32f; 1 Corinthians 1:18, 30, 31; 2 Corinthians 5:14-21; Hebrews 9:15-28; 10:4-18; 1 Peter 2:24; 3:18; Revelation 1:5), the surety of the gift the Father gives the Son for his obedience unto death (Isaiah 53:10-11;

John 13:2-3; John 17; Ephesians 1:14; Titus 2:13-14), and, consequently, the perseverance to a consummated salvation of all the *born again* (Romans 8:35-39; 1 Corinthians 1:4-9; Ephesians 1:13-14; Philippians 1:6; 1 Thessalonians 5:23f; Hebrews 3:14; 6:9-12). These issues will not go away. Their clarity in Scripture along with their God-centered emphasis makes any attempt to escape the doctrines of grace a wobbly and treacherous flight.

A second factor is the conflict over what was pejoratively called "creedalism." Much energy focused on article one of the 1963 *Baptist Faith and Message* that said Scripture has "God for its author, salvation for its end, and truth, without any mixture of error, for its matter." Fervor for inerrancy was equated with creedalism; creedalism was denominated as a bad thing. Any belief system imposed on the human mind, so they claimed, including an affirmation of inerrancy, amounted to a rape of the human soul. Such restriction of human freedom amounted to a denial of historic Baptist values. In light of the stridency and destructive tendency of these objections, many began to wonder why conscientious adherence to a publicly adopted confession was a violation of conscience. Soon, many began to argue that it was entirely legitimate to state what one believed in an organized fashion. The answer that Baptists had never done that and considered it an infringement of soul competence seemed on the face of it to be an absurdity. Systematic study proved that it was indeed an absurdity.

Within the last two decades, Southern Baptists, particularly seminary students, have learned to appreciate the value of historic Baptist confessions. Individuals, churches, associations, denominations, and denominational institutions have adopted confessions and used them constructively. The remarkable zeal with which previous generations of Baptists embraced Christian orthodoxy, along with Protestant evangelical thought, provides a solid foundation for that which is peculiarly Baptist. As one learns the confessional fabric of Baptist theology, he sees that Baptist distinctives, such as a regenerate church membership, separation of church and state, and liberty of conscience, make sense only in this larger context. Given the derivative nature of Baptist distinctives, adherence to the doctrines of grace (or shall we call them as this book does, the "Five Points") does not seem at all *unbaptistic*.

Baptist churches and associations of the mid-nineteenth century followed most closely the Second London Confession of the English Particular Baptists. The Philadelphia Association, the Charleston Association, Baptists in Georgia and Virginia, all used this confession. Shortened versions and abstracts went with settlers from those states into Kentucky, Alabama, Mississippi, Louisiana, and North Carolina. The first Southern Baptist seminary adopted the *Abstract of Principles*, distilled from the confession used in Charleston, South Carolina, the *Second London Confession*. It defines election as "God's eternal choice of some persons unto everlasting life–not because of foreseen merit in them, but of His mere mercy in Christ–in consequence of which choice they are called, justified and glorified." Regeneration has the same flavor of sovereign grace being defined as "a change of heart, wrought by the Holy Spirit, who quickeneth the dead in trespasses and sins enlightening their minds spiritually and savingly" and is called a "work of God's free and special grace alone." Repentance is an "evangelical grace," and "saving faith...is wrought in the heart by the Holy Spirit."

The *New Hampshire Confessions of Faith*, as developed by J. Newton Brown, serves as another confessional tradition strongly influential in Baptist doctrinal views. It constitutes the foundation for all three rescensions of the *Baptist Faith and Message*. Though shorter than the *Second London Confession,* its reformed emphasis is just as warm and clear. Election, regeneration, repentance, faith and perseverance all are set within the framework of free grace given to sinners whose sinful choices come from a "nature utterly void of that holiness required by the law of God, wholly given to the gratification of the world, of Satan, and of their own sinful passions, therefore under just condemnation to eternal ruin, without defense or excuse." Election, therefore, is the "gracious purpose of God, according to which He regenerates, justifies, sanctifies, and glorifies sinners." Election includes all the means by which sinners are called and is consistent with the free agency of man. As such, it is a "glorious display of God's sovereign goodness, and is infinitely wise, holy, and unchangeable." Increasingly familiar with this confessional heritage and increasingly delighted in it, many Southern Baptists view it as the "faith once delivered to the saints." Continue to decry "creedalism" and, thus, continue to foster a return to the doctrine of Baptist confessions.

A third factor in this observable doctrinal recovery, not unrelated to the first two, is the availability of biblical exposition in sermonic and commentary form that argues textually for the doctrines of grace. Among the leading evangelical scholars who write scholarly commentaries and who do expository preaching is no small number of Calvinists. Reprints of works by the reformers of the sixteenth century, the Puritans of the seventeenth century, the evangelical awakeners of the eighteenth century, and the confessional polemicists of the nineteenth century have made available a rich and convincing source of well-argued biblical interpretation. The line of biblical argument extending from Martin Luther, John Calvin, and Zachary Ursinus, through John Owen, John Bunyan, and John Flavel, extended into the ministries of George Whitefield and Jonathan Edwards, was verified in the theological arguments of Archibald Alexander, A.A. Hodge, Charles Hodge, B. B. Warfield, and found to be effective in the expository ministries of D. Martyn Lloyd-Jones, James Montgomery Boice, John MacArthur and others, is shown to be so clear, natural, and powerful, that caricature cannot survive in the light of truth. Alarmists who trade in half-truths and misrepresentation and who hurl half-baked anathemas will soon be discredited. Hopefully they will be forced to deal with Scripture with greater reverence and candor.

The fourth factor helping in this transformation is the irrepressible witness of Baptists, who, being dead, yet speak. Many students in the last twenty-five years received gift copies of J.P. Boyce's *Abstract of Systematic Theology* and learned for the first time that leading Baptist thinkers believed the doctrines of grace. One of the authors of this book, Ernest Reisinger, was largely responsible for the distribution of Boyce's theological work. The fruits of his labor were not lost. Baptists began to learn also of the lovely and inspiring work of John L. Dagg and found great encouragement in the warm exposition of the doctrines of grace in his *Manual of Theology.* They began to learn of the ministries and theology of leaders like Richard Furman, John Gano, Richard Fuller, Jesse Mercer, Basil Manly, Patrick Hues Mell, and others.

They learned that the theology and ministries of Andrew Fuller, William Carey, Adoniram Judson, Luther Rice, and C.D. Mallary did not constitute a revolt from Calvinism but an expression of the true burden of the doctrines of grace. They have seen that the General Baptists declined rapidly into heresy and lost their theology of conversion and the cross, while Particular Baptists maintained orthodoxy and were the fountainhead for missions and church planting. They have learned that Baptist Calvinists had hearts hot for holiness, minds zealous for truth, visions which saw Christ's atoning work as embracing people of all nations and tongues and tribes, spirits submissive to the mysterious and inflictive providences of God, and lives that found their meaning in being consumed to the glory of God.

Today it is impossible to picture Baptist theology as intrinsically opposed to Calvinist theology. That misrepresentation simply will not work, for it is patently false and has been demonstrated to be so. Even the most ardent anti-Calvinist, if he is informed at all on the current state of historical knowledge, seldom makes the argument that Baptists were not historically Calvinistic. Should he do so he would be embarrassed and chagrined at how easily a sermon of Charles Spurgeon, an observation of John A. Broadus, a book by James P. Boyce, a commentary by B. H. Carroll, or the confessions of Abraham Booth, Andrew Fuller, John Clarke, Obadiah Holmes, John Leland, and Isaac Backus would correct him.

Kate Harvey tells the story of how she came to be a Baptist. In attending the First Baptist Church of Providence, Rhode Island, she asked several members what they believed about election. Unsuccessful after several attempts at getting a response, one member of the church finally told her: "What we believe about election is that you cannot vote until you join the church." She knew that she had found her home. Later she became pastor of the church and eventually the Executive Director of the Ministers Council of the American Baptist Churches USA.[1] Roger Williams, the founder of the church in 1639, would find the answer terribly disturbing. While he would agree with the congregational polity implied in the answer, he would cry over the lack of doctrinal knowledge and conviction it indicated. This Baptist-turned-Seeker remained a convinced Calvinist until the end of his life and saw the doctrine of election as the chief underpinning to his view of liberty of conscience. A knowledge of Baptist history that includes the doctrinal part makes one feel right at home in being a Calvinist and a Baptist. Where is the contradiction?

For this reformation of historic doctrine to continue, a healthy combination, under God, of several key ingredients is needed. One, theological instruction and information on the doctrines of grace should be kept before the eyes of Baptist people, clergy and laity alike. We have seen how decline comes. Open hostility does little damage compared to the debilitating effect of mere indifference. The doctrines of grace are doctrines of the biblical revelation. They do not come naturally. If left outside the domain of teaching, people gravitate toward a man-centered theology. God will share his glory with no one. Divine revelation is given to us that we might "know the things freely given to us of God" (1 Corinthians 2:12). These God-honoring, sinner-debasing truths paradoxically hold forth the sinner's only hope and drive him to take refuge from deserved wrath in the perfect satisfaction of Christ's atoning work. We must not grow slack in the proclamation and distribution of gospel truth.

Second, the doctrines of grace must be seen within the context of a comprehensively biblical theology. As the title of this book indicates, the theological concerns and context go far beyond five points. The doctrines of grace extend from and give beautiful symmetry to the full range of categories of traditional systematic theology. Divine revelation which produces an inerrant written text makes perfect sense within a world view that sees human responsibility as operating concurrently with divine sovereignty.

The purposing, the completing, and the sealing of redemption in a Calvinistic system fits perfectly with an orthodox development of the doctrine of the Trinity expressed in categories of ontological equality and economic subordination. The sovereignty of God in salvation is a fit expression of mercy and justice for a God who creates according to wisdom and purpose and mysteriously governs his creation, both material and moral, in order to reveal his own glory. The doctrine of a last Adam who communicates to his people efficaciously and by imputation the salvation he has wrought, coincides perfectly with the first Adam who brought to ruin all his posterity by his disobedience. The centrality of Jesus Christ is highlighted in the doctrines of grace as the one in whom, by the eternal covenant (Hebrews 13:20-21), we have redemption through his blood and in whose character we know the Father and through whose work we receive the gift of the Holy Spirit. The ideal of a regenerate church and liberty of conscience correspond perfectly with the new covenant and the necessity of the Spirit's work in circumcision of the heart. The doctrines of grace effectively preserve conservative doctrine because they alone provide the fullest, most consistent manifestation of every aspect of Christian truth. Insinuating the doctrines of grace into the larger framework of Christian theology should be an ongoing task of this generation of Baptist Calvinists.

A third vital ingredient for continued recovery is courage on the part of those who see these truths. Joseph of Arimathea and Nicodemus showed up in time to bury Jesus, but for fear of the Jews did not befriend him during his lifetime. Some friends of the doctrines of grace may be useful only in giving them a decent burial unless they demonstrate the courage of their convictions. This book issues a call for closet Calvinists to become visible and active in the proclamation of truth. None should let the fear of man inhibit their faithfulness to the truth of God. Ministry and apparent success built on error will neither glorify God nor benefit man. For the love of God and the glory of Christ and the honor of the Spirit, all embarrassment and hesitance about the truth of God's Gospel must be cast away. Sinners should be made to feel safety in no other refuge than the mere mercy of a sovereign God.

The fourth aspect of further reformation is spiritual humility and deference. The authors point out well the danger of haughtiness, spiritual pride, and intemperate zeal. It is so easy to mistake spiritual pride and officiousness for zeal and a willingness to suffer. Both zeal and suffering are gifts of God, but Satan delights to fool the saint and discredit the truth by subtle and self-centered substitutes. The guidance provided by these authors in this important area might save many an unnecessary confrontation.

The present volume embodies virtually all of the ideas set forth in this preface. Biblical exposition, systematic theology, Baptist history, dealing with vital objections, and encouragement for faithfulness and sobriety are all done well and integrated beautifully into a holistic defense of the doctrines of grace. The authors provide a most pleasing combination of two orientations. One is a seasoned preacher and evangelist, a long time defender of these truths, an experienced author and purveyor of literature. His knowledge of literature, his balance, and his battles give a depth and warmth of heart that should be attractive and inviting to all readers. The second author brings the skill of a lawyer's cogency and facile vocabulary. He also provides the energy of a mind newly engaged and a soul profoundly transformed by these truths. The power of orderly arrangement, deep-comprehension, and finely tuned argument provide a vehicle of communication worthy of the exalted purpose for which the authors write.

Tom J. Nettles
The Southern Baptist Theological Seminary
Louisville, KY

Chapter 1

A Conversation About Calvinism

For well over two decades, evangelical Calvinists and conservative Arminians have stood side by side in a "battle for the Bible" against liberalism and neo-orthodoxy in the Southern Baptist Convention. They have disagreed as to their understanding of the nature and workings of God's grace in salvation and yet have put aside their differences over the doctrines of grace in order to jointly defend a high view of the inspiration and authority of Scripture. For the most part, the battle over the authority of the Bible in Southern Baptist life has been won. In his remarkable providence, God has been pleased to turn the Southern Baptist Convention back to orthodoxy.

Now that the inerrancy battle is largely complete, a conversation over the sufficiency of Scripture in Baptist life has begun. Topics of the conversation include the grounds for God's election, whether Christ died for believers only or for all humanity, whether God's grace is irresistible, whether Christians can lose their salvation, the extent of God's sovereignty, the nature of man's free will, and the relationship between one's views of salvation and evangelism. Baptists of Calvinist and Arminian persuasions are now engaged in public discourse on these things. We wish to enter the conversation as proponents of the historical Baptist view, what John A. Broadus called "that exalted system of Pauline truth which is technically called Calvinism."[1]

It is important to underscore that this (in contrast to the fight for the inerrancy of the Bible) is, and should remain, a conversation, not a battle. Evangelical Calvinists and conservative Arminians are Christians alike. They are brothers and sisters in Christ. As of late, this unity has been forgotten by some. One influential, evangelical Arminian Baptist derisively referred to Baptist Calvinists as "cheese and wine theologians." Another labeled the beliefs held by Calvinist Baptists as "doctrines for dunghills." Of course, some Calvinists doubtlessly have been guilty of equally excessive rhetoric. Despite these lapses, our duty to love one another should be kept in mind as the discussion proceeds forward. The Bible commands Christians to speak the truth in love (Ephesians 4:15). The requirement to speak the truth means the conversation must take place. The requirement to speak it in love places limits on how the conversation is to take place. And if this biblical reminder is not enough for the more hot-headed debaters on both sides, perhaps the practical reminder that those who adhere to Baptist liberalism and neo-orthodoxy would like nothing better than for conservatives to take up arms against one another would do the trick. We hope both sides will sheathe their daggers, shake hands, and sit down at a table together to share a good, strong pot of coffee and frank dialogue in front of an open Bible.

This does not mean hard words will not be spoken in the course of the conversation. Both Calvinist and Arminian leaders of the Southern Baptist denomination agree that it is not possible for the two sides to hold their persuasions with relative quietness. They agree that the subject of salvation is no minor matter, but is a weighty and vital part of the Christian message, and indeed, the doctrinal foundation for worship and witness.

This means the conversation which must occur will not always be comfortable. The fact is, Calvinism divides. Those who hold to a Calvinistic system will therefore be divisive whether they wish to be or not. The great Victorian Baptist preacher Charles Spurgeon once said that "these old doctrines either make a man so angry that he goes home and cannot sleep for very hatred, or else they bring him down into lowliness of thought, feeling the immensity of the things which he has heard."[2]

Perhaps we should start out by defining our topic.

What is Calvinism? There are broad and narrow definitions, but for our present purposes, Calvinists have something to say about two critical points of theology: *sovereignty* and *salvation*.

With respect to God's sovereignty, Calvinism says that nothing is outside God's control. Patrick H. Mell, the nineteenth century president of the University of Georgia, seventeen year president of the Southern Baptist Convention and twenty-four year president of the Georgia Baptist Convention, amplified this point in a sermon preached well over a century ago:

> The distinctive characteristic of Calvinism is that it maintains God's sovereignty over all things, sin not excepted; and that His will is shown either efficiently or permissively in all existences and all events on earth. He is not only a creator and preserver, but a sovereign and efficient ruler. His providence and His grace, therefore, control all things and events, great and small, good and bad, material and mental. From intelligent choice, He permits everything in men that is morally wrong, and by His grace, efficiently works in them everything that is morally right. As a creator, an upholder, and a governor, He has intelligence enough to know what objects he would accomplish; and His wisdom and power are adequate to all the demands of the undertaking in its incipiency, its progress, and its consummation. The world, therefore, in all its physical and moral details, is just as He designed it to be; and in all the items of its history—in its special as well as its general results, He will accomplish that which He designed in its creation, in its preservation, and in its government. He did not err in His plan; therefore nothing operates in His system unexpectedly to Him. He is not deficient in power, therefore, nothing operates there in spite of him. God disposes of and directs to some particular end, every person and thing in which he has given or is yet to give, being; and makes the whole creation subservient to and declarative of his own glory.[3]

When this perspective is applied to salvation, Calvinism teaches simply that "salvation is of the Lord" (Jonah 2:9). It is by God's grace, and his grace alone, that we are saved. This aspect of Calvinism is popularly expressed through the so-called "Five Points of Calvinism," the headings of which make up the acronym T-U-L-I-P:

> Total depravity
> Unconditional election
> Limited atonement
> Irresistible grace
> Perseverance of the saints

The essential principle inherent in each of these points is that declared by Paul in Ephesians 2:8-10: "For by grace you have been saved through faith, and that not of yourselves; it is the gift of God, not of works, lest anyone should boast. For we are His workmanship, created in Christ Jesus for good works, which God prepared beforehand that we should walk in them." In other words, salvation is by God's grace from beginning to end.

In the beginning, God the Father chose to save sinners. He made his choice from before the creation of the world. In the fullness of time, God the Son died for sinners on Calvary's tree because of his great love for his people. Up until the time of Christ's return, God the Spirit calls and saves sinners by his grace. He regenerates and grants faith and repentance to those the Father chose and for whom the Son shed his blood. And in the end, God sustains the faith he created in those sinners who are saved by his grace. He preserves his people unto the glory for which they were chosen and created. Hence, it is by grace that we are saved, through faith—and neither one came from ourselves. As Charles Spurgeon once proclaimed: "If anyone should ask me what I mean by a Calvinist, I should reply, 'He is one who says, *Salvation is of the Lord.*' I cannot find in Scripture any other doctrine than this. It is the essence of the Bible... Calvinism is the gospel and nothing else."[4]

Some people may ask: *Why another book on Calvinism?* Aren't books on the doctrines of grace a dime a dozen? Aren't there a number of resources available to discuss these topics? A number of excellent books do address and defend the doctrines of grace. In 1932 Lorraine Boettner wrote his classic work, *The Reformed Doctrine of Predestination*. In 1963 David Steele and Curtis Thomas wrote a fine book still used by many called *The Five Points of Calvinism*. In 1972, Edwin Palmer wrote a study guide called *The Five Points of Calvinism*. More recently, James White wrote a definitive response to Norman Geisler's Arminian polemic *Chosen But Free* called *The Potter's Freedom*. A number of other helpful resources are also in print.

We think there is room for one more, however, from a uniquely Baptist perspective. In the larger evangelical world, Baptists commonly are caricatured as adhering to Arminian beliefs. This caricature has a ring of truth to it. Revivalist practices such as the altar call are part of the rhythm of many Southern Baptist churches. In addition, certain Arminian Baptist ministers are well-known and well-respected. But at least historically speaking, most Baptists were full-blown Calvinists.

Great men like John Bunyan, Charles Spurgeon, Andrew Fuller, John Dagg and James P. Boyce spoke with more or less harmonious voices on issues related to salvation. What we bring to the table here is a refutation of the most common Arminian objections to the Calvinistic system by drawing on the works of these Baptist giants. Though these men are long dead, they still speak through their writings, and in those writings, they have answered virtually every objection Arminians have come up with to oppose Calvinism. We hope renewed attention to their answers will kindle a desire among the readers to go "back to the sources" (*ad fonts*) to read their writings directly. This book also differs from Tom Nettles' excellent work on Calvinism in Baptist history, *By His Grace and For His Glory*, recently back in print, in that it is arranged more as a defense of the doctrines of grace rather than a historical treatment of their development in Baptist life.

In any event, our small volume is not intended to supplant any of the other fine works on Calvinism, but to complement them. In this way, we seek nothing more than to make a modest contribution to the ongoing conversation in Southern Baptist circles about the doctrines of grace.

Lying in Procrustes' Bed

In ancient Greek mythology, a man named Procrustes lived in a house beside a well-traveled road. He offered lodging to weary travelers passing by. He had two beds in his house, one small and the other large. Procrustes would lay short men on the large bed and rack them out to fit it. He would lay tall men on the small bed, sawing off as much of their legs as projected beyond it. It's somewhat of a grisly story. But the Greeks invented Procrustes to make a point. He and his bed symbolize the cost of conformity at any price, even the expense of truth.

Our thesis is that too many evangelical Christians, including a significant number of Southern Baptists, are lying in Procrustes' bed when it comes to the Bible's teachings about sovereignty and salvation. They have lopped off the legs of inconvenient doctrines and hard words about God's grace in order to make modern evangelicalism fit better into the Procrustesian bed of pragmatism, expediency, or cultural appeal. They have abandoned their birthright in the Bible's teaching that salvation is by grace alone for a pottage of worldly rationalism.

We advocate a throwing off of the Arminian rationalism that has so firmly gripped large parts of our Southern Baptist denomination since the conservative resurgence. In the last twenty years a biblical foundation of inerrancy has been recovered in the Southern Baptist Convention, and we praise God for that; but the biblically necessary corollary of the sufficiency of Scripture remains obscure. Because the doctrines of grace are true and biblical, we contend they should be believed and taught and shared and spread in our churches today, just as they were believed and taught and shared and spread in Baptist churches a century ago. If those doctrines were true then, they are equally true today. Thus, this book is offered as a biblical, and biblicist, defense of Calvinism in Baptist life.

A Biblicist Approach

As just mentioned, we adopt a biblicist, not rationalist, approach to our discussion of the doctrines of grace. To describe what we mean by this, we need to back up a bit and start with the meaning and source of true wisdom. John Calvin rightly observed at the beginning of *The Institutes of the Christian Religion* that true wisdom consists of two things: knowledge of God and knowledge of ourselves. But man never achieves a clear knowledge of himself unless he has first looked upon God's face, and then descends from contemplating God to scrutinize himself. When we look in the mirror, we too often see ourselves through a fog, and in the fog, we see ourselves as righteous, upright, wise and holy, because pride exists in all of us. Only by looking to the Lord does the fog dissipate, and we see ourselves as we really are, unrighteous, foul, foolish, and impure. It is as we raise our thoughts to God and ponder his nature, and see how completely perfect are his righteousness, wisdom, and power, that our vileness, masquerading as righteousness, will grow filthy in its consummate wickedness. As Calvin put it, when we look to an infinitely perfect God, what before so wonderfully impressed us about ourselves under the name of wisdom "will stink in its very foolishness."[5]

How, then, does one get true wisdom and knowledge? There are two fountains from which people can drink in search of these things: the fount of Scripture or the wellspring of human reason. True wisdom comes from Scripture as God's authoritative and inspired words of revelation. Calvin said the Bible operates for us as "spectacles" which show us the true God, the God upon whom we are to look.[6] Not so when we look to human reasoning. All humanity has degenerated from the true knowledge of God. Without the spectacles of Scripture, men's sight of God is distorted. Through their own reasoning abilities, men do not apprehend God as he offers himself, but imagine him as they have fashioned him in their own presumption. As Calvin said, man's nature is a "perpetual factory of idols."[7]

In other words, when seeking knowledge of God and knowledge of self, one can be either a biblicist or a rationalist. What is a biblicist? The term "biblicist" has sometimes been used pejoratively to refer to: (1) one who believes God's truth is found only in the Bible, not in general revelation; (2) one who has no respect for confessions, creeds, or the work of past theologians; or (3) one who employs a "proof-texting" method of biblical argumentation, rather than bringing the whole of Scripture to bear on a topic and viewing a Scripture passage in its historical, cultural, logical, and literary context in interpreting it.[8]

We do not mean any of these things. We believe God's truth is to be found especially in the Bible, but also in creation; we have great respect for the creeds, confessions, and theologians of the past; and we hold to the grammatical-historical method of Scripture interpretation, as well as the analogy of Scripture (which says Scripture interprets other Scripture). No, we refer to a biblicist as someone who approaches Scripture as the written Word of God, inspired, inerrant, sufficient, and authoritative, with an attitude of reverence, humility and submission, determined to accept, adopt, agree with, and advocate all its teachings with devotion and passion.

A biblicist believes and declares that "all Scripture...is profitable for doctrine, for reproof, for correction, for instruction in righteousness, that the man of God may be complete, thoroughly equipped for every good work" (2 Timothy 3:16). He is determined to bring every thought into captivity to the obedience of Christ (2 Corinthians 10:5). He recognizes that he is of earth and God is of heaven. Therefore, his basic approach to knowledge is to accept and submit to the teachings of God's Word, whether he understands them or not. "The fear of the Lord is the beginning of knowledge, but fools despise wisdom and instruction" (Proverbs 1:7).

Anselm spoke for the biblicist when he said, in a celebrated phrase: "I do not seek to understand that I may believe, but I believe in order to understand. For this also I believe—that unless I believed, I should not understand."[9]

What is a rationalist? Iain Murray has insightfully noted:

> The use of the mind is not "rationalism"; it all depends on whether that use is right or wrong. Rationalism is a use of the mind which trusts in its own ability to arrive at truth about God without his aid and apart from revelation: it treats the mind as a source of knowledge rather than as a channel. The Enlightenment was a classic demonstration of innate human pride in the exaltation of the human intellect. To equate that spirit with the teaching of the Princeton men, who believed that it is the grace of God alone which sets men free to understand, is to stand truth on its head.[10]

The rationalist, then, approaches the text differently than the biblicist. He comes to the Bible with a willingness to stand in judgment over it. His general attitude is: "I will not believe unless I understand." Concomitantly, his basic interpretive method is to allow human reason to determine what the Bible says or does not say, or what it means or does not mean, based on his own subjective judgment that "God can't do this" or "God doesn't do that."

A perceptive reader might ask: Isn't everyone a rationalist at times? To be sure, because of the presence of indwelling sin, even the best of Christians is a rationalist at some point as we approach the Word of God. Be honest. How many times have you come to a passage in the Bible that calls for obedience in a particular area of life and closed the book or shut out its teaching simply because you do not want to do what God is telling you to do? All of us, including the authors, have done so many times, more than we care to consider.

But the true biblicist does not remain a rationalist indefinitely. At some point the biblicist will relent and quit kicking against the goads, so that Holy Spirit conviction and heartfelt repentance for rebellion follow. Sooner or later, his general attitude becomes one of submission to Scripture and the God of the Bible.

The reverse is not true. A rationalist does not become a biblicist simply by accepting the Bible's teaching on a particular matter. He may accept, for example, portions of the Sermon on the Mount (say, the Beatitudes) as belonging to authentic Christianity, but that is only because he has stood in judgment of the text and found that it met his approval.

In any event, despite the rationalistic tendency in all of us, it can still be said as a generalization that everyone adopts one basic perspective or the other when approaching the Bible. Everyone has a predisposition in favor of one or the other approach, and with each encounter with God's Word, everyone has a choice to make: Submit to its teachings or rationalize them away. In Matthew 7:24-27, Jesus put the point squarely to the hearers of the Sermon on the Mount:

> Therefore whoever hears these sayings of Mine, and does them, I will liken him to a wise man who built his house on the rock: and the rain descended, the floods came, and the winds blew and beat on that house; and it did not fall, for it was founded on the rock. But everyone who hears these sayings of Mine, and does not do them, will be like a foolish man who built his house on the sand: and the rain descended, the floods came, and the winds blew and beat on that house; and it fell. And great was its fall."

This is no small matter. Jesus repeatedly enjoined those who heard his words to submit to them. "Blessed are those who hear the word of God and keep it!" (Luke 11:28). So did the apostles. Paul told the Roman believers: "Not the hearers of the law are just in the sight of God, but the doers of the law will be justified" (Romans 2:13). James admonished believers scattered throughout the Roman empire: "Be doers of the word, and not hearers only" (James 1:22). True Christians who desire true knowledge of themselves and of God want to believe exactly what Christ taught and follow precisely what the Scriptures say.

These general principles apply with force when it comes to the subjects of God's sovereignty and salvation. Biblicists seek answers to difficult questions about the nature of God's providence and his provision of salvation in the Bible, not in rational speculation or philosophy or preconceived notions about God's nature. They scour the Bible to learn the whole truth about the entire topic. Rationalists, simply put, bring their own preconceptions and expectations to the biblical text and read the Bible in view of those expectations. They eisogete (read into the text one's own ideas) rather than exegete (explain the text). As will be made clear in the coming pages, we believe the consistent biblicist will walk away from the text of Scripture as a committed Calvinist.

A Polemical Approach

Along with a biblicist approach, we also adopt a polemical approach in this book. True religion, said Beza, is no cold matter—it must be fiery if it is true faith. Hence, we are not neutral. We are advocates for Calvinism, which is historical Baptist Christianity. Our viewpoint is simple: If it were true when our Baptist forefathers believed it, it must be true now, because God does not change!

Historically, of course, engaging in polemical theology was risky business at best. In centuries past, it could have most unfortunate consequences—like getting one's head lopped off or one's body burned at the stake. It did for John Hus, fourteenth century Bohemian reformer, who was martyred for his faith because he accepted the doctrines of Christ over the teachings of the pope. It did for William Tyndale, who dared to translate the Holy Scriptures into the English language for the first time and paid for this audacity with his life in 1536. It did for Anne Askew, a godly woman who was burned at the stake after being cruelly tortured by the Lord Chancellor of England during the reign of Henry VIII of England in order to get her to recant her Protestant "heresies." But for God's providential safekeeping, the martyr's end would have resulted for Martin Luther, who stood before Holy Roman Emperor Charles V, his advisors, the Spanish military, electors, princes, territorial representatives, and church envoys (basically the entire known world) at the Diet of Worms in 1517 and refused to recant his writings, declaring, "Here I stand, I can do no other. God help me, Amen."

Even in our own day, taking a Christian worldview (and attempting to spread it) can have dire consequences in some parts of the world. In recent days, Christians have been kidnapped in the Philippines, imprisoned in Afghanistan, and burned to death in India. These are just the ones we know about. Countless others give their lives for their faith quietly, unknown, their voices unheard this side of heaven.

In the Western world, the society in which we live, engaging in vigorous theological debate will not create martyrs. It will, however, divide churches, get preachers fired, get groups barred from seminary campuses, and stir up passions. This often gives rise to a question: Is it worth the candle?

Shouldn't Christians avoid controversy? This is an important and serious question. After all, did not our Lord pray in the Garden of Gethsemane just before going to the cross: "I do not pray for these alone, but also for those who will believe in Me through their word; that they all may be one, as You, Father, are in Me, and I in You; that they also may be one in Us, that the world may believe that You sent Me. And the glory which You gave Me I have given them, that they may be one just as We are one: I in them, and You in Me; that they may be made perfect in one, and that the world may know that You have sent Me, and have loved them as You have loved Me." (John 17:20-23).

It should be said at the outset that we deeply respect our evangelical Arminian Baptist brothers with whom we disagree on these vital issues. Both of the authors were saved in Arminian churches. One of us has family roots in a prominent Arminian Baptist church in Memphis, Tennessee, and still remembers with deep gratitude the gracious prayers of the pastor of that church when his grandfather, a long-time member, went home to be with the Lord. God greatly used a number of Arminian Baptists (and Calvinists as well) to bring about the conservative resurgence in the Southern Baptist Convention. We believe Arminians are wrong on important issues but they are still Christians and brothers and sisters in Christ. We prefer to think that they have a better Christian experience than they do a doctrinal understanding.

At the same time, controversies with those whom we respect are often unavoidable. They are even beneficial when they revolve around the truth of God's Word.

Perhaps the question should be asked differently: *Should Christians avoid controversy at any cost, including the cost of truth?* Here we say no. Truth matters! In the same high priestly prayer where Jesus prayed for unity among his followers, he also proclaimed: "Your word is truth" (John 17:17). In a quest for unity, it should not be forgotten that God requires our assent to his own doctrines. Even more so, he requires our devotion to his character. Douglas Wilson said it well, albeit in a slightly different context:

> When we turn to God's Word as the standard, as we must do, we discover that more is expected than simple propositional assent. When we are operating within biblical categories, we see that orthodoxy involves far more than mere head-nodding, mere intellectual going-along. Orthodoxy requires all our faculties, our reason, our imagination, our bodily habits, our affections...True orthodoxy is lovely and involves the whole man.[11]

The fact is, there has never been reformation without controversy. When Martin Luther nailed his Ninety-Five Thesis to the door of the Wittenberg Church, no small controversy began. It was a healthy controversy, but a painful one nonetheless. Yet we would not be protestants without it. Closer to our day, when the conservatives (Calvinist and non-Calvinist alike) began the battle for the Bible in the Southern Baptist Convention, they created real and necessary controversy. Accordingly, it behooves all who care for the truth to engage in cordial yet vigorous public debate on those issues that matter.

A Charitable Approach

In this book, along with a biblicist and polemical approach, we also hope to adopt a charitable approach. In a Summer 1998 *Founders Journal* article entitled "Polemical Theology or How to Deal with Those Who Differ From Us," Dr. Roger Nicole provides some helpful advice on how to engage in polemical theology without being either contentious or compromising.[12] Dr. Nicole asked and answered three questions: (1) What do I owe the person who differs with me? (2) What can I learn from the person who differs from me? (3) How can I cope with the person who differs from me?

With respect to the first question, he answered that we have an obligation to make a serious effort to know the person with whom we differ. If the person has published books or articles, we have an obligation to be acquainted with them. It is not appropriate for us to express disagreement if we have failed to read what the person has said. In addition, we have an obligation to attempt to understand what the other person means. Further, we should not quibble about language just in order to criticize our opponent for not using more accurate wording. We should try to understand the other person's aims. What are they looking for; what makes them tick; what are they recoiling against? All these things show our opponent that we have a real interest in him or her as a person and that we are not simply trying to win an argument.

With respect to the second question, Dr. Nicole said we must argue in humility. We must be prepared to learn that we are wrong and that the other side is right. This does not apply to basic truths of the faith like the Deity of Christ or salvation by grace. To question those fundamental tenets of orthodox Christianity is to destabilize the faith, not exemplify broad-mindedness. Nonetheless, on secondary issues, we must be willing to acknowledge our own fallibility. A failure to do so reveals that we are more interested in winning a discussion than discovering the truth. He also said we may learn from our opponents that there are blind spots in our own position. We may also learn that there are ambiguities in our viewpoint or communication breakdowns so that we are not understood as clearly as we might otherwise think. As Charles Spurgeon once said, "Believe in Calvinism; but if there be a single truth which only the Arminians hold, believe that too. Do not put your feet into Chinese shoes to be squeezed after the current fashion into an orthodox shape; be willing to have a broad understanding: receive anything which God has revealed, and be content to take the whole of God's truth, whether you can make it into a system or not."[13]

With respect to the third question, we should avoid a pugnacious attitude that injects bitterness into controversies. We must forever keep in mind Paul's injunction that we speak the truth in love (Ephesians 4:15). The goal of polemical theology, then, is not to win an argument but to focus biblical light on a subject to assist those still caught in some darkness. Biblical debate should be a dialogue or conversation, not a shouting match.

Our goal in this work is to abide by all three of these precepts as we discuss the doctrines of grace. We also want to deal directly with the concerns and objections that Arminians have regarding Calvinism. We do not wish to talk past our evangelical Arminian brothers and sisters in this book. We want to directly answer their arguments with both Scripture and the Scripture-saturated statements of historical Baptists. We therefore seek to avoid *Sturm und Drang*, sheer rhetoric, shorn of substance, that heretofore has too often infected the Baptist conversation of the doctrines of grace. We believe most Baptists find such an argumentation style neither helpful nor persuasive anyway. We seek to engage the mind, not the emotions.

The fact is, the topics of sovereignty, salvation and free grace are worthy of nothing less than serious, careful contemplation. As Charles Mallary, a mid-nineteenth century Georgia and South Carolina pastor and early Southern Baptist leader, warned in a sermon on the doctrines involving God's sovereignty:

> They are revealed, and are therefore to be contemplated and believed; yet they are mysterious and awful, and should never therefore be approached in the spirit of cavailing, of levity and pride. With what sacred awe, with what holy reverence, with what deep humility should we gaze at those grand revelations which exhibit God in the sovereignty of his grace and the glory of this dominion...[14]

As an aside, one of the reasons why God has blessed the efforts of the publishers of this book, Founders Ministries, is that it has always operated within the parameters of its stated purpose. Its leaders have not operated out of haste, anger, or passion of ecstasy. It remains incumbent upon us, and all who discuss disputed or controversial matters, to do so in a constructive way, engaging opposing ideas and not personalities. We seek to do that here. We pray that what was said of Herman Witsius may characterize us:

> His zeal for 'the faith once delivered to the saints' conspicuously appeared in his discourses and writings. When dangerous opinions in philosophy and divinity prevailed, and when reason was extolled to the prejudice of faith and to the overthrow of the essential doctrines of the Christian religion, he vindicated the cause of truth with pious ardor and unshaken fidelity, most happily blended with meekness and prudence. With regard to the less important differences of sentiment which took place among sound and faithful theologians, no one could exercise greater mildness and forbearance. He was an admirer of that excellent saying: 'Unanimity in what is necessary, liberty in what is not necessary, in all things prudence and charity.' To heal the breaches of Zion and promote peace and concord

amongst brethren, was to him a delightful office.[15]

A Word About Terminology

Perhaps this is a good place to say something about terminology. Some people have a knee-jerk reaction to any mention of John Calvin's name. They ask something like: *Wasn't John Calvin a heartless purveyor of religious intolerance and how can you associate yourself with such a man?* We recognize, of course, that to some, use of the term "Calvinist" is like waving a red flag at a snorting bull in a Spanish bullfight. Baptist Calvinists frequently are tarred with the fact that John Calvin believed in infant baptism and supported the execution of a Unitarian heretic named Michael Servetus.[16] This is not valid argumentation but an attempt at guilt by association—in much the same way that Christian fundamentalists unfairly are tarred with the brush of Islamic extremism. Andrew Fuller said that even if we assume for the sake of argument that Calvin was a wicked man, destitute both of religion and humanity, "what would all this prove as to the tendency of the system that happened to be called after his name but which imatters allowed to have existed long before he was born?"[17]

Like John Broadus, we are admirers of Calvin, but we have no interest here in slavishly following the man or defending everything he said or did.[18] The terms "Calvinist" and "Calvinism" are theological shorthand for what the Bible says about grace. As Mell said, "this term [Calvinism]...is used merely for convenience as a designation, and not, to imply, either that these doctrines owed their origin to the Genevan Reformer, or that Calvinists are responsible for all the sentiments advanced by him."[19] Spurgeon also said:

> The word Calvinism, is frequently used here as the short word which embraces that part of divine truth which teaches that salvation is by grace alone, but it is not hence to be imagined that we attach any authority to the opinion of John Calvin, other than that which is due to every holy man who is ordained of God to proclaim his truth. We use the word simply for shortness of expression, and because the enemies of free grace will then be quite sure of what we mean. It is our firm

> belief, that what is commonly called Calvinism, is neither more nor less than the good old gospel of the Puritans, the Martyrs, the Apostles, and of our Lord Jesus Christ.[20]

Of course, the fact that Calvin was a sinner should not come as a surprise to anyone. Who among us is immune from that charge? No one. Nor does the fact that Calvin was wrong on some things mean he was wrong on everything, or even most things, much less the major premises of his theological system. In any event, the term "Calvinism" is merely a label for the doctrines of grace revealed by God, taught by Jesus and expounded by Paul and the other apostles. We accept and use the labels "Calvinist" or "Calvinism" for convenience's sake. The terms are too entrenched in theological thought to turn back now. At the same time, as we have pledged to respect our opponents enough to take their concerns honestly and treat their views seriously, we hope our opponents will respect us enough to confine their comments to the merits of our theological system and not tar us with the brush of guilt by association because Calvin happened to accept infant baptism and may have had some role in the judicial execution of a sixteenth century heretic. Calvin is not the issue; the grace of God is!

Organization of What Follows

A few words about the organization of this book are in order.

First, from a formatting perspective, the book is arranged in a loose catechetical fashion. The discussion in each chapter is organized around a series of what we believe are commonly asked questions about the topic matter at hand. These questions are marked in italics. We believe this format enhances readability.

Second, in terms of structure, the book is divided into three uneven parts. The threefold division is along the lines of the classical goals of Christian education: instruction in truth, goodness and beauty.

TRUTH. The first part deals with truth. Here we discuss and defend not only the so-called "five points of Calvinism," but also the underlying foundational principles beyond those points. In Chapter Two, we provide a brief summary of the five points and discuss briefly their historical origin. In Chapters Three and Four, we analyze the five points from a biblical perspective.

Obviously, this is the nub of the argument with respect to the five points. For if the five points are biblical, they are therefore true and worthy of belief. If they are not biblical, they are not true, but false, and worthy of the vigorous condemnation given them by so many non-Calvinists. We are convinced from biblical evaluation that they are true and worthy of devotion. In Chapter Five, we go beyond the five points to examine the foundational principles underlying those points that make up the Calvinistic system.

GOODNESS. The second part deals with God's goodness. Can a Calvinistic God who elects some to salvation and passes over others be a good God? Is he a just God? Chapter Six seeks to answer those important questions. Chapter Seven addresses several other "hardball objections" and "heartfelt questions" some non-Calvinists may have with respect to the Calvinistic system.

BEAUTY. The last part deals with the beauty of God's truth regarding his sovereignty and salvation. Even if someone believes election is true, how can that person actually love what God has to say on these issues? God requires that man not just grudgingly accept who he is and what he does, but that his disciples be zealous witnesses of those things. Hence, in this experiential or practical part of the book, we defend the view that the doctrines of grace are not only worthy of acceptance, but also worthy of passionate approval. A corollary of this is that these doctrines are also worthy of being taught to others. We seek to convince timid Calvinists who believe the doctrines of grace but keep them to themselves that the truth matters. Too many "closet Calvinists" say that they believe the truth of the doctrines of grace but they are afraid to teach and preach them. Chapter Eight addresses those issues.

In Chapter Nine, we seek to warn over-zealous Calvinists against being *personally* offensive as they teach and preach the truth they know and love. We know too well that not all divisions and controversies over Calvinism center upon a genuine disagreement over biblical doctrine. Too frequently, abrasive personalities and over-zealous tactics lead to disputes. On these occasions, when divisions and controversies revolve around personalities and human excesses, they are not beneficial and good, but destructive and evil. Our message to over-zealous Calvinists is this: Let your doctrine do the dividing.

Yes, Calvinism cuts. But then, so does every biblical doctrine, in one way or another. The Word of God is not called the "sword of the Spirit" (Ephesians 6:17) in vain. "For the word of God is living and powerful, and sharper than any two-edged sword, piercing even to the division of soul and spirit, and of joints and marrow, and is a discerner of the thoughts and intents of the heart" (Hebrews 4:12). Thus, even though we have stated that we are engaged in a conversation, not a battle, the battle analogy is not altogether inappropriate. For behind the conversation at the human level is a spiritual battle, in which our only sword is the sword of the Spirit. That battle, however, belongs to the Lord, not to us.

With these things in mind, let's begin our conversation.

Truth

Chapter 2

The Five Points of Calvinism: Where Did They Come From?

Although Calvinism as a system extends beyond the so-called "five points of Calvinism," an understanding of the five points is a good starting place for explaining the broader system. As already noted, the five points are commonly thought of according to an acronym—TULIP. The "T" stands for "total depravity," the "U" for "unconditional election," the "L" for "limited atonement," the "I" for "irresistible grace," and the "P" for "perseverance of the saints." At the risk of tearing apart a beautiful flower, we think the five points better can be summarized in the following way:

1. *Total Depravity.* Because of the fall, man is unable, of himself, to believe the gospel (Romans 3:10-18). The sinner is dead, blind and deaf to the things of God (2 Corinthians 4:3-4; Ephesians 2:1-2). His heart is deceitful and desperately wicked (Genesis 6:5; Jeremiah 17:9). As the first writing Southern Baptist theologian, John Dagg, said, "Depravity exists at the very fountain from which all human action flows. The depravity of man is total." Calvinists call this "total depravity."

2. *Effectual Calling.* As a consequence of man's depravity, it is only by the Holy Spirit's special inward call that sinners can come to salvation (John 6:37, 44; 10:16; Romans 8:29-30). The founder of the first Southern Baptist seminary, James P. Boyce, put it like this: the external call of the Gospel "meets with no success because of the willful sinfulness of man, although, in itself, it has all the elements which should secure its acceptance." But God, knowing this is true even of those he has chosen to save, "gives to these such influences of the Spirit as will lead to their acceptance of the call." Calvinists call this "effectual calling" or "efficacious grace." The person does nothing to initiate the saving process (John 15:16). Indeed, faith itself is a gift of

God (Ephesians 2:8-9).

3. *Unconditional Election.* Moreover, God's choice of individuals unto salvation occurred before the foundation of the world and rested solely in his sovereign will (Ephesians 1:4-5, 11; Romans 8:29-30; 9:6-26; 2 Thessalonians 2:13; Acts 13:48). Calvinists call this "unconditional election." As Boyce carefully put it: "God...of his own purpose (in accordance with his will, and not from any obligation to man, nor because of any will of man), has from Eternity...determined to save...a definite number of mankind...as individuals...not for or because of any merit or work of theirs, nor of any value to him of them (not for their good works, nor their holiness, nor excellence, nor their faith, nor their spiritual sanctification...nor their value to him...); but of his own good pleasure (simply because he was pleased so to choose)."

4. *Particular Redemption.* In addition, Christ's redeeming work was designed to save the elect, and it actually secured salvation for them. Christ came not to advise or urge or induce or assist the elect to save themselves. No! He came to actually save the ones he chose (John 10:15; Romans 3:25; 5:10). Thus, in Boyce's words, although the atonement of Christ "is abundantly sufficient to secure the salvation of all who will put their faith in him," Christ died "in an especial sense for the Elect; because he procured for them not a possible, but an actual salvation." Many Calvinists call this "particular redemption" (our preferred term) or "definite atonement." Others often call it "limited atonement."

5. *Perseverance of the Saints.* Finally, all who are chosen by God, redeemed by Christ, and given faith by the Holy Spirit are eternally saved (Romans 8:38-39; John 6:39; John 10:28-29; Ephesians 1:13-14). The truly redeemed cannot fall from grace. In Dagg's words, "whatever struggles it may cost, and whatever temporary departures from the straight line of duty may mark their course, they are graciously preserved from total and final apostasy." Indeed, grace in the heart is "incorruptible and abiding." This is called the "preservation of the saints," and its flip side, the "perseverance of the saints."[1]

In the next two chapters, we will flesh out each of these "petals" in significantly more detail. For now, this summary is sufficient to take us to our next point—a brief historical overview of where these points came from.

Where Did The Five Points Come From?

The Synod of Dort

In 1603 a Dutch theologian named Jacob van Hermanns (anglicized, Jacob Arminius) was named professor of theology at Leydon. This quickly proved to be a controversial appointment, since Arminius, who had studied at the feet of Theodore Beza, parted company with his Reformed mentors. He objected to John Calvin's doctrines of predestination and reprobation. He sought to modify Calvinism so that man, in his words, would not be viewed as "an automaton in the hands of God." He advocated conditional election, affirming that God's predestination of the elect is based on his foreknowledge of the way in which they will freely accept Christ. He asserted that man has an ability to initiate and cooperate with God in salvation. The ensuing controversy soon spread over all Holland.[2]

Arminius asked the Dutch government to convene a synod to resolve the dispute, but he died in 1609 before a council could be formed. His followers, however, picked up his torch and carried on his teachings. They called themselves the "Arminians." In 1610 the Arminians formulated a creed in five articles, which was called the "Remonstrance." The five articles of the Remonstrance outlined what has remained, until recently, the heart of Arminian theology:

> **Article One**. [*Conditional election*]. That God, by an eternal, unchangeable purpose in Jesus Christ his Son, before the foundation of the world, hath determined, out of the fallen, sinful race of men, to save in Christ, for Christ's sake, in and through Christ, those who, through the grace of the Holy Ghost, shall believe on this his Son Jesus...
>
> **Article Two**. [*Universal atonement*]. That...Jesus Christ, the Savior of the world, died for all men and for every man, so that he has obtained for them all, by his death on the cross, redemption and the forgiveness of sins; yet that no one actually enjoys this forgiveness of sins except the believer...

Article Three. [*Natural inability*]. That man has not saving grace of himself, nor of the energy of his free will, inasmuch as he, in the state of apostasy and sin, can of and by himself neither think, will, nor do any thing that is truly good (such as saving Faith eminently is); but that it is needful that he be born again of God in Christ, through his Holy Spirit...

Article Four. [*Prevenient grace*]. That this grace of God is the beginning, continuance, and accomplishment of all good, even to this extent, that the regenerate man himself, without prevenient or assisting, awakening, following and co-operative grace, can neither think, will, nor do good...so that all good deeds or movements, that can be conceived, must be ascribed to the grace of God in Christ. But as respects the mode of the operation of the grace, it is not irresistible...

Article Five. [*Uncertainty of perseverance*]. That those who are incorporated into Christ by a true faith, and have thereby become partakers of his life-giving Spirit, have thereby full power to strive against Satan, sin, the world, and their own flesh, and to win the victory;...But whether they are capable, through negligence, of forsaking again the first beginnings of their life in Christ, of again returning to this present evil world, of turning away from the holy doctrine which was delivered them, of losing a good conscience, of becoming devoid of grace, that must be more particularly determined out of the Holy Scripture, before we ourselves can teach it with the full persuasion of our minds.

The Arminians deemed these articles "agreeable to the Word of God."[3] On November 13, 1618, partly at the behest of King James I of England, the government of Holland convened the National Synod of Dort to resolve the controversy.[4] Present at the Synod were 58 Dutch theologians and representatives of the churches of England, Scotland, the Palatinate, Heidelberg, Hess, the major cities of Switzerland (Zurich, Berne, Basle and Geneva), and Bremen. At the Synod, the five articles of Arminianism were unanimously rejected, and five counter-articles adopted. The counter-articles adopted by the Synod were abbreviated and then reported as follows:

> **First Head of Doctrine** [*Of Divine Predestination*]. Since all men sinned in Adam and lie under the curse, God would have done no injustice if he had left them to their merited punishment; but in his infinite mercy he provided a salvation through the gospel of Christ, that those who believe in him may not perish, but have eternal life. That some receive the gift of faith from God and others not, proceeds from God's eternal decree of election and reprobation...Election is absolute and unconditional. It is not founded upon foreseen faith and holiness, as the prerequisite condition on which it depended; on the contrary, it is the fountain of faith, holiness and eternal life itself...
>
> **Second Head of Doctrine** [*Of the Death of Christ*]. According to the sovereign counsel of God, the saving efficacy of the atoning death of Christ extends to all the elect, so as to bring them infallibly to salvation. But intrinsically, the sacrifice and satisfaction of Christ is of infinite worth and value, abundantly sufficient to expiate the sins of the whole world...
>
> **Third and Fourth Heads of Doctrine** [*Of the Corruption of Man, his Conversion to God, and the Manner thereof*] ...All men are conceived in sin, and are by nature children of wrath, incapable of any saving good, prone to evil, dead in sin, and in bondage thereto; and without the regenerating grace of the Holy Spirit, they are neither able nor willing to return to God, to reform the depravity of their nature, nor to dispose themselves to reformation. What, therefore, neither the light of nature nor the law could do, that God performs by the operation of his Holy Spirit through the word or ministry of reconciliation...so he calls them effectually in time, confers upon them faith and repentance, rescues them from the power of darkness, and translates them into the kingdom of his own Son...Faith is therefore the gift of God.
>
> **Fifth Head of Doctrine** [*Of the Perseverance of the Saints*]. Whom God calls, according to his purpose, to the communion of his Son our Lord Jesus Christ,

> and regenerates by the Holy Spirit, he delivers also from the dominion and slavery of sin in this life; though not altogether from the body of sin and from the infirmities of the flesh, so long as they continue in this world...But God is faithful, who having conferred grace, mercifully confirms and powerfully preserves them therein, even to the end.

Nineteenth century church historian, William Cunningham, said the Synod of Dort, "representing as it did almost all the Reformed churches, and containing a great proportion of theologians of the highest talents, learning, and character, is entitled to a larger measure of respect and deference than any other council recorded in the history of the church."[5] As a result of the Synod, the Arminians were banished and their doctrines condemned. The judgment of the Synod was that the five points of Calvinism, as the counter-articles became known in summary form, not the five points of Arminianism, consisted of doctrine "drawn from the Word of God."

The Pelagian Controversy

The Synod of Dort may have been the origin of the five points of Calvinism but it certainly was not the origin of Calvinistic doctrine. But then, neither was the theology of John Calvin. Calvin's theological views, and those of the other sixteenth century Protestant reformers, in fact, were a revival of Augustinian theology. Calvin scholars have commented that the Genevan's views on predestination presented little new from medieval Augustinianism. That, in turn, derived from the doctrines of Augustine, the fourth century church leader, as forged in his Pelagian controversies.[6]

Pelagius was a simple monk born in the fourth century in Britain. He was well-respected as a pious man, but as church historian Phillip Schaff put it, "his morality was not so much the rich, deep life of faith, as it was the external legalism, the ascetic self-discipline and self-righteousness of monkery."[7] Pelagius took great offense at Augustine's prayer in his *Confessions*: "Give what thou commandest, and command what thou wilt." He rejected the idea that God would have to give anyone the power to obey what God commanded. "God has not willed anything impossible," he asserted. In other words, he believed that because God commands people to obey his laws, *a fortiori*, they must have the ability to do so. Put another way, Adam's fall must have affected only himself and not humanity as a whole. Thus, he believed human nature has a permanent capability for sinlessness; people are not born with a sin nature but are born neutral. He denied the notion of original sin.[8]

Flowing from Pelagius' view of man's condition was his view of God's grace. He taught that God's grace is helpful to living a godly life, but it is not necessary for salvation. Pelagius also believed that predestination was based on foreseen qualities in a person's life. The touchstone of Pelagian theology was a belief in the supremacy of human freedom. As Schaff summarized, to Pelagius and his followers:

> Freedom is the supreme good, the honor and glory of man, the *bonum naturae*, that cannot be lost. It is the sole basis of the ethical relation of man to God, who would have no unwilling service. It consists according to Pelagius, essentially in the *liberum arbitrium*, or the *possibilitas boni et mali*; the freedom of choice, and the absolutely equal ability at every moment to do good or evil.[9]

Augustine recognized the acute danger of Pelagianism. If the human will is uncorrupted by sin and people actually have the capacity not to sin, therefore having no need of regeneration, there also is no need for a redeemer to give new life. Although he was an old man by the time of the Pelagian controversies, Augustine arose to do battle against this dangerous heresy. He responded by arguing that the original man, Adam, was indeed able not to sin (using what subsequently became a famous Latin phrase, *posse non peccare*, or able not to sin). However, Adam's fall pervasively affected all subsequent humanity, such that man now has lost his freedom of choice (in Latin, *non passe non paccare*, or not able not to sin). Thus, all of humanity is infected with original sin and original guilt. All humanity is a mass of sin or lump of perdition. Moreover, sin radically corrupts. It has its seat in the moral character of the will. Thus, good works of man avail nothing to salvation. From a Godward perspective, unregenerated man is incapable of doing good.

Augustine also asserted that grace is the antidote to sin. As humanity inherited sin and death from the first Adam, from the second Adam, Christ, we receive eternal life. In grace, the will has the power and ability to do good and the capacity for faith. In his *Retractions*, Augustine rejected his immature view that faith is a work of man, concluding instead that faith itself is a result of grace. He taught that grace is absolutely necessary, unmerited, and irresistible. The result of grace in eternity will be the inability to sin (*non passé peccare*).[10]

Augustine did not stop here, though. He grounded his soteriology on a strong view of predestination. For him, grace is efficacious only in the elect. As Schaff summarized Augustine's views:

> The election of grace is conditioned by no foreseen merit, but is absolutely free. God does not predestinate His children on account of their faith, for their faith is itself a gift of grace; but He predestinates them to faith and to holiness.[11]

Augustine taught that God's choice in election is according to his secret and inscrutable justice. Moreover, to the elect, the final grace of perseverance is given. Those to whom it is not given are "left in the mass of ruin."[12] The following chart[13] compares the two views:

PELAGIAN AND AUGUSTINIAN VIEWS OF SIN

	Pelagius	**Augustine**
Effect of Fall	Only Adam effected	All humanity effected
Original Sin	No	Yes
Hereditary Sin	No	Yes
Humans at Birth	Born neutral	Born with fallen nature
Man's Will	Free	Enslaved to sin

	Pelagius	**Augustine**
Fact of Universal Sin	Due to bad examples	Due to innate sinfulness
Turning to God in salvation	Is possible independent of God's grace	Is only possible through God's grace

We can safely say, then, that Pelagianism is the ancestor of Arminianism and Augustinianism is the ancestor of Calvinism. However, calling the theological system which we follow Augustinianism does not mean we are following Augustine into the Roman Catholic Church any more than calling it Calvinism means we believe in baptizing infants or burning heretics. It simply means we are in agreement with the theological beliefs that Augustine taught on the nature of God's grace in salvation.

Was Augustine, then, the beginning of Calvinistic doctrine? Once again, the answer is no. Augustine found his views in the theology of the apostle Paul. John A. Broadus, a great Southern Baptist of the last century, was right when he said that this system goes back to the Apostle Paul. Broadus called Calvinism "*that exalted system of Pauline truth*."[14]

Charles Spurgeon made the same point when he observed that "Calvin found his doctrine in the Scriptures. Doubtless he may have also received some instruction from the works of Augustine, but that mighty doctor of grace learned it from the writings of St. Paul; and St. Paul, the apostle of grace, received it by inspiration from Jesus the Lord. We can trace our pedigree direct to Christ himself."[15] The origin of Calvinism, therefore, lies in the teachings of our Lord himself. Augustine preserved those teachings through the Middle Ages. Calvin systematized them, and the Synod of Dort codified them. Our Baptist forebears believed them and taught them as true. The question for us is whether we will learn from those who went before us. If those doctrines were true then, they are equally true today.

The Calvinism-Arminianism Debate

After the Synod of Dort, for centuries the debate between

Calvinism and Arminianism remained essentially frozen, perpetually framed in terms similar to those described above. From a formal perspective, Calvinism had the ascendancy in most Protestant denominations. Even today, the doctrines of Calvinism are contained in the creeds and confessions of most evangelical churches. The official creeds of the Presbyterian, Reformed and Congregational churches, the Westminster Confession of Faith, the Belgic Confession, and the Savoy Declaration, are thoroughly Calvinistic. The Anglican Church has a Calvinistic creed in the Thirty-Nine Articles. Arminianism was not adopted by an organized church until 1784 as part of the beliefs of the Methodist Church of England.

Moreover, most of the outstanding leaders of the church throughout its history believed in the doctrines of grace. Augustine, whose doctrines we have seen, was likely the greatest theologian outside the Bible. Martin Luther, the founder of Protestantism, wrote *The Bondage of the Will* as a diatribe against the belief that people can come to Christ as a matter of their own free will without divine intervention. Wycliffe, Zwingli, John Owen, George Whitefield, Jonathan Edwards, Charles Hodge, B.B. Warfield, D. Martyn Lloyd-Jones, J.I. Packer, and R.C. Sproul are all Calvinists. The English and American Puritans, Particular Baptists, Presbyterians and Reformed denominations followed in their Calvinist fathers' footsteps.

More recently, Arminianism has prevailed, at least in popular thought, fed by the preaching of such men as John Wesley, Charles Finney and modern revivalists. Denominationally, the Wesleyan-holiness movement and Pentecostals carried the torch for the Arminian system.

What about the Baptists? Most Baptists historically have been Calvinists. The English Particular Baptists, from whom modern-day Southern Baptists trace our roots, had their start as an offshoot of the Separatists, a radical branch of English Puritanism. One of the earliest traces of Baptist life was in 1644, when several London Baptist churches got together and published a Calvinistic confession of faith. That *First London Confession* states: "God had in Christ before the foundation of the world, according to the good pleasure of his will, foreordained some men to eternal life through Jesus Christ, to the praise and glory of His grace, leaving the rest in their sin to their just condemnation, to the praise of His justice."[16]

Benjamin Keach, who pastored a church in England in the late 1660s, introduced hymn singing (as opposed to exclusive psalmody) into Baptist life, and wrote the first Baptist catechism for children, was a thorough-going Calvinist. John Bunyan, the writer of the immortal classic *Pilgrim's Progress*, was a Calvinist. John Gill, who lived in the eighteenth century and wrote the first Baptist systematic theology, was the foremost Calvinist of his era. Andrew Fuller, who wrote a book entitled *The Gospel Worthy of All Acceptation*, moved Baptists toward a warm missionary-minded Calvinism. William Carey, the first missionary Baptist and a close friend of Fuller, was a strong Calvinist. Roger Williams and Isaac Backus, prominent early American Baptists, were Calvinists. Baptist missionaries Adoniram Judson, Luther Rice and Lottie Moon were Calvinists. Of course, Charles H. Spurgeon, arguably the greatest Baptist preacher to ever live, was an ardent Calvinist.

In looking back to the rock from which we are hewn, we cannot overlook some of our great Southern Baptist Convention fathers and leaders who were committed, articulate Calvinists. Take Basil Manly, Sr. for example. Instrumental in the formation of the Southern Baptist Convention, Manly was a Calvinist of the first order. Consider James P. Boyce, the principal founder of the first Southern Baptist seminary (Southern Baptist Theological Seminary). Long after Boyce's death, one of his former students, Dr. David Ramsey, gave a Founders Day address, on January 11, 1924, entitled "James Petigru Boyce: God's Gentleman." A few lines from Dr. Ramsey's address will tell the story that Boyce was a committed Calvinist and that, at the same time, he loved the souls of men:

> My contention is that no other theology than that of an overwhelming and soul consuming love for men will account for James P. Boyce and his career. This passionate love was the motif that directed his thinking in those early conferences and in the preparation of those papers which led to the establishment of the seminary. This purpose to help his fellow men ran through all his plans, through his conversation, his writings and his preaching and teaching as the scarlet thread that runs through every foot of cable of the English Navy. This zeal for souls called out the finest of his being as the morning sun causes the dew-laden flowers and plants

> to bend toward the god of day.[17]

His love for his fellow man was such that, after Boyce died, Rabbi Moses of Louisville said about him: "Before I came to Louisville, I knew Christianity only in books, and it was through such men as Boyce that I learned to know it as a living force. In that man I learned not only to comprehend, but to respect and reverence the spiritual power called Christianity." Boyce not only loved men, but he loved God. Ramsey said, concerning this point:

> "Let the thought embrace both the subjective and objective love; man's love for God and God's love for man." Boyce's close friend and fellow founder of the seminary, John A. Broadus, expressed his own feelings about the theology of Boyce which we call Calvinism: "It was a great privilege to be directed and upborne by such a teacher in studying that exalted system of Pauline truth which is technically called Calvinism, which compels an earnest student to profound thinking, and when pursued with a combination of systematic thought and fervent experience, makes him at home among the most inspiring and ennobling views of God and the universe He has made."[18]

Boyce's legacy to us and to our posterity is the biblical theology expressed in the *Abstract of Systematic Theology*, which is nothing other than his classroom teaching. It is pure Calvinism.

In defense of Boyce's Calvinism, William A. Mueller, author of *A History of Southern Baptist Theological Seminary*, said:

> As a theologian, Dr. Boyce is not afraid to be found "in the old paths." He is conservative, and eminently scriptural. He treats with great fairness those whose views upon various points discussed, he declines to accept, yet in his own teaching is decidedly Calvinistic, after the model of "the old divines." Difficulties as connected with such doctrines as the federal headship of Adam, election and the atonement he aims to meet, not so as to silence the controversialist, but so as to help the honest inquirer.[19]

Rev. E. E. Folk, in the Baptist Reflector commented on Boyce's abilities and fruits as a teacher of theology:

> You had to know your systematic theology, or you could not recite it to Dr. Boyce. And though the young men were generally rank Arminians when they came to the seminary, few went through this course under him without being converted to his strong Calvinistic views.[20]

Boyce and Manly were strong Calvinists. But they were not alone. Their theology was no anomaly in early Southern Baptist life. W.B. Johnson, first president of the Southern Baptist Convention, was a Calvinist. R.B.C. Howell, second president of the convention, also was a Calvinist. Richard Fuller, third Southern Baptist Convention president, was a Calvinist. Charles Dutton Mallary, first recording secretary of the Southern Baptist Foreign Mission Board, was a Calvinist. So was B.H. Carroll, founder of Southwestern Baptist Theological Seminary. Patrick Hues Mell, president of the convention for seventeen years, longer than any other man, was a polemic defender of Calvinism.

Mrs. D.B. Fitzgerald, a member of Mell's Antioch Church in Oglethorpe, Georgia and a resident in Mell's home for a number of years, recalls Mell's initial efforts at the church:

> When first called to take charge of the church, Dr. Mell found it in a sad state of confusion. He said a number of members were drifting off into Arminianism. He loved the truth too well to blow hot and cold with the same breath. It was a Baptist church and it must have doctrines peculiar to that denomination preached to it. And with that boldness, clearness, and vigor of speech that marked him, he preached to them the doctrines of predestination, election, free-grace, etc. He said it was always his business to preach the truth as he found it in God's Word, and leave the matter there, feeling that God would take care of the results.[21]

We could go on and on giving names and biographical sketches of our Southern Baptist founding fathers who were equally committed Calvinists and ardent evangelists, but will name just one more. Dr. John A. Broadus, a great preacher and one of the founders of Southern Seminary said:

> The people who sneer at what is called Calvinism might as well sneer at Mont Blanc. We are not bound in the least to defend all of Calvin's opinions or actions, but I do not see how anyone who really understands the Greek of the Apostle Paul, or the Latin of Calvin or Turretin, can fail to see that these latter did but interpret and formulate substantially what the former teachers taught.[22]

Yes, it is Calvinistic blood that runs through the veins of today's Southern Baptists. Spurgeon was not hesitant to credit Calvinism with the preservation of the Baptist denomination: "It is that vein of free-grace, running through the sermonizing of Baptists, which has saved us as a denomination. Were it not for that, we should not stand where we are today."[23] As Southern Baptists, we stand on the shoulders of some giant Calvinists. The opposing view of Arminianism did not begin seriously taking hold in the denomination until the late nineteenth or early twentieth century.

The point is that we would do well to listen to the words of our forefathers. They certainly were not infallible. Each of them had his own separate faults and blind spots. Yet they were all in agreement on the issues discussed in this book. Thus, if a historically-minded Southern Baptist is going to reject Calvinism, he must do so in the face of the overwhelming tide of church history and Baptist history. The fact that the best and brightest church leaders throughout the ages were Calvinists does not make Calvinism automatically true, but it does mean that the person who will oppose it should be very sure about his position.

The historical debates between Calvinists and Arminians were often heated, yet the arguments, at least in evangelicalism, seldom moved far beyond the discussions crystallized in the Dutch Arminian controversy. Not anymore.

Open Theism - A New Arminianism

Within the last twenty years, a new, pernicious variant of Arminianism has arisen. This new theology is called the "openness of God" theology or "open theism." Its proponents agree with the traditional Arminian notion that God does not affirmatively control everything. Yet they go beyond the traditional Arminian view to add that God does not even *know* everything. In the "openness of God" view, God lacks exhaustive foreknowledge. He "knows everything that can be known," but humanity's free decisions cannot be knowable—even by God—"because they are not yet settled in reality." In other words, decisions not yet made are "potential—yet to be realized but not yet actual" and so God cannot know them. Thus, "God can predict a great deal of what we will choose to do, but not all of it, because some of it remains hidden in the mystery of human freedom."[24] To the open theists, God is not fully omniscient, but is limited in his knowledge.[25]

While this radical view that God lacks exhaustive foreknowledge has only recently burst upon the contemporary scene, it actually is not new. A heretical sixteenth century group called the Socinians also denied that God can know what a free agent does before he acts.[26] James P. Boyce, the first president of Southern Baptist Theological Seminary, in his nineteenth century systematic theology textbook, called Socinianism a "most objectionable theory." He wrote that the "objections to this theory are obvious": (1) It is based on a wrong conception of the nature of free will because it fails to account that even free agents are influenced by motives. (2) It is opposed to the independence of God for it supposes that God's actions and will must depend on human actions and will. (3) It is opposed to the omniscience of God for it says God is limited in his knowledge. (4) It does not account for prophecy by which God predicts beforehand even the bad actions of men.[27]

In 2000, the Southern Baptist Convention explicitly repudiated the current version of this "most objectionable theory" by adding the following clarifying language to the Southern Baptist confessional statement, *The Baptist Faith and Message*: "His perfect knowledge extends to all things, past, present, and future, including the future decisions of His free creatures."[28] Jack Graham and Daniel Akin commented on this amendment:

> Surveys reveal 95% of all Americans believe in God. That is the good news. What they think that God, gods or goddesses are like may take many shapes and forms. Unfortunately, the evangelical community is not speaking with one voice on this crucial point. Following the teachings of Scripture, we affirm the absolute perfections of the eternal God who is a Trinity of three persons –Father, Son and Holy Spirit. He is all-powerful and all

> knowing with "His perfect knowledge extend[ing] to all things past, present, and future, including the future decision of His free creatures." There is no place in the theology of Southern Baptists for a "finite theism" that limits God's omnipotence or an "open theism" that limits God's omniscience. This "user-friendly" deity may be more comfortable for a culture that values its personal autonomy more than it ought, but it is certainly not the God we discover in the Bible.[29]

Moreover, in November 2001, the Evangelical Theological Society, an influential gathering of evangelical scholars, also repudiated open theism's denial of God's exhaustive foreknowledge, passing a resolution declaring: "We believe the Bible clearly teaches that God has complete, accurate, and infallible knowledge of all events past, present, and future including all future decisions and actions of free moral agents."[30]

Our purpose here is not to focus on the heretical views of "openness of God" theology per se. A number of fine works ably refute the major tenets of this dangerous new belief set.[31] Our goal here is instead to focus on the old Calvinist vs. Arminian debate in light of the new Arminian (that is, "openness of God") objections to the traditional Arminian counterpoints to Calvinism. We take this tack because openness of God proponents, at least, are honest in recognizing many of the fallacies inherent in the evangelical Arminian objections to Calvinism. The proponents of this new radical brand of Arminianism openly proclaim that their views are shaped by both a rejection of Calvinism and an inability to accept traditional Arminian teachings.

The leading openness theologian Clark Pinnock is very upfront about this. In the 1960s, Pinnock was a Baptist and a theology professor at New Orleans Baptist Theological Seminary. At that time he was a leading light of conservative theology, criticizing the then-leadership of the Southern Baptist Convention for failing to hold to the inerrancy of Scripture. Today, Pinnock has long left behind both New Orleans Seminary and the conservatism he held when he taught there. A professor at McMaster Seminary in Canada, he now rejects and attacks the inerrancy he once believed and defended. He also denies an exclusive salvation in Christ, along with vociferously rejecting the orthodox belief that God has exhaustive foreknowledge of future events.

In a book he edited entitled *The Grace of God and the Will of Man*, Pinnock traced his theological evolution to a rejection of Calvinism. He called it a pilgrimage "from Augustine to Arminius" (although he later acknowledged it should have been called a journey from Augustine to Arminius and beyond"). He recounted that, in 1970, after he left New Orleans Seminary, "one of the links in the chain of the tight Calvinian logic broke," and he rejected the view that Christians cannot lose their salvation. Upon this change, "the thread was pulled, and the garment must begin to unravel, as indeed it did."[32]

An embracing of the view that humans have a "wonderful capacity to relate or decline to relate to God, to love or not to love him" led him to the "morally intolerable" and "morally loathsome" doctrine of "double predestination." He then decided "upon reflection" that the New Testament texts speaking of God's election "could indeed be read corporately" so that election spoke of "a class of people rather than specific individuals."[33] He concluded that "this model has the distinct advantage of construing election as a divine decision and not the pale notion of God's ratifying our choices as in the standard Arminian interpretation."

His rejection of what he called the "morally loathsome" Calvinistic view of election brought Pinnock "considerable relief." He had no difficulty accepting the interpretation of verses suggesting that Christ's death was on behalf of the entire human race because "they fitted so obviously into the doctrine of God's universal salvific will, which I had already come to accept." But this required him to also "reduce the precision" in which he understood Christ's death to be substitutionary.[34] And so it goes.

The thread of orthodoxy has unraveled, all beginning with the strand that Christians are eternally secure in their salvation. Pinnock himself believes that his new reading of Scripture is "more evangelical and less rationalistic."[35] We rather think his new perspective, commencing with his a priori rejection of Calvinism, shows he has metamorphosed foursquare into a theological rationalist rather than biblicist.

For all it has against it, however, as noted, openness theology does point out the bankruptcy of the evangelical Arminian position. For example, Pinnock says his new theology "makes the choices even sharper and clearer" and offers "a more coherent alternative to Calvinism than Arminians have presented before."[36] John Sanders, another "openness of God" theologian, said:

> It is no accident that the doctrines of unconditional election, limited atonement, and irresistible grace developed. They are all logical corollaries with the absolutistic conception of God. The soteriological doctrines of Augustine and Calvin are quite correct if God actually is as the absolutistic view claims he is. The covenant has to be seen as unilateral on God's part. There can be no reciprocity or conditionality to it. The working out of the covenant is necessarily monegerstic: faith is a solely divine work in us.[37]

In light of these rather remarkable admissions, one wonders whether the forceful critique of the "openness of God" theology will end up driving a death nail in the coffin of traditional Arminianism. Pinnock has well pointed out the logical flaws of evangelical Arminians; unfortunately, he has taken those errors to a new and dangerous extreme. Our hope is that the more orthodox non-Calvinists, the evangelical Arminians, would see the error of their own rationalism and turn back to biblical Christianity.

Chapter 3

The Five Points of Calvinism: Was Paul a Calvinist?

We now turn to a brief examination of the biblical evidence for the five points of Calvinism. As we discuss the five points, the reader should keep in mind that these five great doctrines are not the totality of Calvinism. They are, as Charles Spurgeon cautioned, "in some degree, a summary of the rest; they are distinctive points wherein we differ from those who 'have erred from the faith, and pierced themselves through with many sorrows.'"[1] Because the five points present a point of contact with those who disagree with us, they are an appropriate place to begin our defense of the Calvinistic system.

This chapter consists of five sections, each of which takes as its subject one of the five points of Calvinism. In each section, we briefly restate the Calvinist position, and then describe the traditional Arminian objections to that position, followed by the openness of God rejoinder. Because we believe the Calvinist position to be the traditional Baptist position, we frequently draw upon the thoughts of historic Baptists to summarize the point in discussion. We then look to Scripture to resolve the issue. This involves a short exegetical study of key passages.

For the sake of space, we have limited our examination here to Paul's Epistle to the Romans. Hopefully, this limitation will not present a stumbling block; after all, surely evangelicals who hold to the inspiration of the Bible will agree that if Calvinism is true in Romans, it is true in the rest of the Scriptures. Why Romans? We have chosen that book because it contains many of the critical passages addressing the five points of Calvinism. As Martin Luther said, "This epistle is really the chief part of the New Testament, and is truly the purest gospel."[2] John Calvin likewise said: "If we have gained a true understanding of this Epistle, we have an open door to all the most profound treasures of Scripture."[3]

We depart from this approach only with respect to the issue of "limited atonement" (the "L" in "tulip") or, as we prefer to call it, "particular redemption." Although we examine the critical passages in Romans in this chapter, we postpone until the next chapter a more detailed look at this controversial issue. We do so for two reasons. First, the most salient passages cited both in support and in opposition to the Calvinistic position are not contained in Romans. Second, this issue deserves a closer review because it is particularly controversial in Baptist circles, even among men and women who otherwise claim to hold to the Calvinist position.

It finally should be noted that we have modified the usual order of the five points (once again tearing apart the tulip) to better fit a chronological perspective. We begin, then, before time itself, deep in the recesses of eternity past.

Before Time Began – Election to Life

The Calvinist View

R.C. Sproul has provocatively stated that all Christians believe in predestination. He is absolutely right. Bible-believing Christians really have no choice. The word "predestined" (Gr. *proorizo*) is used six times in Scripture. In Acts 4:28 the early church believers lift up a prayer of praise to God because the Roman and Jewish leaders who had Christ crucified did "whatever Your hand and Your purpose determined before to be done." Romans 8:29 plainly states that "those God foreknew he also predestined to be conformed to the likeness of his Son." Romans 8:30 adds: "Moreover whom He predestined, these He also called; whom He called, these He also justified; and whom He justified, these He also glorified." Ephesians 1:4-5 similarly declares that "he predestined us to be adopted as his sons through Jesus Christ, in accordance with his pleasure and will" (NIV). Ephesians 1:11 adds: "In Him also we have obtained an inheritance, being predestined according to the purpose of Him who works all things according to the counsel of His will."

1 Corinthians 2:7 says: "but we speak God's wisdom in a mystery, the hidden wisdom which God predestined before the ages to our glory" (NASB).

The word "predestinate" means simply "to decide beforehand." In predestination, God decides beforehand the final destination of humans. There are two aspects of it: election and reprobation. In election, God decides beforehand that heaven will be the final destination of some individuals. In reprobation, he decides beforehand that hell will be the final destination of others. However, as we will subsequently see, Calvinist Baptists are quick to insist that there is a difference between these two decisions: election to salvation is an active decision on God's part; God's decision to reprobate is not active but passive. The Bible speaks of both but emphasizes election over reprobation.

Just as all Christians must believe in predestination, all Christians must also believe in election. To "elect" means simply "to choose." References to election occur throughout the pages of Scripture. Some are: Deuteronomy 7:6 ("For you are a holy people to the Lord your God; the Lord your God has chosen you to be a people for Himself, a special treasure above all the peoples on the face of the earth); 1 Samuel 10:24 ("And Samuel said to all the people, 'Do you see him whom the Lord has chosen, that there is no one like him among all the people?' So all the people shouted and said, "Long live the king!"); and John 15:19 ("If you were of the world, the world would love its own. Yet because you are not of the world, but I chose you out of the world, therefore the world hates you.").

Because predestination and election are so clearly biblical concepts, the nub of the dispute between Calvinists and Arminians is not over their existence but rather over the basis of God's election, or choice, of sinners to salvation. Thus it is that a former president of the Southern Baptist Convention could adopt a hostile stance toward Calvinism and yet proclaim, "I believe in foreordination. I believe in predestination....I believe in election. I believe in all that. Why do I believe that? Because I can read the Bible."[4] What Calvinists and Arminians mean by those terms is entirely different.

In his monumental work, *The Institutes of the Christian Religion*, John Calvin declared: "Scripture clearly proves that God, by his eternal and unchanging will, determined once and for all those whom he would one day admit to salvation....His decision about the elect is based on his free mercy with no reference to human deserving."[5] He wrote "If you say that God could foresee who would be holy and therefore elected them, you invert Paul's order. So we may safely infer that if he elected us to make us holy, he did not elect us because he saw that we would be holy. The two things are obviously contradictory..."[6] In a later treatise, *Concerning the Eternal Predestination of God*, Calvin responded to critics of his earlier published views on predestination by elaborating on his view of foreknowledge:

> To make faith the cause of election is quite absurd and at variance with the words of Paul. For, as Augustine wisely observes, he does not call them elect because they are about to believe, but in order that they may believe; he does not call them elect whom God foresaw would be holy and immaculate, but in order that they might be made so. Again, God did not choose us because we believed, but in order that we might believe, lest we should seem first to have chosen Him. Paul emphasizes that our beginning to be holy is the fruit and effect of election. Hence, they act most preposterously who place election after faith.[7]

Calvin continued: "I know the objections which many make here: when Paul says that those are predestined whom God foreknew, he means that each is elected in view of his faith. But I cannot allow them this false supposition. God is not to be understood as foreseeing something in them which procures grace for them; rather they are foreknown because they were freely chosen."[8] In short, Calvin believed the root of predestination must come before the fruit of regeneration!

Like Calvin, Baptists who bear the name of his theology hold that the basis of election is God's sovereign purpose, not anything in man. Charles Mallary said that election is "God's free, sovereign, eternal and unchangeable purpose to glorify the perfections of his character in the salvation of a definite number of the human family by Jesus Christ without regard to any foreseen merit or good works on their part, as the ground or condition of this choice."[9]

Article III of the *Baptist Confession of 1644* states: "God had in Christ before the foundation of the world according to the good pleasure of his will foreordained some men to eternal life through Jesus Christ to the praise and glory of his grace leaving the rest in their sin to their just condemnation to the praise of his justice." The *Baptist Confession of 1689*, carried over to America as the *Philadelphia Confession* and to the American South as the *Charleston Confession*, following the *Westminster Confession*, states in chapter 3, sections 3 and 5:

> By the decree of God, for the manifestation of His glory, some men...are predestined, or foreordained to eternal life through Jesus Christ, to the praise of His glorious grace; others being left to act in their sin to their just condemnation, to the praise of His glorious justice.
>
> Those of mankind that are predestined to life, God, before the foundation of the world was laid, according to His eternal and immutable purpose, and the secret counsel and good pleasure of His will, hath chosen in Christ unto everlasting glory, out of His mere free grace and love, without any other thing in the creature as a condition or cause moving Him thereunto.

Article V of the *Abstract of Principles*, the founding—and still governing—document of Southern Baptist Theological Seminary and Southeastern Baptist Theological Seminary states: "Election is God's eternal choice of some persons unto everlasting life—not because of foreseen merit in them, but of his mere mercy in Christ—in consequence of which choice they are called, justified and glorified."

John Gill comprehensively addressed the doctrine of predestination in several works, including his multi-volume systematic theology, his commentaries, and his treatise on the subject, *The Cause of God and Truth*. (He wasn't called Dr. Voluminous for nothing!) He said "predestination is usually considered as consisting of two parts, and including the two branches of election and reprobation, both with respect to angels and men." Some angels are elect (1 Tim. 5:21); others are said to be "reserved in chains" until the day of judgment (2 Pet. 2:4). Some people are likewise "vessels of mercy, afore prepared for glory; others vessels of wrath, fitted for destruction." Some are "the elect persons, that obtain righteousness, life, and salvation; and others are the rest that are left in, and given up to blindness, Romans 9:22,23 11:7."[10] He defined "election" as an ordination to eternal life:

> As many as were ordained to eternal life, believed; by which ordination is meant no other than the predestination, choice, and appointment of men to everlasting life and salvation by Jesus Christ; and from whence it appears that this is of particular persons, of some and not all, though many; that it is not to temporary privileges and enjoyments, but to grace and glory; and that faith is not the cause, but the sure and certain fruit and effect of it; and that both eternal life through Christ, and believing in him, are infallibly secured by this act of grace.[11]

Moreover, to Gill, the basis of election is not foreknowledge of foreseen faith, but God's own purpose: Election does not find men in Christ, but puts them there; it gives them a being in him, and union to him.[12] It is "wholly owing to the will and pleasure of God; and not to the faith, holiness, obedience, and good works of men; nor to a foresight of all or any of these."[13]

Although Gill is often viewed as a hyper-Calvinist, he denied the idea of a positive decree of reprobation. In fact, in his systematic theology, he gave up use of the term "reprobation" entirely, commenting that it "through wrong and frightful ideas being affixed to it, carries in it with many a sound harsh and disagreeable."[14] In *The Cause of God and Truth*, he said, "What is called reprobation is no other than non-election."[15] He asserted: "The true state of the question before us, and what ought to be attended to, is this, that as God, of his sovereign good will [and] pleasure, has, from all eternity, chosen some men unto salvation by Jesus Christ, through sanctification of the Spirit, [and] belief of the truth, so he has, of his sovereign will and pleasure, from all eternity, passed by others, and determined to leave them to themselves, and deny them that grace which he gives to others, and damn them only for their sin."[16]

Andrew Fuller, the English Baptist theologian whose writings ignited the great Baptist missionary movement of the late eighteenth and early nineteenth centuries argued: "If any are saved, it must be by an act of free grace. If some are brought to believe in Christ, while others continue in unbelief...the difference between them must be altogether of grace. But if God make a difference in time, he must have determined to do so for eternity; for to suppose God to act without a purpose is depriving him of wisdom; and to suppose any new purpose to arise in his mind would be to accuse him of mutability. Here, therefore, we are landed upon election—sovereign, unconditional election. And does not this accord with the Holy Scriptures?"[17]

The first writing American Baptist, John Dagg, also treated the topic of election extensively in his popular nineteenth century systematic theology text, *A Manual of Theology*.

He made eight claims about the topic. First, "the Scriptures clearly teach that God has an elect or chosen people." Second, "the Scriptures teach expressly that God's people are chosen to salvation." Third, "the Scriptures plainly teach that election of grace is from eternity." Fourth, "election is part of God's eternal purpose." "Had it been his purpose to save all the human race, there would have been no elect from among men; no peculiar people, no redeemed out of every nation. But his purpose to save did not include all the race; and therefore, on some principle yet to be inquired into, some of the race have been selected, who will receive the kingdom prepared for them from the foundation of the world." Fifth, "the Scriptures teach that election is of grace, and not of works." In the last day, God will discriminate between the righteous and the wicked, but the purpose of God includes an earlier discrimination "made at the time of calling," which is "not according to men's works." This discrimination is made "for reasons wholly unknown to mortals; not according to the works of men, but on a ground which infinite wisdom approves." Sixth, "election is not on the ground of foreseen faith or obedience." The elect are chosen "not because of their holiness, but that they may be holy; not because of their obedience, but unto obedience." Seventh, God's choice of the elect is "with reference to Christ, and that they might be given to him, and rendered accepted in him." The elect are said to be "chosen in Christ." Finally, those not included in the election of grace are called in Scripture "the rest" or "vessels of wrath."

Dagg was quick to point out that "reprobation, as a positive act of God, is no other than the condemnation under which all believers lie." Why are they not included? Dagg humbly admitted, we are unable to explain this, and therefore we must let the matter rest in God's sovereignty.[18]

The Evangelical Arminian View

Evangelical Arminians disagree. James Arminius was asked:

> "Which is first, Election, or Faith Truly Foreseen, so that God elected his people according to faith foreseen?"

He responded:

> If therefore "Election" denotes "the decree which is according to election concerning the justification and salvation of believers." I say Election is prior to Faith, as being that by which Faith is appointed as the means of obtaining salvation. But if it signifies "the decree by which God determines to bestow salvation on some one," then Faith foreseen is prior to Election. For as believers alone are saved, so only believers are predestinated to salvation. But the Scriptures know no Election, by which God precisely and absolutely has determined to save anyone without having first considered him as a believer. For such an Election would be at variance with the decree by which he hath determined to save none but believers.[19]

Arminius also declared: "This decree [of election] has its foundation in the foreknowledge of God, by which he knew from all eternity those individuals who would, through his preventing grace, believe..."[20]

John Wesley similarly affirmed that election is based on the foreknowledge of God. In a 1740 sermon entitled *Free Grace*, he exclaimed, "I abhor the doctrine of predestination!"—which he attributed to the devil.[21] He contended that the Calvinist view of predestination is "flatly contrary to which is the whole tenor of Scripture."[22] He said, "Flatly contrary to this are all the scriptures; and those in particular, 'Elect according to the foreknowledge of God' (1 Peter 1:2;) [and] 'Whom he did foreknow, he also did predestinate.' (Romans 8:29.)."[23] He concluded that the Calvinist doctrine of predestination was "a doctrine full of blasphemy."[24]

A modern traditional Arminian, Jack Cottrell, also articulates this classic view. He declares that God's foreknowledge enables him to monitor people's plans and act as they will. He affirms "that God has a true foreknowledge of future free-will choices without himself being the agent that causes them or renders them certain." To him, this foreknowledge is grounded in and conditioned by the choices themselves as foreknown.[25] William MacDonald likewise asserts that "God foresaw the actual situation with all its contingencies, interrelationships, and hidden motives of hearts."[26]

Contemporary Baptist evangelical Arminians hold that election is based on foreseen faith. Herschel Hobbs, for example, in an early work, called the doctrine of election "one of the most vital in the Bible—and one of the least understood."[27] He observed that the term "elect" appears several times in both Old and New Testaments. He affirmed God's sovereignty in the abstract and agreed with Calvinists that "the initiative in election is with God, not man." Nonetheless, he called it an error to say that "election depends merely upon God's will or good pleasure." In his view, such a conclusion would "magnif[y] some aspects of God's nature to the neglect of all others." He believed the Calvinist perspective erroneously "emphasizes God's will and power and minimizes his righteousness and love" and "ignores the human will and power of choice."[28]

In fact, Hobbs candidly stated his view that the free will of man must be put over against the sovereignty of God. "We know that divine sovereignty must not cancel human freedom, else man becomes a mere machine, incapable of fellowship with God."[29] He said: "But the free will of man is involved, for he must either accept or reject the saving overtures of a righteous and loving God. Even the sovereignty of God is limited to God's moral and spiritual laws and by the nature of the free will of man."[30] Hobbs therefore believed that the doctrine of election referred to a "plan of salvation for all men and not simply the capricious choice of some men and the rejection of others."[31] Although this seems to imply a corporate view of election, in the same section of the book in which this discussion takes place, Hobbs reverted to the foreknowledge perspective, stating: "The foreknowledge of God simply means that God knows all things before they happen. God knew beforehand who would accept or reject his overture of grace."[32]

In a later work, Hobbs quoted E.Y. Mullins to the effect that "Election is not to be thought of as a bare choice of so many human units by God's action independently of man's free choice and the human means employed. God elects men to respond freely. He elects men to preach persuasively and to witness convincingly. He elects to reach men through native faculties and through the church, through evangelism and education and missionary endeavor. We must include all these elements in election."[33] This statement is ambiguous in many respects. Calvinists, of course, believe both that the elect respond freely to the gospel and that God uses means such as evangelism, education and missionary efforts to bring about the salvation of the elect. Hobbs, however, clearly took Mullins to mean that election is based upon nothing more and nothing less than the foreknowledge of a salvation decision by individuals. He added to Mullins' statement: "Whether it be in God's offer of salvation or his call to be a propagating people, we may say yes or no to him." "The final choice lay with man. God in his sovereignty set the condition. The final choice lay with man."[34]

A current Southern Baptist leader voiced a popular version of this position when he said, "I also reject the hyper-Calvinist's [sic] view of unconditional election....God puts no condition, but there's always a condition from...our viewpoint. That condition is faith; you've got to believe." He continued: "Election is based on foreknowledge. God gave you a will and God has already known what you are going to do with it because God knows what you do with that will."

Wiley Richards quotes Wayne Ward in support of another popular Baptist articulation of this view. Ward asserts: "By his vote alone God has chosen us in Christ from before the foundation of the world (Eph. 1:4)" but "the circle of election is complete only when the individual believer puts in his vote and tips the balance against Satan and for Christ."[35] Richards does not explain how this statement avoids being nonsensical, that is, asserting two inherently contradictory propositions in the same breath.

Other Arminians adopt a view that election in Romans 9 has nothing to do with salvation, but is (1) corporate in nature, dealing solely with the election of the nation of Israel and (2) oriented to service rather than salvation. For example, one former

Southern Baptist Convention president said that Paul in that chapter "is talking about his dealing with the nation Israel. This is national, not personal. He is not talking about personal salvation here. And I defy you to show me where he mentions personal salvation, heaven or hell here; it does not...Paul is explaining the nation Israel." Another said: "Romans 9 doesn't have anything to do with the election of individuals....Romans 9, 10, 11 is about the election of Israel and not about the election of individuals. You can go on and read it; see if it is not true." These individuals may hold this view simultaneously with or separate from a foreseen faith view of foreknowledge.

The Openness of God View

As we have seen, evangelical Arminians want to hold on to God's foreknowledge and even use it affirmatively as the basis for God's election. Openness of God theologians see the irrationality of this position. Richard Rice and Clark Pinnock reject the traditional Arminian view of divine foreknowledge. Rice flatly stated that Arminius had "no coherent explanation" for God's exhaustive foreknowledge.[36] He sees the problem with traditional Arminianism's view on divine foreknowledge as being: "If human beings are really free, and their actions are not determined by God, how can he know in advance everything they are going to do?"[37] His implicit conclusion is that God cannot know in advance what humans will do if their actions are not determined by God. He concludes that this problem is insurmountable:

> The concept of absolute foreknowledge renders meaningless any notion of divine freedom and therefore of divine decision. To know exactly what you are going to decide is to have made the decision already. There is nothing left to be decided. Consequently, it makes no sense to speak of divine decisions if we attribute absolute foreknowledge to God, for he must know everything that he is ever going to decide....If God's foreknowledge is infallible, then what he sees cannot fail to happen. This means that the course of future events is fixed, however we explain what actually causes it. And if the future is inevitable, then the apparent experience of free choice is an illusion.[38]

Pinnock has similarly written with respect to his journey from Calvinism to "openness" theology:

> I found that I could not shake off the intuition that such a total omniscience would necessarily mean that everything we will ever choose in the future will have been already spelled out in the divine knowledge register, and consequently the belief that we have truly significant choices to make would seem to be mistaken. I knew the Calvinist argument that exhaustive foreknowledge was tantamount to predestination because it implies the fixity of all things from "eternity past," and I could not shake off its logical force.[39]

Thus, to Arminians who are determined to remain orthodox (by accepting God's complete omniscience and exhaustive foreknowledge), open theists pointedly observe that "exhaustive divine omniscience needs strong predestination to explain how it works."[40] Open theists agree with Calvinists: "If you start with exhaustive foreknowledge, you go straight to predestination."[41] Because he denies exhaustive foreknowledge, Pinnock, therefore, has been constrained to adopt a different view as to the basis of God's election. He, along with other open theists, believes that election is a "corporate category and not oriented to the choice of individuals for salvation."[42]

The Biblical View

Andrew Fuller made a bold claim that sovereign, unconditional election accords with the Holy Scriptures. Was he right? Ultimately, it matters not what Calvin and Hobbs (or Fuller or anyone else) thinks about predestination. The real question is: What does Paul, writing through the inspiration of the Holy Spirit, say? A good starting place is Romans 8:29.

ROMANS 8:29. This verse states: "For those God foreknew he also predestined to be conformed to the likeness of his Son, that he might be the firstborn among many brothers." This passage teaches a clear relationship between God's foreknowledge and his predestination. But what is the nature of that relationship? What is the meaning of this crucial word "foreknew" (*progi-*

nosko)?[43] Is God's predestination based on a "foreknowledge" of what will occur in the future, i.e., whether one will accept Jesus Christ as Savior, as evangelical Arminians believe? Or does "foreknowledge" refer to something else?

"Foreknowledge" in both Greek and English merely means "to know beforehand, in advance."[44] But the bare linguistic meaning does not answer the critical question of precisely what it was God knew in advance and the basis on which he knew it.

The real question is, what about believers is known beforehand? Godet and other commentators adopting the Arminian line supply the content of God's beforehand knowledge, supposing that he foresees future faith.[45] It is certainly true that God foresees faith; he foresees all that comes to pass. The problem with this solution, however, is that faith itself is something that God creates in and grants to a person. (John 3:3-8; 6:44-45, 65; Ephesians 2:8; Philippians 1:29; Hebrews 12:2; 2 Peter 1:2). Therefore, under this proposal, God would foresee something that he himself grants. This ends up being circular.

Foreseen faith certainly is not in view in Romans 8:29. The text does not state that the content of God's foreknowledge is faith. To the contrary, it says "for *those* God foreknew he also predestined to be conformed to the likeness of his Son." It is the *person* that God foreknew, not the person's future faith. The number of commentators observing this point is legion.[46]

How did God know beforehand those persons he predestined? There are several theoretical possibilities. If Paul had used the word *epistamai*, which refers to reasoned out knowledge, one could say God knew the elect rationally. If Paul had used the word *oida*, which refers to intuitive knowledge, one could say God knew the elect intuitively. But Paul used the term *proginosko*, which referred to experiential or relational knowledge. God knew the elect experientially; he knew them intimately.

Virtually all reputable commentators reach this conclusion. Dunn says *proginosko* "obviously means more than simply foreknowledge, knowledge before the event....It has in view the more Hebraic understanding of 'knowing' as involving a relationship experienced and acknowledged...hence commentators regularly and rightly refer to such passages as Gen. 18:19, Jer. 1:5, Hos. 13:5, Amos 3:2...whose influence elsewhere in the Pauline correspondence is evident."[47] Schreiner observes that the background of the term *proginosko* should be located in the Old Testament, where for God "to know" (Hebrew, *yada*) referred to his covenant love for his people. He sees the parallel terms "consecrate" and "appoint" in Jeremiah 1:5 to be noteworthy in that God did not merely "foresee" that Jeremiah would be a prophet; he lovingly chose him for the role. Similarly, in Amos 3:2, God "knew" Israel in that he set his covenant love upon only Israel.[48] Murray also states:

> Although the term "foreknow" is used seldom in the New Testament, it is altogether indefensible to ignore the meaning so frequently given to the word "know" in the usage of Scripture; "foreknow" merely adds the thought of "beforehand" to the word "know." Many times in Scripture "know" has a pregnant meaning which goes beyond that of mere cognition. It is used in a sense practically synonymous with "love," to set regard upon, to know with peculiar interest, delight, affection, and action....It means "whom he set regard upon" or "whom he knew from eternity with distinguishing affection and delight" and is virtually equivalent to "whom he foreloved."[49]

F.F. Bruce and Robert Haldane are of essentially the same view.[50] Hodge adds:

> God is represented as looking on the fallen mass of men, and fixing on some whom he predestines to salvation. This is the *proginosko*, the foreknowledge, of which the apostle here speaks. It is the knowing, fixing upon, or selecting those who are to be predestinated to be conformed to the image of the Son of God.[51]

Indeed, this is the only interpretation that makes sense when the context is kept in mind. Verses 29-30 declare that it is God who predestinates, God who calls, God who justifies, and God who glorifies. In these things, God's determinative action is at work. In this light, foreknowledge of man's faith—making salvation ultimately a product of the person's decision and not of God's independent action—is incongruous with God's determinative action as stated in the rest of the verse.[52] Accordingly, from an exegetical standpoint, it simply cannot be said that foreknowledge of future faith is the basis of God's election to salvation.

ROMANS 9:6-18. If foreknowledge of future faith is not the basis of God's election, what is? This question is answered in Romans 9:6-18:

> It is not as though God's word had failed. For not all who are descended from Israel are Israel. Nor because they are his descendants are they all Abraham's children. On the contrary, "It is through Isaac that your offspring will be reckoned." In other words, it is not the natural children who are God's children, but it is the children of the promise who are regarded as Abraham's offspring. For this was how the promise was stated: "At the appointed time I will return, and Sarah will have a son." Not only that, but Rebekah's children had one and the same father, our father Isaac. Yet, before the twins were born or had done anything good or bad—in order that God's purpose in election might stand: not by works but by him who calls—she was told, "The older will serve the younger." Just as it is written: "Jacob I loved, but Esau I hated." What then shall we say? Is God unjust? Not at all! For he says to Moses, "I will have mercy on whom I have mercy, and I will have compassion on whom I have compassion." It does not, therefore, depend on man's desire or effort, but on God's mercy. For the Scripture says to Pharaoh: "I raised you up for this very purpose, that I might display my power in you and that my name might be proclaimed in all the earth." Therefore God has mercy on whom he wants to have mercy, and he hardens whom he wants to harden.

Paul wrote Romans 9 through 11 to address the problem of Israel's unbelief. Here, Paul wrestles with the implications of the gospel for the Jews, God's chosen people of the Old Testament: Why did they not experience the salvation offered in Christ? The unbelief of Israel seemed to call God's word into question. As John Piper has observed, "ultimately, God's own trustworthiness is at stake."[53] Paul's point then is to show that God is faithful to his people and that, eventually, "all Israel will be saved" (Romans 11:26).

Paul's argument hinges in large part, however, upon one critical assumption—that "not all who are descended from Israel are Israel" (Romans 9:6). In other words, even in the Old Testament, salvation was never promised to all biological descendants of Abraham; it was always a gift of God's electing love.[54]

Paul elaborates in verses 7-12. In verse 7, he distinguishes between physical Israel and spiritual Israel: "For they are not all Israel who are descended from Israel" (NASB). In verse 8, he repeats: "It is not the children of the flesh who are children of God, but the children of the promise are regarded as descendants" (NASB). Hence, Paul is attacking the assumption that to be a child of Abraham in the physical sense automatically makes one a child of Abraham in the spiritual sense.[55] Physical Israel is not synonymous with spiritual Israel.

Paul illustrates his point with two important examples from Jewish history. First, citing Genesis 21:12, he asserts that there is a fundamental distinction between Abraham's two sons, Isaac and Ishmael. Both were physical descendants of Abraham, but only Isaac was a spiritual descendant of Abraham: "It is through Isaac that your offspring will be reckoned" (Romans 9:7; NIV). Isaac's advantage was in the spiritual realm; it was to him, not his brother, that God's covenant promises would fall.

Second, citing Genesis 25:23, Paul asserts the same distinction with respect to Isaac's sons, Jacob and Esau. Before the twins were born, God told their mother, "the older will serve the younger" (Rom. 9:12). Piper states that these words are more than a "wish or even a statement of foreknowledge," but that they "express a decision on God's part to intervene in the lives of Jacob and Esau in such a way that those words come true." They constitute an act of *predestination* rather than *prerecognition*.[56]

Here, Paul's language, a quotation of Malachi 1:2-3, is striking: "Just as it is written: 'Jacob I loved, but Esau I hated'" (Rom. 9:13). Paul is referring to individuals here, not the nations they represented. As Schreiner points out, the view that Paul refers only to the temporal destinies of the nations Jacob and Esau represented "ignores the fact that the issue in the context of Rom. 9 relates to the salvation of the Jews, and a discussion of historical destiny apart from salvation is irrelevant to the issue that called forth this discussion."[57]

Does this passage refer to double predestination? Yes, but the two decrees are not identical. God's hatred of Esau is best viewed as referring to his passive decision not to bestow his elective love on Esau.[58] This was the position taken by John Bunyan long ago—that reprobation "is a leaving or passing by, not a cursing of the creature."[59] It was also the position of John Gill. Although his commentary on this passage is somewhat convoluted, it is nonetheless worth quoting: "'Esau have I hated'; that is, had not loved him, as he had Jacob; for it cannot be understood of positive hatred, for God hates none of his creatures, as such, only as workers of iniquity; but of negative hatred, or of not loving him; which, in comparison of the love he bore to Jacob, might be called hatred."[60]

In any event, the point is that both Jacob and Esau were physical descendants of Isaac, but only Jacob was a spiritual descendant. The purpose of this second example was to silence the hypothetical objector who argued that Isaac was preferred over Ishmael simply because they had different mothers; Jacob and Esau, of course, had the same mother.[61] Indeed, Esau would ordinarily have been the preferred child since he was the first born. The choice of Jacob over Esau was thus against the grain.

Why did God choose Isaac and not Ishmael; Jacob and not Esau? Human merit certainly had nothing to do with it. Paul plainly declared in verse 11: "Yet, before the twins were born or had done anything good or bad—in order that God's purpose in election might stand: not by works but by him who calls—she was told, 'The older will serve the younger.'" God's electing decision is independent of works. "There was nothing within the persons of Jacob and Esau that could have been the basis for God's choice of the one over the other."[62]

Nor is foreseen faith the basis of election in these verses. Godet refers back to Romans 8:29 and tries to draw a distinction between foreseen works and foreseen faith.[63] Schreiner rightly comments, however, that if Paul had wanted to say that election and calling were dependent on human faith, he could have easily done so. His failure to insert human faith as the decisive and ultimate basis for God's election indicates that God's call and election are prior to and the ground of human faith.[64] And as we have seen, an exegetical examination of Romans 8:29 demonstrates that God's election is not based on either foreseen works or foreseen faith.

To the contrary, "election is based on God's mercy, and God

will have mercy on whom God will have mercy (Romans 9:15-16). It is "not by works" but simply "by him who calls" (Romans 9:12). In other words, election is by the "determinate will of God."[65] As Murray concludes, "sovereignty pure and simple is the only reason for the differentiation by which some are consigned to hardening while others equally ill-deserving are made the vessels of mercy."[66]

As an aside, an exegetical examination of Ephesians 1:11 conclusively confirms this view. In that verse Paul states: "In Him also we have obtained an inheritance, being predestined according to the purpose of Him who works all things according to the counsel of His will." John Feinberg makes this verse the centerpiece of his argument in favor of a specific sovereignty model of providence. He states that the focus of the verse is that "we have obtained an inheritance." The rest of the verse amplifies how this has happened. To show this, Feinberg breaks the verse out into its component terms, "purpose," "counsel," and "will." "Purpose" refers to the goal God intended to accomplish. Thus, our predestination to salvation was done according to a specific design or aim. This suggests "that his decision was based solely on his desires, i.e., it was unconditional." Predestination was according to a divine pattern. God deliberated about the best way to reach his goal and from that deliberative process sprang forth a plan (counsel) that he deemed best. He willed that plan and then brought it to pass. The important point is that the purpose, the deliberating, and the choosing of the plan is based on nothing other than God.[67]

But what about the belief that election is corporate, not individual, in nature, and oriented to service, not salvation? Predictably, some commentators have sought to avoid the obvious conclusion that God personally elects some individuals to salvation by his sovereign will and in accordance with his good pleasure by arguing that Paul is speaking in Romans 9 of God's election of the nations Israel and Edom as a whole, not the election of the individual Jacob (and not Esau).[68] Kasemann rightly calls this an unacceptable "softening" of Paul's argument.[69] Moo says that Paul clearly is thinking of Jacob and Esau as individuals in Romans 9:10-11 when he mentions their conception, birth and works, language that is not easily applied to nations. Moo and Schreiner also observe that Paul uses language here that he commonly uses when referring to salvation ("election" (11:5, 7); "call" (8:28), "not of works" (4:2-8; 11:6)).[70] Finally, as we have already noted, to make election corporate runs counter to the entire thrust of the argument Paul is developing as to why some Jews who belong to physical Israel do not belong to spiritual Israel.

What about the view that election is to service, not to salvation, and what Paul has in mind here is simply that God has used some individuals rather than others in the furtherance of his plan? This also makes a hash out of the passage. As Moo and Schreiner pointed out, key words in the paragraph ("children of God" (v. 8); "descendents" (vv. 7, 8); "children of promise" (v. 8); "call" (v. 7, 12), "not of works" (v. 12)) are "consistently applied by Paul" to refer to the salvation of individuals. Moreover, as we have seen, Paul's whole argument is offered as an explanation of why some Jews were being saved and others were not. The entire passage concerns salvation. To wrench an inconvenient verse here or there out of its context in order to refer to something else is simply unnatural. That this passage concerns salvation is born out by a reading of verses 24 to 29, which clearly concern salvation of individuals. There is no reason to break the flow of the entire argument, artificially assigning some of it to one purpose, temporal service, and other portions to another, salvation.

There is thus no escaping the meaning of Romans 9:6-16. At the conclusion of his analysis of this passaage, Douglas Moo writes:

> This passage gives strong exegetical support to a traditional Calvinistic interpretation of God's election: God chooses those who will be saved on the basis of his own will and not on the basis of anything—works or faith, whether foreseen or not—in those human beings so chosen." He thus concludes that "the introduction into this text of any basis for God's election outside God himself defies both the language and the logic of what Paul has written. The only logical possibility, then, would seem to be to reverse the relationship between God's choosing and faith: as Augustine stated it: 'God does not choose us because we believe, but that we may believe.'[71]

This is strong language for an erudite theologian writing a scholarly commentary! Yet, as we have seen, it is entirely borne out by sound exegesis. Thus, we may conclude that John Calvin was entirely right when he said with respect to Romans 8:29 and its use of *proginosko*:

> The foreknowledge of God, which Paul mentions, is not a bare prescience, as some unwise persons absurdly imagine, but the adoption by which he had always distinguished his children from the reprobate....It hence follows, that this knowledge is connected with God's good pleasure; for he foreknew nothing out of himself, in adopting those whom he was pleased to adopt; but only marked out those whom he had purposed to elect.[72]

Christ's Work – Actual Redemption

We now move from the beginning of time to the fullness of time. For whom did Christ die? The debate over the extent of the atonement has been especially contentious among evangelicals. And, on this issue, many who otherwise join the Calvinists switch sides.[73]

The Calvinist View

The Calvinist view of the extent of the atonement has been known by various terms. The "L" in "tulip" stands for "limited atonement." But most Calvinists prefer the term "particular redemption" or "definite atonement" over "limited atonement." John Gill said: "The doctrine of particular redemption is the doctrine of the Scriptures. Christ died not for all men, but for some only; who are called his people, his sheep, his church..."[74] John Dagg likewise declared: "The Scriptures teach that the Son of God, in coming into the world and laying down his life, had the salvation of a peculiar people in view...The Scriptures also teach that the expectation of the Redeemer will be fully realized, and that not one of all whom the Father gave him will fail to be saved.[75]

Andrew Fuller expounded the doctrine of particular redemption at length in a number of writings. His treatment of that doctrine comprises a great bulk of volume two of his three volume

Collected Works. Here is a sampling:

> Calvinists in general have considered the particularity of redemption as consisting not in the degree of Christ's suffering...or in any insufficiency that attended them, but in the sovereign purpose and design of the Father and the Son, whereby they were constituted or appointed the price of redemption, the objects of that redemption ascertained, and the ends to be answered by the whole transaction determined. They suppose the sufferings of Christ, in themselves considered, are of infinite value, sufficient to have saved all the world, and a thousand worlds, if it had pleased God to have constituted them the price of their redemption, and to have made them effectual to that end. Further, whatever difficulties there may appear in these subjects, they in general suppose that there is in the death of Christ a sufficient ground for indefinite calls and universal invitations, and that there is no mockery or insincerity in the Holy One in any of these things.
>
> These views of the subject accord with my own.[76]

Fuller thus emphatically believed that "there was a certain, absolute, and consequently limited, design in the death of Christ, securing the salvation of all those, and only those, who are finally saved."[77]

Louis Berkhof says that the appropriate question is: "Did the Father in sending Christ, and did Christ in coming into the world, to make atonement for sin, do this with the design or for the purpose of saving only the elect or all men?"[78] Dagg answers for Calvinistic Baptists: "Redemption cannot have been universal in its purpose; otherwise the purpose will fail to be accomplished, and all, for which the work of redemption was undertaken, will not be effected."[79]

Wayne Grudem argues that Berkhof misframes the debate by focusing on the purpose of the Father and the Son rather than on what actually happened in the atonement. He says the question "rightfully asked" is: "Did Christ pay for the sins of all unbelievers who will be eternally condemned, and did he pay for their sins fully and completely on the cross?"[80] Grudem answers his own question: no—Christ did not pay for the sins of unbelievers who will never come to salvation, but he "died for particular people (specifically, those who would be saved and whom he came to redeem), that he foreknew each one of them individually...and had them individually in mind in his atoning work."[81]

The Non-Calvinist View

Charles Ryrie rejects Berkhof's formulation of the question to be answered with respect to the extent of redemption. He reframes the question as follows: "Did Christ purpose by coming into the world to make provision for the salvation of all people, realizing that the Father would mysteriously draw the elect to Himself and allow others to reject the provision made?"[82] As a proponent of unlimited atonement, also known as general redemption, Ryrie answers his own question: yes—Christ "provided the payment for the sins of all people—those who accept that payment and those who do not."[83] He thus interprets the most celebrated verse ostensibly supporting unlimited atonement, 2 Peter 2:1, as meaning that "the Lord in His sacrifice paid the price of redemption for these non-elect people."[84] Robert Shank, a Baptist Arminian, adopted the same view: "An objective reconciliation has been accomplished for all mankind. Jesus 'gave himself a ransom for all'...and 'by the righteousness of Jesus the free gift came upon all men unto justification of life.'"[85]

Herschel Hobbs, another contemporary Baptist advocate of general redemption, was not willing to go this far. He said: "Because of Christ's mediatorship, the entire human race may be saved. This does not mean universal salvation. Redemption from sin is offered to all people, but it is effected only in those who receive Christ as their Savior."[86] At the same time, he believed there is no differentiation between God's love for his people and God's love for the reprobate. He said: "[t]he whole tenor of the Bible is that God loves all men equally and endeavors to save them equally."[87] The attitude of other Southern Baptist proponents of general redemption is, quite frankly, that the Bible is so clear on the issue that there is no need to argue for their position, biblically or otherwise. One prominent Southern Baptist leader undoubtedly spoke for many when he dismissed the Calvinist position with the caustic statement:

Jesus died "not just for the frozen chosen."

Terry Miethe adopts a bit more sophisticated analysis. He asserts that "the redemptive events in the life of Jesus provided a salvation so extensive and so broad as to potentially include the whole of humanity, past, present and future." He believes the Bible teaches that Christ died for all and "it means just that." In passages suggesting that "all" are saved, he repeats, all really means all. Once again for good measure: "The atonement—the suffering of Christ—of Christ is said to be on behalf of all." In passages suggesting that Christ takes away the sins of the world, not surprisingly, he asserts that "world" really means "world." "Jesus paid the price of sin for all people."[88]

The Openness of God View

Pinnock takes a different view, questioning the substitutionary nature of the atonement altogether. He recognized the difficulties involved in the traditional Arminian view. After describing the traditional unlimited atonement perspective that "Christ really took away the guilt of the sins of the race," he queried: "Is the whole race then not now justified by virtue of that fact? Has not Christ actually achieved their salvation for them?...What kind of substitution, if unlimited in scope, does not entail absolute universalism in salvation?" The problem of universalism inherent in the unlimited atonement view led Pinnock to "reduce the precision in which [he] understood the substitution to take place."[89]

The Biblical View

Once again, it does not matter what any theologian has to say on the subject of the extent of the atonement. The important question is, What does Scripture have to say? Several verses in Romans bear on the topic of the atonement.

ROMANS 5:8. Paul wrote in Romans 5:8: "But God demonstrates his own love for us in this: While we were still sinners, Christ died for us." This verse is simple yet sublime. For whom did Christ die? He died for sinners who have departed from the way of righteousness. He died for the ungodly (Rom. 5:6). He died for his enemies (Rom. 5:10). He died for *us*. What amazing love our Savior demonstrated!

Some commentators focus on the fact that "sinners" and "the ungodly," as raw categories, encompass everyone in existence, and they therefore conclude that Christ must have died in place of the elect and non-elect alike. However, this is an argument from silence. It does not inexorably follow that indiscriminate categories such as "ungodly" or "sinners" must always refer to everyone who may fit within those classes of persons.

Romans 5:8 says that "Christ died for us." The *us* for whom Christ died must refer to believers, and not to the world. This is clear from the context; verse 9 says the "us" for whom Christ died is those who "have now been justified by his blood." Hence, Schreiner rightly concludes that this verse refers to a unique love of God for his people.[90] As Moo additionally observes, there is a "basic unity" and even "identity" between the love of God as it is shown in the event of Christ's death on the cross and as it is experienced by the believer. "A cold, sober historical interpretation that indeed God 'loved the world' on the cross is of little benefit to a person until that love is experienced" as two aspects of "one great love, ultimately indivisible."[91] This verse, then, provides clear support for the view that the suffering of our Lord on the cross did not make salvation merely available, but it "accomplished atonement for sinners, in that he took the punishment we deserved."[92]

ROMANS 8:32-34. Paul echoed the point in Romans 8:32-34:

> He who did not spare his own Son, but gave him up for us all. How will he not also, along with him, graciously give us all things? Who will bring any charge against those whom God has chosen? It is God who justifies. Who is he that condemns? Christ Jesus, who died, more than that, who was raised to life, is at the right hand of God and is also interceding for us.

Here as well, the extent of "us all" in this passage is defined by the context. The "us all" of verse 32 cannot be more inclusive than the "us" of verse 31 ("What, then, shall we say in response to this? If God is for us, who can be against us?"). This is those who are foreknown, predestined, called, justified and glorified.[93] Likewise, the "us" in verse 32 cannot be more inclusive than "those whom God has chosen" in verse 33 and those on behalf of whom Christ makes intercession in verse 34. Hence, according to Murray, "the sustained identification of the persons in these terms shows that this passage offers no support to the notion of universal atonement."[94] Other passages in Paul's writings support the same conclusion. In Ephesians 5:25, Paul wrote: "Husbands, love your wives, even as Christ also loved the church, and gave himself for it."

Proponents of general redemption are quick to cite Scripture passages appearing to suggest that Christ died for "all" or "the world"—which would include those who will not be saved. Two are Romans 5:18 and Romans 14:15.

ROMANS 5:18. Romans 5:18 says: "Consequently, just as the result of one trespass was condemnation for all men, so also the result of one act of righteousness was justification that brings life for all men." Godet reads this verse to mean, not that all will be individually justified, but that "all may be so, on condition of faith."[95] Moo disagrees, stating that it is "questionable" whether Paul's language can be taken that way:

> For one thing, Paul always uses "justification" language of the status actually conferred on the individual, never of the atonement won on the cross itself....Second, it is doubtful whether Paul is describing simply an "offer" made to people through the work of Christ; certainly in the parallel in the first part of the verse, the condemnation actually embraces all people. But perhaps the biggest objection to this view is that it misses the point for which Paul is arguing in this passage. This point is that there can be an assurance of justification and life, on one side, that is just as strong and certain as the assurance of condemnation on the other. Paul wants to show, not how Christ has made *available* righteousness and life for all, but how Christ has actually secured the benefits of that righteousness for all who belong to him.[96]

Thus, Paul's point is that Christ affects those who are his just as certainly as Adam does those who are his. Every person without exception is within Adam, but only those who "receive the gift" (Romans 5:17) are in Christ. Accordingly, Romans 5:18 does not support the notion that Christ died for the non-elect.

ROMANS 14:15. What about Romans 14:15? There, Paul says:

> If your brother is distressed because of what you eat, you are no longer acting in love. Do not by your eating destroy your brother for whom Christ died.

In this verse, Paul is warning the strong believer not to use his Christian liberty to be a stumbling block to a weaker "brother for whom Christ died." It would seem that he is protecting the faith of a weaker believer. Yet, his phraseology is interesting. He warns against conduct that "destroy[s]" the weaker brother. Some say the word "destroys" here likely refers to "ultimate spiritual ruin—failure to attain final salvation."[97] For example, Moo observes that virtually every time Paul used the verb "destroy" with a personal object, he referred to spiritual ruin.[98] General redemption proponents seize upon this interpretation to say that the "brother for whom Christ died" will ultimately come to spiritual ruin and not be saved.

Murray more accurately believes the destruction mentioned here "should not be construed as eternal perdition." He says: "all sin is destructive and the sin of the weak in this instance is a serious breach of fidelity which, if not repaired, *would* lead to perdition."[99] Paul, in essence, is using "loaded language" to drive home to the strong that causing a fellow believer to stumble is a serious offense. The strong believer should "not take refuge behind the security of the believer and the final perseverance of the saints."[100] Moreover, as Hodge has incisively pointed out, "believers (the elect) are constantly spoken of as in danger of perdition. They are saved only, if they continue steadfast unto the end. If they apostatize, they perish...Saints are preserved, not in despite of apostasy, but from apostasy."[101] In the end, this verse as well cannot support the notion of general redemption.

These passages should be enough to at least cast doubt on the notion that Christ's atonement is general rather than particular. Because this is the most controversial of the "Five Points of Calvinism," however, we have marshalled additional support for the Calvinistic view in the next chapter. For now, we ask the reader to suspend judgment as we move on to the next point.

The Human Condition—Pervasive Depravity

The Calvinist Position

John Calvin wrote in *The Institutes of Christian Religion* that "the contamination of parents is transmitted to their children so that everyone, without exception, is depraved from their earliest moment."[102] It reaches every part of the soul, makes us abhorrent to God's wrath and produces in us what Scripture calls "works of the flesh." Moreover, "because we are crooked and corrupt in every part of our nature, we are rightly condemned by God, who can accept nothing but righteousness, innocence and purity."[103]

In keeping with these statements, the theology that bears Calvin's name declares that all persons are fundamentally evil and that nothing that a person does is good. This concept of "total depravity" teaches that the natural man is never able to do any good that is fundamentally pleasing to God, and in fact, he does evil all the time. As Calvin himself declared, "our nature is not only completely empty of goodness, but so full of every kind of wrong that it is always active" and "everything which is in man, from the intellect to the will, from the soul to the body, is defiled and imbued with this lust."[104] Thus, no part of a person escapes the devastation of sin. Southern Baptist Charles Mallary put it this way:

> Man, by nature, is destitute of all holy principles and desires; that there is nothing in his character which is pleasing in the sight of God; that being alienated in his heart from God, corrupt in the very foundation of action, in the temper and spirit of his mind, all the actions that he performs, even those which are in themselves excellent and lovely, are still the service of an alien and a rebel, and consequently an abomination in the sight of heaven. Every imagination of the thoughts of his heart is only evil continually.[105]

There are three common misconceptions about the doctrine of total depravity.

First, total depravity is not the same as absolute depravity.

Total depravity refers to an entire absence of holiness, not the fullest measure of sin. For this reason, perhaps a better term than "total depravity" is "pervasive depravity." Absolute depravity, in contrast, would mean that a person expresses his depravity to the fullest degree at all times. Perhaps we might think that people like Hitler, Stalin and Judas Iscariot are candidates for absolute depravity. But even these terribly evil men could have done more evil. As R.C. Sproul has noted, Hitler could have murdered his own mother.[106] Judas, the betrayer of Jesus, was sent out by the Lord to proclaim the gospel, heal the sick, and cast demons out of the oppressed. It is likely that some people were healed or delivered as a result of his "ministry." Thus, absolute depravity was not even true for Judas Iscariot. As Charles Mallary said, "The scriptural doctrine of depravity is not that every man is as bad as he possibly can be, for there may be indefinite progression in guilt—nor that one man is necessarily wicked as another—for there may be as many shades of depravity as there are sinners in the universe."[107] As Edwin Palmer illustrates, when children hurt each other, they often do it by mocking one another or calling one another names. This is wrong. But they could be worse. They could gouge out one another's eyes with scissors or drive needles under one another's fingernails. What they do is evil, but it is not as evil as it could be.[108] Thus, Calvinists affirm that humanity's depravity is pervasive but not absolute.

Second, total depravity does not teach that unregenerate man is incapable of doing any good, relatively speaking. This last qualifier is vitally important. Question 91 of the Heidelberg Catechism asks: "But what are good works?" The answer is, "those only which are done from true faith, according to the Law of God, for His glory; and not such as rest on our own opinion, or the commandments of men." Therefore, from a theological perspective, good works cannot be performed by non-believers. John Gill states:

> They must be believers in him, before they are capable of doing that which is spiritually good. And even believers themselves are not able to think a good thought or perform a good work of themselves; it is God who works in them both *to will and to do of his good pleasure.* Sometimes when they have a will to that

> which is good, yet how to perform they know not; they can do nothing without Christ, though all things through him, who strengthens them; much less then have unregenerate persons either a power or a will to that which is spiritually good.[109]

On the other hand, Calvinists affirm that non-believers can perform what humanity commonly calls "good works" in a non-theological sense apart from true faith. As Calvin stated, "in everyday speech we say that one man is good and another bad, but we must also maintain that both are depraved like everyone else."[110] Hence, a devout Moslem can donate a million dollars to a children's hospital and do relative good but from a theological perspective remain totally depraved. Similarly, an elderly gentleman who lives across the street and keeps a neat home, cuts the grass, loves his wife, gives candy to the neighborhood children, and does not swear, but who refuses to go to church or have anything to do with God, is relatively good but totally depraved.[111] "The virtues which deceive us may be acclaimed in society and daily life, but before God's judgment seat they will be useless in establishing a claim to righteousness."[112]

Third, total depravity does not mean that human nature is inherently wicked. God created man in his image. It was only after Adam introduced sin into the world that the human will became antagonistic to God. As Jonathan Edwards so cogently explained in *The Freedom of the Will*, humanity's inability to believe is a moral inability, not a natural inability. Incidentally, Edwards' explanation deeply influenced the theology of the great missionary Baptists William Carey, Andrew Fuller and John Sutcliffe.[113] Fuller revealed his reliance on Edwards when he asserted: "It is not a want of ability, but of inclination that proves his [man's] ruin."[114]

This last point gives rise to a corollary to total depravity: the doctrine of "total inability." Calvinists believe that humans are unable to free themselves from their depravity. Since the fall of man, an unsaved person is under the curse of sin, unable to love God, and wholly unable to do anything meriting salvation. Chapter 6, section 3 of the London Baptist Confession of 1689 thus declared:

> Man, by his fall into a state of sin, hath wholly lost

> all ability of will to any spiritual good accompanying salvation; so as a natural man, being altogether averse from that good, and dead in sin, is not able by his own strength to convert himself, or to prepare himself thereunto.

John L. Dagg also declared that humans lack the necessary disposition to free themselves: "By nature we love darkness rather than light, sin rather than holiness." The unbelieving mind is at enmity with God. Humans lack the power, along with the disposition, to flee the way of transgression. "If any man thinks he has the power to be holy at will, let him try it, and he will find his mistake."[115] Patrick Mell similarly said: "Calvinism teaches man's utter helplessness. Being sinners in character and conduct, none are able to renew their hearts, nor make atonement for their sins. Even after the atonement of Christ is offered in the gospel to their acceptance, none, without divine influence, are willing to accept Christ as a Savior, nor are able to understand experimentally the truth as it is in Jesus."[116]

It is important to understand, however, that in Calvinist doctrine, this moral inability to believe does not translate into a lack of responsibility to believe. Charles Mallary addressed this topic in a nineteenth century sermon on the doctrine of election. After surveying John 6:44 ("No man can come unto me, except the Father which hath sent me draw him") and John 6:65 ("no man can come unto me, except it were given unto him of my Father"), he warned:

> Do not for a moment suppose, my friend, that the inability to which the Savior refers involves in it any thing which furnishes a just excuse for rejecting him. Its real nature is explained in another declaration, 'Ye will not come unto me that ye might have life.' Nothing is more common than for men to say that they *cannot* do that which they *will not* do. The scriptures nowhere say that men cannot come to Christ, if they would; on the contrary, their language is 'whosoever will, let him take of the water freely.' The want of power is the want of will. Therefore the sinner is utterly inexcusable.[117]

Mallary reiterated this point later in his sermon: "Nothing hinders a compliance with the requisitions of the gospel but the sinner's rebellious will. That will remain inexorably. All rush madly on to the brink of death."[118]

The Arminian View

Interestingly, Jacob Arminius agreed with the Calvinists on the issue of total depravity. He wrote that man's free will "is not only wounded, maimed, infirm, bent, and weakened; but it is also imprisoned, destroyed, and lost." He continued: "The mind of man, in this state, is dark, destitute of the saving knowledge of God, and, according to the Apostle, incapable of those things which belong to the Spirit of God." And finally: "nothing can be spoken more truly concerning man in this state, than that he is altogether dead in sin. (Romans 3:10-19.)"[119] John Wesley also adopted a more or less Calvinist viewpoint of "total depravity."[120] Herschel Hobbs quoted Romans 3:23 ("for all have sinned") in support of the total depravity of man. He correctly stated: "The doctrine of the 'total depravity' of man does not mean that all are equally vicious in their sins," but it means that "all men are sinners in that they have transgressed the will of God." He added that the doctrine does not mean "that there is not some good in all men," but he failed to add the Calvinistic qualifier that this is from the human rather than divine perspective.[121] Nuances aside, Lewis Johnson was certainly correct in observing that "it is doubtful that one can find greater agreement on any doctrine in the abstract than on the doctrine of the universality of sin."[122]

Of course, consensus does not mean unanimity. Charles Finney stood outside the consensus. In *Lectures on Systematic Theology*, he claimed to have been "embarrassed" by the Calvinistic position on man's depravity:

> The doctrines of a nature, sinful *per se*, of a necessitated will, of inability, and of physical regeneration, and a physical Divine influence in regeneration, with their resulting and kindred dogmas, embarrassed and even confounded me at every step.[123]

He wrote:

> This doctrine is a stumbling block both to the church

> and to the world, infinitely dishonorable to God, and an abomination alike to God and to the human intellect, and should be banished from every pulpit and from every formula of doctrine, and from the world. It is the relic of heathen philosophy, and was foisted in among the doctrines of Christianity by Augustine, as everyone may know who will take the trouble to examine for himself.[124]

He called the doctrine of total depravity "absurd," "anti-Scriptural and nonsensical dogma," and claimed that it made the gospel "a farce."[125] Finney instead drew a distinction between "physical depravity" and "moral depravity," calling physical depravity the "physiological states of disease, decay, and degeneration" and moral depravity the existence of sin in the life of a person.[126] He thus, denied the existence of a sin nature.

Clark Pinnock likewise questions total depravity "as a possible ambush designed to cut off non-Augustinians at the pass." Yet at the same time, he confuses total depravity and absolute depravity. In his essay "From Augustine to Arminius" he asked the question: "Does the Bible generally not leave us with the impression that one can progress in sin as in holiness, and...how total one's depravity is varies from person to person and is not a constant?" He then answered his own question: "Surely 'total' depravity biblically would be the point beyond which it is not possible to go in realizing the full possibilities of sinfulness and not the actual condition of all sinners at the present time."[127] This, of course, is a definition of absolute depravity, not total depravity, and as such, it is an easy straw man for Pinnock to knock down, since Calvinists are careful to distinguish the two concepts, holding to the one, total depravity, and acknowledging that not everyone (if anyone) ever reaches the other, absolute depravity.

The relative consensus (Finney and Pinnock aside) falls apart when it comes to the Calvinistic corollary of total inability. On the one hand, Grant Osborne, an evangelical Arminian, says that "the world is indeed totally depraved and always chooses to reject Christ."[128] Herschel Hobbs likewise said that there is enough knowledge of God in the lost to walk in the will of God and be saved but "his sinful nature makes that impossible."[129] On the other, Robert Shank flatly asserted, "All theologians to the contrary notwithstanding, the Scriptures declare that, with respect to the saved and the lost, God takes fully into account the faculty of spiritual initiative and decision with which he endowed man in creation."[130] A prominent Southern Baptist leader perhaps spoke for many non-Calvinists when he said: "Man is totally depraved but he can hear God even if he is a raw pagan like Romans 1...So therefore, I reject the hyper-Calvinist's view of total depravity" [he meant total inability]. He added: "Of course the dead can hear. The dead can understand. And unsaved people can know truth."

The Biblical View

Did Paul agree?

ROMANS 3:10-18. Romans 3:10-18 reads:

> What shall we conclude then? Are we any better? Not at all! We have already made the charge that Jews and Gentiles alike are all under sin. As it is written: "There is no one righteous, not even one; there is no one who understands, no one who seeks God. All have turned away, they have together become worthless; there is no one who does good, not even one." "Their throats are open graves; their tongues practice deceit." "The poison of vipers is on their lips." "Their mouths are full of cursing and bitterness." "Their feet are swift to shed blood; ruin and misery mark their ways, and the way of peace they do not know." "There is no fear of God before their eyes."

Here, Paul is asserting that there is no difference between Jew and Gentile in respect of sin and condemnation. Jews and Gentiles "alike are all under sin" (Romans 3:9). As Murray points out, all are "under the dominion of sin."[131] Calvin adds that all "are justly condemned as sinners before God" and that all "are held under the curse which is due to sin."[132]

Paul then provides a litany of Old Testament paraphrases and quotations designed to support his point. As Calvin put it, he "now begins to reason from authority."[133]

These quotations cover the "wide range of human character and activity."[134] They provide a "unified summary of the witness of the Old Testament to the pervasive sinfulness of mankind."[135]

Verses 10 through 12 discuss "general characteristics" about human corruption.[136] Verse 10 is a paraphrase of Psalm 14:3: "there is no one who does good, not even one." Paul makes an important change, however, that refutes Finney's view that there is no sin nature, but only sinful conduct. Paul changes the Psalm from "there is no one who does good" to "there is no one who is righteous." What he means is that, as Moo puts it, "there is not a single person who, apart from God's justifying grace, can stand as 'right' before God."[137] Thus, humanity, in its nature, is corrupted. Verse 11 is a paraphrase of Psalm 14:2: "The LORD looks down from heaven on the sons of men to see if there are any who understand, any who seek God." The implication in the Psalm, which Paul makes explicit, is that there is none. Thus, humanity, in its cognition as well as its nature, is depraved. Verse 12 is a verbatim quotation of Psalm 14:3. There is no loophole here: "All have turned aside, they have together become corrupt; there is no one who does good, not even one." Thus, humanity, in its conduct, is depraved.

Verses 13 through 17 are more concrete, if no less sweeping, in their indictment. In verses 13-14, using quotations from Psalm 5:9 and Psalm 10:7, Paul condemns the organs of speech: the throat, the tongue, the lips, the mouth. In verses 15-16, using quotations from Isaiah 59:7-8, he condemns the feet, which are swift to shed blood.

In verse 18, using quotations from Psalm 36:1, Paul condemns the eyes, which do not fear God. Murray says about this verse: "To be destitute of the fear of God is to be godless, and no indictment could be more inclusive and decisive than the charge here made."[138]

The conclusion, then, is that humanity is evil "from head to toe." Our corruption is wholly extensive. There is no part of universal humanity or any human in particular that is excepted from corruption.

Some commentators, however, have challenged the thesis that Romans 3:10-18 applies to all humanity. Instead, they seek to confine Paul's condemnation to Jews by noting that the Old Testament passages quoted here distinguish between the wicked and the righteous, confining the wicked to a particular group in opposition to the righteous.[139] That is exegetically untenable. First, as Moo has pointed out, Paul is not speaking here of righteousness in a relative sense. Rather, "Paul appears to be looking at all human beings as they appear before the Lord apart from his saving grace" and in this theological sense, even Abraham and David were, in themselves, unrighteous.[140] Second, in quoting these Old Testament passages, "Paul's actual intention is probably more subtle; by citing texts that denounce the unrighteous and applying them, implicitly, to all people, including all Jews, he underscores the argument of 2:1-3:8 that, in fact, not even faithful Jews can claim to be 'righteous.'"[141] Third, Paul says in verse 9 that "all" are under sin, both Jew and Gentile, so "we can be assured that Paul intends to say that all without exception, including the Jews, are sinners and guilty before God."[142] Finally, the universality of sin is emphasized in the very next verse, Romans 3:19 ("whatever the law says, it says to those who are under the law, so that every mouth may be silenced and the whole world held accountable to God").[143]

This is only one passage, but it is sufficient to prove the point. We could add a number of others. In Romans 5:6, for example, Paul says the ungodly are "without strength." In Romans 6:16-17, he says believers were formerly slaves to sin from which they had been delivered. In 2 Timothy 2:26, Paul says unbelievers have been taken captive by the devil to do his will. In Ephesians 2:1 and Colossians 2:13, he says they are dead in trespasses and sins. In 1 Thessalonians 5:6, he says unbelievers "sleep." In Ephesians 5:14, he combines both metaphors, exhorting the lost to "awake, you who sleep, arise from the dead, and Christ will give you light." In 2 Peter 2:19, Peter says the wicked are slaves of corruption and brought into bondage. When the biblical data is examined carefully, the conclusion of Jonathan Edwards becomes inescapable: "All mankind are corrupt." "Every one is wholly and altogether corrupt; and also extremely and desperately corrupt."[144] As John Murray also concluded: "the verdict of Scripture is one of universal and total depravity."[145]

The responsibility of the biblicist is to accept the Scripture's teaching that the unbeliever is pervasively depraved and unable to come to Christ on his own. Even more so, his duty is to follow the advice that Robert Murray M'Cheyne gave to a young minister before his ordination as a missionary in 1840: "Pray for more knowledge of your own heart—of the total depravity of it, of the awful depths of corruption that are there."[146] To recur to Calvin again, to know God we must know ourselves.

The Spirit's Call—Irresistible Grace

If, as we have seen, the human condition without Christ is one of total depravity, with no one being righteous, no one being good, no one seeking God, all having turned away, where is the hope for salvation? Once again, Calvinists and Arminians have different answers.

The Calvinist View

Grace is the fountainhead of our salvation. A sweet theme it is that runs throughout the pages of Scripture. Spurgeon said the Bible speaks of the fall of man and the depravity of the human heart only in order that we may see that grace forgives sin and overcomes the depravity of our nature.[147] Grace is so sweet because it is free and it is free because it comes to those who do not seek it. The Prince of Preachers never tired of proclaiming the grace of God:

> When we sought the Lord, though we did not know it, the Lord had sought us long before. There had been a work of His Spirit upon our hearts when we did not know it. We thought that *we* said, "*I* will arise and go unto my Father." So we did; but there was another parable, if you remember, before the one that speaks of the return of the prodigal son, and that tells us of a piece of money that was lost, which could not find itself, and the house had to be swept and the candle to be lit that it might be found; we are told of a sheep that never thought of coming back, as sheep seldom do, but the shepherd had to go after it and find it and lay it upon his shoulder. Yes, in all cases when we come to God it is because God first came to us.[148]

Calvinists assert that grace is a gift from God. A necessary corollary of this is that grace is effective in those whom are of the elect. Another way of putting this is that the Holy Spirit effectively (or to use the older term, effectually) calls those ordained to eternal life so that they freely come to Christ in faith and repentance. The *Second London Baptist Confession* states in chapter 10, section 1:

> Those whom God hath predestined unto life, He is pleased in His appointed and accepted time, effectually to call, by His Word and Spirit, out of that state of sin and death in which they are by nature, to grace and salvation by Jesus Christ; enlightening their minds spiritually and savingly to understand the things of God; taking away their heart of stone, and giving unto them a heart of flesh: renewing their wills, and by His almighty power determining them to that which is good, and effectually drawing them to Jesus Christ; yet so as they come most freely, being made willing by His grace.

It continues in chapter 10, section 2:

> This effectual call is of God's free and special grace alone, not from anything at all foreseen in man, nor from any power or agency in the creature, being wholly passive therein, being dead in sins and trespasses, until being quickened and renewed by the Holy Spirit; he is thereby enabled to answer this call, and to embrace the grace offered and conveyed in it, and that by no less power than that which raised up Christ from the dead.

Calvinists thus believe that a special work of God, an effectual calling, is necessary because humanity is dead in sin and nothing short of a supernatural, lifesaving power of the Holy Spirit will ever cause a person to do what is spiritually good. B.B. Warfield observed: "If men were not dead, possibly they might be saved by something else than power. By good advice, say; by pointing out to them something, some good thing, to do, by which they might inherit eternal life. That is what the law does. And that is why the law cannot save, cannot, that is, save dead men. The law tells us what we ought to do...But grace is power. It does not instruct, it energizes; and what dead men need is energizing, such energizing as raises the dead. Only God's grace, which is almighty power, can do that."[149]

In the Calvinist scheme, salvation is wholly of the Lord, not man. Faith itself is a gift of God and the result of grace (Eph. 2:8-9). Spurgeon said:

> Grace is the first and last moving cause of salvation;

> and faith, essential as it is, is only an important part of the machinery which grace employs. We are saved "through faith," but salvation is "by grace." Sound forth those words as with the archangel's trumpet: "By grace are ye saved." What glad tidings for the undeserving![150]

Historical Baptists expressed wholehearted agreement with these precepts. For example, John Dagg wrote in his *A Manual of Theology* that the Holy Spirit effectually calls all the elect to repent and believe. He distinguished between an outward call and an inward call. In the outward call, "the gospel calls all who hear it to repent and believe." It proceeds from the Holy Spirit, who qualifies the ministers of the gospel for their work and gives them the written word to preach. Men resist and disobey this outward call of the Spirit and thus remain under condemnation. Yet along with this external, often ineffectual outward call, there is another call which is internal and effectual. This inward call always produces repentance and faith and therefore secures salvation. The outward call comes in word only. The inward call comes in word and with power.[151]

B.H. Carroll, founding president of Southwestern Baptist Seminary, said: "Every one that God chose in Christ is drawn by the Holy Spirit."[152] Can this inward call be resisted? Dagg says yes—in a sense. In the process of conversion, "the Holy Spirit is violently resisted." However, "the internal grace softens and subdues the heart, and brings it into peaceful subjection to the gospel of Christ." This internal grace which renders the outward call effectual is the grace of regeneration.[153] Gill had said the same thing a hundred years earlier:

> The things of the Spirit of God are disagreeable to a natural man: it is no wonder that the external ministry of the word and ordinances are despised, opposed, and resisted. The external call may be rejected; yea, some inward motions and convictions may be overruled, stifled, and come to nothing: nay, it will be granted, that there may be and is an opposition and resistance to the work of the Spirit of God in conversion; but then the Spirit cannot be so resisted, in the operations of his grace, as to be obliged to cease from his work, or to be overcome or hindered in it; for he acts with a

> design which cannot be frustrated, and with a power which is uncontrollable; were it otherwise, the regeneration and conversion of every one must be precarious, and where the grace of the Spirit is effectual, according to the doctrine of free-will, it would be more owing to the will of man than to the Spirit of God.[154]

Does the effectiveness of the inward call of the Holy Spirit make God the equivalent of a divine rapist, as some non-Calvinists have charged? No! Mallary said in his sermon on the doctrines of grace: "Dare we assert that [God] cannot so operate on the minds and hearts of men as effectually to incline them to that which is good, without annihilating the established laws of intellect, conscience and will? Under the operations of grace, as we have before intimated, the individual freely repents and obeys, just as freely as before he rejected the calls of mercy."[155] As he later said in doxology: "I love him because he first loved me. He turned me and I was turned. He drew me, and I ran after him; he quickened me, and I called upon his name…"[156]

The Arminian View

John Wesley had a very different viewpoint on the nature of God's grace. He believed there are three types of grace: prevenient, justifying and sanctifying grace.[157] With respect to prevenient grace (or as Wesley put it, "preventing" grace):

> Salvation begins with what is usually termed (and very properly) *preventing grace;* including the first wish to please God, the first dawn of light concerning his will, and the first slight transient conviction of having sinned against him. All these imply some tendency toward life; some degree of salvation; the beginning of a deliverance from a blind, unfeeling heart, quite insensible of God and the things of God.[158]

To Wesley, prevenient grace is a gift of God. "Every man has a greater or lesser measure" of it.[159] It is given universally.

With respect to justifying grace, Wesley believed this grace could be resisted. According to Rakestraw:

> Wesley writes, "You can do something, through Christ strengthening you. Stir up the spark of grace which is now in you, and he will give you more grace." You must be "workers together with him—otherwise he will cease working." Wesley, because of his insistence on the universality of prevenient grace, is forced to ascribe to the sinner, operating under the influence of that grace, some element of active responsiveness. Before even faith can be bestowed there must be the "first wish to please God," which is possible because of prevenient grace. By actively responding to grace in this way (which response includes repentance and works meet for repentance when there is opportunity) one is brought to desire faith and to seek fervently to be justified.[160]

Thus, for Wesley, "even though one cannot in any sense save oneself by good works or by any inherent goodness, that one is ultimately the determining factor in the decision of his or her justification. Faith is offered as God's free gift, but the sinner must then actively respond to that offer and reach out with the arms of true repentance to receive the gift."[161] To Wesley, salvation ultimately is up to man, not God.

A current Southern Baptist leader said of the Calvinistic view of irresistible grace: "I don't find any verse in the Bible that speaks of that. I thoroughly believe that any man or woman who resists coming to Christ can do that and so I don't buy irresistible grace for a moment." Fritz Guy, a modern Arminian, likewise states that "grace is never, strictly speaking, 'irresistible.'" To him, "grace is the offer of a gift, not the imposition of another's will; and it is in the nature of a gift that it can be rejected."[162] One former president of the Southern Baptist Convention expressed his agreement with this sentiment in more provocative language. He said about the Calvinist position: "You're going to get saved no matter what if you are elect. God's going to get you; God's going to zap you, that you can't resist the Holy Spirit of God." He repeated: "If God is going to save you, there's nothing you can do about it. I mean his Holy Spirit is going to zap you and you are gone…And so if you are one of the elect, you are going to be saved; there's nothing you can do about it. And if you are not one of the elect, there's nothing you could do about that either." He then equated God to a young man who takes a liking to a girl who does not reciprocate his affection. Upon being spurned, he ominously tells her: "I'm going to make you love me." This leader then commented: "Now friend, coerced love is a contradiction in terms. There is no such thing as forced love...That's not love at all. You become a robot."

This same Southern Baptist leader also rejected the notion of a special call that draws the elect to salvation. He apparently accepts only a general call to every person, conflating Jesus' reference to the drawing power of the Holy Spirit in John 6 with a general gospel invitation: "How many does he draw? Just the elect? John 1, verse 9: Christ is that light that lighteth every man that cometh into the world. He's the light that lights every person."

The Openness View

Pinnock comments on Wesley's view that the adoption of prevenient grace "allowed him to retain his belief in total depravity and still avoid the Calvinistic consequences in terms of particularist election and limited grace." Yet he candidly acknowledged "that the Bible has no developed doctrine of universal prevenient grace, however convenient it would be for us if it did."[163] The only way around the problem for Pinnock was to reject the notion of total depravity.

The Biblical View

Would Paul agree with Wesley?

ROMANS 8:28-30: This beloved passage states:

> And we know that in all things God works for the good of those who love him, who have been called according to his purpose. For those God foreknew he also predestined to be conformed to the likeness of his Son, that he might be the firstborn among many brothers. And those he predestined, he also called; those he called, he also justified; those he justified, he also glorified.

This passage first makes evident that believers have been "called" according to God's purpose. Wesley sought to sever the links of this "golden chain" of salvation. He asserted that "many are called who never are justified."[164] However, this is not sound exegesis. The "calling" (*kletos*) mentioned by Paul must be seen as effectual. Haldane has noted that "calling" is "solely the effect of grace; for when it is said to be a calling according to God's purpose, it is distinguished from a calling according to works."[165] Indeed, Schreiner's comment on this point is worth quoting in full:

> It is not merely an invitation that human beings can reject, but it is a summons that overcomes human resistance and effectually persuades them to say yes to God. This definition of "calling" is evident from Rom. 8:30, for there Paul says that "those whom he called (...*ekalesen*) he also justified." The text does not say that "some" of those called were justified. It fuses the called and justified together so that those who have experienced calling have also inevitably received the blessing of justification. Now if all those who are called are also justified, then calling must be effectual and must create faith, for "all" those who are called are justified and justification cannot occur without faith (3:21-22, 28; 5:1)...The foundational reason why all things work for believers' good begins to emerge: God's unstoppable purpose in calling believers to salvation cannot be frustrated, and thus he employs all things to bring about the plan he had from the beginning in the lives of believers.[166]

Murray likewise points out that there is an "unbreakable bond" between the actions mentioned here.[167] All who are foreknown are predestined. All who are predestined are called. All who are called are justified. All who are justified are glorified. Thus, "it is made abundantly clear that there cannot be one element without the others and that the three elements which are temporal [calling, justification and glorification] flow by way of consequence from the eternal counsel, particularly from predestination."[168]

F. F. Bruce similarly states: "They are 'called,' not in the general sense in which 'many are called, but few are chosen,' but in the sense of that 'effectual calling' which is the work of God's Spirit, whereby, convincing us of our sin and misery, enlightening our minds in the knowledge of Christ, and renewing our wills, he doth persuade and enable us to embrace Jesus Christ, freely offered to us in the gospel."[169]

Godet equivocates on the point, conjoining the outward call of the Holy Spirit in the preaching of the gospel and the inward drawing by the Spirit. He can thus say (incorrectly) that "Paul does not mean that God addresses this call only to those whom He has predestined to glory."[170] Yet this is precisely what Paul means. As Hodge, Moo, Murray and others have observed, Paul always uses the verb *kaleo* and the noun *kletoi* as referring to "God's effective summons by which people are brought into relationship with himself."[171] (Cf. Rom. 1:1, 6-7).

Therefore, calling, justification and glorification are all "set forth as acts of God."[172] God called. God justified. God glorified. In this context, it makes as much sense to speak of resisting God's calling as it does to speak of resisting God's justification or his glorification. The very idea is unthinkable! Hence, Romans 8:29-30 remains an unbroken "golden chain" of salvation.

What about free will? Arminians object that the notion of irresistible grace vitiates man's free will.[173] Calvinists, however, affirm that God opens the will in the act of regeneration and makes it truly free to voluntarily come to Christ. Grudem says:

> It is important that we not give the impression that people will be saved by the power of this call apart from their own willing response to the gospel...Although it is true that effective calling awakens and brings forth a response from us, we must always insist that this response still has to be a voluntary, willing response in which the individual person puts his or her trust in Christ.[174]

We will say more about the will in a subsequent chapter.

Preservation of the Saints—Kept By God's Hand

Can Christians lose their salvation? Not surprisingly, here as well, Calvinists and Arminians reach differing conclusions to this all-important question.

The Calvinist View

Calvinists have a two-fold emphasis when it comes to the doctrine of the eternal security of the believer.

The first emphasis is on the notion of *preservation*. Calvinists thus affirm that God's grace is the ultimate basis of the believer's security. Lewis Sperry Chafer, for example, says that "no individual once the recipient of the saving grace of God will ever fall totally and finally from that estate, but that he shall be 'kept by the power of God through faith unto salvation' (1 Peter 1:5)."[175] This doctrine flows directly from the other four points of Calvinism. For if God unconditionally elects certain persons to salvation, if Jesus atoned for the sins of the elect on the cross, if the Spirit effectually calls the elect to salvation and opens their hearts through regeneration to make them willing to come to Christ, then the same Father, Son and Spirit that did the saving will keep the elect preserved in his grace until the believer reaches glory.

In addition, the eternal security of the believer rests on the character of the one doing the saving. As Calvin said, "when we are his, we are saved forever."[176] Spurgeon likewise said: "Where the grace of God begins—effectually begins and the heart of the man is really changed, the work which has been begun will be completed. There will be much opposition to that completion from the flesh and from temptations from without and from Satan; but he that began to build is not a vain builder who cannot finish...The only grace worth having is the grace which, when it takes hold of us, never lets us go, but lands us safely in glory."[177]

The preservation of the saints further rests on the character of the life bestowed on the believer. It is eternal life. If that is to have any meaning at all, it means it cannot end. As Spurgeon so cogently argued:

> None of you can form an idea of eternity which can grasp all its length of endurance. Only this, you know it has no end, and cannot therefore close. If anybody said that he had eternal life and lost it, he would be flatly contradicting himself...If the life that Christ

> gives us, when we are born again, can die, it is not "eternal" life, or else words have ceased to have any meaning at all.[178]

The second emphasis is on the concept of *perseverance*. Calvin wrote:

> Persevering in God's grace requires, on the human side, "severe and arduous effort." From our human perspective the Christian's circumstances are very uncertain, and the believer at times can feel that his life "hangs only by a thread, and is encompassed by a thousand deaths." The believer needs to continually feed his soul on the preaching of the Word and to grow in faith throughout the whole course of life. Since it is easy for the believer to fall away for a time from the grace of God, there is constant need for "striving and vigilance, if we would persevere in the grace of God."[179]

John Dagg likewise declared:

> They who understand the doctrine of perseverance to imply that God's people will obtain the crown without the struggle, totally mistake the matter. The doctrine is that God's people will persevere in the struggle; and to suppose that they will obtain the crown without doing so is to contradict the doctrine. It is a wretched and fatal perversion of the doctrine, if men conclude that, having been once converted, they will be saved, whatever may be the course of life...
>
> The doctrine of final perseverance, properly understood, gives no encouragement to sluggishness or negligence in duty; much less does it lead to licentiousness. He who takes occasion from it to sin against God, or to be indolent in his service, not only misunderstands and misapplies the doctrine, but has reason to fear that his heart is not right before God. Perseverance in holiness is the only infallible proof that the heart is right; and he who ceases to persevere, on the presumption that his heart is right, believes without the proper evidence, and is woefully hazarding his eternal interests on his presumption. The doctrine is, that grace in the heart

> will produce perseverance to the end; and where the effect is not produced, the cause does not exist.[180]

This second emphasis on perseverance keeps Calvinists from falling into the antinomian trap of teaching that one can be saved and live like the devil for the rest of one's life. Schreiner and Caneday observe that some "radicalize eternal security by insisting that security in Jesus Christ guarantees that even those who fail to persevere in faithfulness to Christ and his gospel will never perish but are saved and will remain saved forever."[181]

Wayne Grudem's definition of "perseverance" incorporates both of these emphases. He says perseverance means that "all those who are truly born again will be kept by God's power and will persevere as Christians until the end of their lives, and that only those who persevere until the end have been truly born again."[182] According to Grudem: (1) all who are truly born again will persevere to the end; (2) only those who persevere to the end have been truly born again; and (3) those who fall away may give many external signs of conversion.[183]

Calvinists adopt differing perspectives on the so-called "warning" passages of Scripture. On the one hand, John Calvin, John Owen and Wayne Grudem, for example, argue that those who fall away were never saved.[184] In a recent ground-breaking work, Thomas Schreiner and Ardel Caneday offer a different view. They assert that the "warning" passages "are a crucial means God uses to protect his people for 'the salvation that is ready to be revealed in the last time.'"[185] In their view, "the warnings serve the promises, for the warnings urge belief and confidence in God's promises. Biblical warnings and admonitions are the means God uses to save and preserve his people to the end."[186]

The Arminian View

Whatever else can be said of Arminius, he did not wholly reject the notion of perseverance. As the Remonstrants' articles quoted in Chapter Two demonstrate, Arminius and his early followers expressed doubt about the perseverance doctrine, but they were not willing to utterly renounce it.[187]

Wesley, on the other hand, did reject the notion of perseverance.

He wrote: "I find no general promise in holy writ, 'that none who once believes shall finally fall.'"[188] Based on his reading of Hebrews 6:4, 6; 10:26-29; 2 Peter 2:20-21, and other warning passages, Wesley was persuaded that a true believer can make a shipwreck of his faith and perish everlastingly.[189] New Testament scholar Howard Marshall is of the same view.[190]

Most non-Calvinistic Baptists accept a version of God's preservation of the saints even if they do not emphasize the flip-side notion of perseverance. From this comes the slogan "once saved, always saved." In recent years, in at least some Baptist circles, this has mutated into the erroneous belief that someone can "walk an aisle" and make a decision for Christ, then fall away from fellowship with Christ and his church, but yet be saved because "once saved, always saved." One Southern Baptist leader mockingly (and erroneously) described the Calvinist perspective on perseverance this way: "If you claim to be a saint and at the end of your life have a spiritual blow-out, you're going to hell because you did not persevere."

However, at least two prominent Baptists, Dale Moody and Robert Shank, have defended the Arminian view that a Christian can lose his salvation. Shank said, "It is the testimony of our Savior and the New Testament writers that an initial reception of the word of the Gospel must be followed by faithful retention, if men are to continue in the saving grace of Christ and the eternal life of God."[191] Hence, "it is indeed possible for us to forfeit eternal life by failing to abide in Him 'who is our life.'"[192] "If we fail to abide in Him, the eternal life continues; but our participation in that life ceases."[193]

The Biblical View

What did Paul have to say? In fact, the eighth chapter of Romans contains two passages that argue emphatically in favor of the eternal security of the believer. The first is founded on the decree or purpose of God (Romans 8:29-30), and the second is based on the love of God (Romans 8:31-39).

Let's return one final time to the "golden chain" of salvation, Romans 8:29-30: "For whom He foreknew, He also predestined to become conformed to the image of His Son, that He might be the first-born among many brethren; and whom He predestined, these He also called; and whom He called, these He also justified; and whom He justified, these He also glorified."

Glorification belongs to the future. Yet the aorist tense is used here. This signifies "the certainty that what God has begun he will finish."[194] No one will drop out in the process. As Moo has said, "Paul is looking at the believer's glorification from the standpoint of God, who has already decreed that it should take place."[195] Hodge has likewise commented: "Paul is speaking of that God, who sees the end from the beginning, and in whose decree and purpose all future events are comprehended and fixed; so that in predestining us, he at the same time, in effect, called, justified, and glorified us, as all these were included in his purpose."[196]

The bond is insoluble. Just as all who are called are justified, all who are justified are glorified. God loses none of those whom he foreknows (i.e., fore-loves), predestines, calls and justifies.

In the next verse, Paul draws a conclusion from the decrees of God of which he has just been speaking. "If God is for us, who can be against us?" (Romans 8:31). No answer need be given. One might respond—If God is for us, who cares who is against us? In verse 35, Paul asks another question: "Who shall separate us from the love of Christ?" He responds with a litany of possibilities: trouble, hardship, persecution, famine, nakedness, danger, or sword. He could have easily included pain, misery, and loss. But as he surveys the possibilities, his answer is unmistakable. None of these things shall separate us from the love of Christ, for "we are more than conquerors through Him who loved us"! (Romans 8:37).

In the next two verses, Romans 8:38-39, Paul drives home his point, and in so doing, he soars to unreached rhetorical heights:

> For I am convinced that neither death, nor life, nor angels, nor principalities, nor things present, nor things to come, nor powers, nor height, nor depth, nor any other created thing, shall be able to separate us from the love of God, which is in Christ Jesus our Lord.

There is a decided poetic cast to this passage. With the exception to the reference to "powers" in verse 38, the items mentioned in verses 38-39 are in pairs. Neither death nor life shall separate believers from the love of God. Neither angels nor rulers. Neither present things nor future things. Neither height nor depth. Paul then throws in "any created thing," lest someone suggest that he has omitted something that could threaten the believer's security. Paul's point, of course, is that *nothing* in creation can separate a believer from the love of God.

In his commentary on Romans, B.H. Carroll recalled hearing a sermon by nineteenth century Landmark Baptist J.R. Graves emphasizing this subject. He said Graves pointed out that the Christian's life is sealed with the impression of the Holy Spirit until the day of redemption. Graves then thundered:

> Who can pluck that life out of the hands of God? If hell should open her yawning mouth and all of the demons of the pit should issue forth like huge vampires darkening water and land, could they break that seal of God? Could they soar to the heights of heaven? Could they scale its battlements? Could they beat back the angels that guard its walls? Could they penetrate into the presence of the Holy One on his eternal throne, and reach out their demon-claws and pluck our life from the bosom of God where it is hid with Christ in God?[197]

Carroll added: "The pages of religious persecution are very bloody; rack, thumbscrews and fagot, have been employed. Confiscation of property, expatriation from country, and hounding pursuit of the exile in foreign lands, exposedness to famine and nakedness and sword and other perils, and yet never has this persecution been able to effect a separation of the believer from his Lord. Roman emperors tried it, Julian the apostate tried it, Ferdinand and Isabella, Charles V, their son, and Philip II, his son, all tried it in their time. The inquisition held its secret court; war, conflagration, and famine wrought their ruin, but the truth prevailed."[198]

Some have argued, however, that, even though nothing in creation can separate believers from the love of God, people themselves can choose to depart from the faith and thereby fall outside the scope of the saving love of Christ.[199] Schreiner ably rebuts this interpretation. First, Romans 8:28-30 constitutes an "unbreakable process" so that all who are foreknown end up being glorified. "The category of the justified is inseparable from the category of the glorified."[201] Second, the interpretation that believers may forsake their salvation is subversive of the text. The very point of this text is to rule out the possibility that believers could lose their salvation. Affliction, persecution, death and so on are mentioned because "these are the sort of things that would cause a believer to renounce faith in Christ." None of these threats will succeed because the love of Christ is stronger than all of them and "he will see to it that what has been started will be finished."[202]

In light of the amazing nature of God's preserving grace, Hodge's closing doxology on this passage is worth repeating:

> How wonderful, how glorious, how secure is the gospel! Those who are in Christ Jesus are as secure as the love of God, the merit, power, and intercession of Christ can make them. They are hedged around with mercy. They are enclosed in the arms of everlasting love. "Now unto Him that is able to keep us from falling, and to present us faultless before the presence of his glory with exceeding joy; to the only wise God our Savior, be glory and majesty, dominion and power, both now and for ever. Amen!"[203]

In this chapter, we have dealt with various asserted objections to the doctrines of grace and found them wanting. In the end, we conclude that Calvinism is nothing more than true biblical doctrine. To quote B.B. Warfield:

> There is no true religion in the world...which is not Calvinistic—Calvinistic in its essence, Calvinistic in its implications. When these implications are soundly drawn out and stated, and the essence thus comes to its rights, we obtain just Calvinism...This is why those who have caught a glimpse of these things love with passion what men call "Calvinism"....It is not merely the hope of true religion in the world: it is true religion in the world—so far as true religion is in the world at all.[204]

In other words, Calvinism is nothing more and nothing less than "religion in its purity."[205] The title of this chapter asks the question: Was Paul a Calvinist? Our answer is, no, he was not. Instead, we say, Calvin and those who follow his theology of grace are Paulists and biblicists.

Chapter 4

An Excursis On The Atonement Particular or General?

In this chapter, we expand on our discussion of particular redemption. As noted in Chapter Three, the Calvinist position on that topic is not the most debated in Southern Baptist circles; it is instead the most ridiculed. We propose addressing the topic more biblically. As we saw in Chapter Three, a number of passages within the Pauline corpus, particularly in Romans, support the notion that Christ died for the elect in a special way. There are also, of course, a number of passages outside the Pauline corpus that speak to this fact. Matthew 1:21: "And she will bring forth a Son, and you shall call His name Jesus, for He will save *His people* from their sins." Matthew 20:28: "just as the Son of Man did not come to be served, but to serve, and to give His life a ransom *for many*." Matthew 26:28: "For this is My blood of the new covenant, which is shed *for many* for the remission of sins." Acts 20:28: "Therefore take heed to yourselves and to all the flock, among which the Holy Spirit has made you overseers, to shepherd *the church of God* which He purchased with His own blood."

Additionally, there are a number of verses in John's Gospel in which Christ, during his earthly ministry, spoke of a particular group of people whom the Father has given to him. In John 6:37-39 he declared: "All that the Father gives Me will come to Me, and the one who comes to Me I will by no means cast out. For I have come down from heaven, not to do My own will, but the will of Him who sent Me. This is the will of the Father who sent Me, that of all He has given Me I should lose nothing, but should raise it up at the last day." In John 10:11 Jesus said: "I am the good shepherd. The good shepherd gives His life for the sheep." In John 10:15 he said: "As the Father knows Me, even so I know the Father; and I lay down My life for the sheep." He also said in John 17:9 "I pray for them. I do not pray for the world but for those whom You have given Me, for they are Yours." Our Lord was very plain on this subject in John 10:26: "You do not believe because you are not of My sheep."

Yet there are some verses that, at face value, seem to suggest that Christ died in some sense for all humanity. John 1:29: "The next day John saw Jesus coming toward him, and said, "'Behold! The Lamb of God who takes away the sin of the world!'" John 6:51: "I am the living bread which came down from heaven. If anyone eats of this bread, he will live forever; and the bread that I shall give is My flesh, which I shall give for the life of the world." 1 Timothy 2:5-6: "For there is one God and one Mediator between God and men, the Man Christ Jesus, who gave Himself a ransom for all, to be testified in due time." 1 John 2:2: "And He Himself is the propitiation for our sins, and not for ours only but also for the whole world."

How do we make sense of this? Everyone committed to the inspiration and inerrancy of Scripture must wrestle with and attempt to make sense out of these seemingly discordant streams of authority. Is there a way out of the conundrum? We believe there is. The question "For whom did Christ die" relates to the extent of the atonement. But questions regarding the *extent* of the atonement cannot fully be answered without first understanding the *nature* of the atonement.

The Nature of Redemption As Determining the Scope of Redemption

The English term "atonement" comes from two other English words "at" and "one-ment." As these words suggest, the atonement refers to the reconciliation that Christ obtained for believers at the cross. The older term for the transaction of the cross is "satisfaction."[1] In these two terms we see a nutshell description of what Christ did when he was one the cross. He satisfied the justice of God by becoming a propitiation, appeasing God's wrath toward sinners by having it redirected to him instead. In addition, he reconciled lost sinners to God, removing their guilt and obtaining for them the forgiveness of sins. Both of these things are foreshadowed in the Old Testament sacrificial system by the scapegoat and the sacrificial lamb.

More specifically, there are essentially five things that Christ did when he was on the cross. The first four of them show how Christ's death met the four needs that we have as sinners. We deserve to die as the penalty for sin. We deserve to bear God's wrath against sin. We are separated from God by our sins. We are in bondage to sin and to the kingdom of Satan.[2]

These needs are met by Christ's death in the following ways:

He was a *SACRIFICE*. The Old Testament sacrifices were expiatory. They had reference to sin and guilt. The sacrifice was the divinely instituted provision whereby sin might be covered and the liability to divine wrath and curse removed. The Old Testament worshipper brought a lamb to the altar. He laid his hands on the animal, symbolically transferring his guilt and liability to the offering. The lamb, the offering, then suffered the death penalty on behalf of the offerer. The Old Testament offering, of course, was but a shadow of the work of Christ. As the Lamb of God, Jesus' sacrifice was fully expiatory. In offering himself, he removed our guilt and purged away our sin. He was the great sacrifice, offered without spot to God. To him were transferred the sins of his people (Hebrews 9:6-15; 13:10-13). "He has appeared once for all at the end of the age to put away sin by the sacrifice of himself" (Hebrews 9:26).

He was a *PROPITIATION*. Propitiation (*hilasterion*) means to placate or appease God's anger.[3] There are four primary references to propitiation in the New Testament: Romans 3:25; Hebrews 2:17; 1 John 2:2; and 1 John 4:10. Romans 3:25 says that "God displayed [Christ] publicly as a propitiation in His blood through faith" (NASB). An appeasement of anger, of course, presupposes that the wrath and displeasure of God rests upon humans in the first place. Paul declared: "The wrath of God is revealed from heaven against all ungodliness and unrighteousness of men who hold the truth in unrighteousness" (Romans 1:18). Yet on the cross, Christ propitiated or appeased the wrath of God toward his people. Those to whom Christ is a propitiation is revealed "through faith." Moreover, propitiation is grounded in love. 1 John 4:10 says: "In this is love, not that we loved God, but that he loved us and sent his son to be the propitiation for our sins."

Humans, of course, cannot placate God's anger toward sin and the sinner. But God in his undeserved love has done for us what we could never do by ourselves. He gave his own Son to die in our place and appease God's wrath. Therefore, we who are justified by faith have peace with God (Romans 5:1). Believers are "saved from wrath" (Romans 5:9; see also 1 Thessalonians 1:10; 5:9).[4]

Yet God's wrath unquestionably remains on the ungodly (Romans 1:18; also Romans 12:19; John 3:36; Ephesians 2:3). They are "storing up wrath against [themselves] for the day of God's wrath" (Romans 2:5; also 2:8). Thus, there is a Scriptural dichotomy between believers, for whom Christ is a propitiation, and for whom God's wrath is removed, and unbelievers, who are still under the wrath of God because of their sin. This Scriptural dichotomy is destroyed by the idea that Christ's death assuaged the wrath of God with respect to the non-elect unbeliever.

He was our *REDEMPTION*. In Romans 3:24-25, Paul declares that believers are "justified as a gift by His grace through the redemption which is in Christ Jesus" (NASB). The idea of redemption here involves far more than the general notion of deliverance.[5] The word "redemption" is a commercial term borrowed from the marketplace. The language of the NT refers not generally to a "deliverance" but specifically to a commercial transaction of purchase, more specifically, ransom. "For the Son of Man also came not to be served but to serve and to give his life as a ransom for many" (Mark 10:45). Ransom is the securing of a release by the payment of a price. (The ransom, of course, was not paid to the devil, but to God.) We were in bondage to the curse of the law, but "Christ hath redeemed us from the curse of the law, being made a curse for us." (Galatians 3:13).

Redemption is release from the guilt of sin and the power of sin. In the Old Testament, redemption was used of slaves who were purchased in order to be set free; they were "redeemed."[6] It has reference to a "price-paying method of release."[7] John Murray notes that redemption is directed to the bondage to which our sin has consigned us—a bondage which is multiform. Christ redeemed his people from the curse of the law (Galatians 3:13). He redeemed his people from sin, both its guilt and its power.[8] "All who believe" were once slaves to sin and utterly unable to liberate ourselves. "But Jesus Christ 'redeemed' us, bought us out of captivity, shedding his blood as the ransom price."[9]

Did Jesus redeem un-elect unbelievers out of slavery through the shedding of his blood? God's Word suggests not. It is believers whom the Father has delivered "from the dominion of darkness" and brought "into the kingdom of the Son he loves" in whom we have "redemption" and "the forgiveness of sins" (Colossians 1:13-14). It is believers who have been "set free from sin and have become slaves to righteousness" (Romans 6:18). It is believers who "are no longer a slave, but a son" (Galatians 4:7).

General redemption proponents often respond that Christ actually redeemed those who will never be saved but that they are responsible for appropriating that redemption that has already been accomplished for them.[10] In other words, unbelievers who have not appropriated their redemption *and who never will* nonetheless remain redeemable. The problem with this is that it is a subtle but impermissible change in the meaning of redemption. Scripture speaks of redemption as an actuality, not a potentiality. As Ephesians 1:7-8 says: "In him we have redemption through his blood, the forgiveness of sins, in accordance with the riches of God's grace." 1 Peter 1:18-19 says: "For you know that it was not with perishable things such as silver or gold that you were redeemed from the empty way of life handed down to you from your forefathers, but with the precious blood of Christ, a lamb without blemish or defect."

Hence, John Murray says:

> What does redemption mean? It does not mean redeemability, that we are placed in a redeemable position. It means that Christ purchased and procured redemption. This is the triumphant note of the New Testament whenever it plays on the redemptive chord. Christ redeemed us to God by his blood (Rev. 5:9). He obtained eternal redemption (Heb. 9:12). "He gave himself for us in order that he might redeem us from all iniquity and purify to himself a people for his own possession, zealous of good works" (Tit. 2:14). It is to beggar the concept of redemption as an effective securement of release by price and by power to construe it as anything less than the effectual accomplishment which secures the salvation of those who are its objects. Christ did not come to put men in a redeemable position but to redeem to himself a people.[11]

A.A. Hodge added:

> Christ did not die simply to make the salvation of those for whom he died possible—i.e., to remove legal obstructions to their salvation—but that he died with the design and effect of actually securing their salvation and of endowing them gratuitously with an inalienable title to heaven.[12]

He was our *RECONCILIATION*. Romans 5:10-11 states: "For if, when we were God's enemies, we were reconciled to him through the death of his Son, how much more, having been reconciled, shall we be saved through his life! Not only is this so, but we also rejoice in God through our Lord Jesus Christ, through whom we have now received reconciliation." This passage, and others like it, set up a clear dichotomy between those who are believers and those who are not. For example, Colossians 1:21-22 states: "Once you were alienated from God and were enemies in your minds because of your evil behavior. But now he has reconciled you by Christ's physical body through death to present you holy in his sight, without blemish and free from accusation." God "through Christ reconciled us to himself" (2 Corinthians 5:18).

The unbeliever is alienated from God. But it is more important that God is alienated from the unbeliever. Although we often focus on and think about our alienation from God, it is more so the case that, through sin, God was alienated from us (Matthew 5:23-24). He has a holy enmity toward those who are not believers. In reconciliation, we are restored to God.

Again, general redemption proponents, to be consistent, have to assert that Christ, in his death, actually reconciled all to God—even un-elect unbelievers, who will never become believers but will reject the God they know with their very last breath. This is profoundly unscriptural. Unbelievers are "by nature children of wrath" (Ephesians 2:3). After reviewing the pertinent passages, Morris plainly says: "There is no disputing the fact that Scripture regards man as constituting himself God's enemy by the fact of his sin."[13] Therefore, it will not do to speak of the non-elect unbeliever as being, in fact, reconciled to God. Nor, once again, will it solve the problem to speak of reconciliation as a possibility rather than an actuality. As Morris has cogently stated: "The New Testament view is that reconciliation was wrought on the cross before there was anything in man's heart to correspond."[14]

In all these things, Christ was our *SUBSTITUTE.* Closely related to the concept of propitiation is the idea of substitution. Christ's death was vicarious. This is sometimes called "vicarious atonement." A "vicar" is someone who stands in the place of another or who represents another. Christ is a "vicar" because he died for the sins of others. Indeed, as Romans 5:8 says: "Christ died for us." Romans 8:32 similarly says God "did not spare his own Son, but delivered him up for us all." The word "for" (*huper*) in these two verses means "on behalf of" or "in the place of."[15] Christ died "in the place of" believers. Spurgeon so eloquently put it this way:

> Christ was an offering for sin, in the sense of a substitute. God longed to save; but, if such a word may be allowed, Justice tied his hands. "I must be just," said God; "that is a necessity of my nature....But then my heart desires to forgive—to pass by Man's transgressions and pardon them. How can it be done?" Wisdom stepped in, and said, "It shall be done thus:" and Love agreed with Wisdom. "Christ Jesus, the Son of God, shall stand *in man's place*, and he shall be offered upon Mount Calvary *instead of man*....Although [God] did not give Christ to drink the actual hells of believers, yet he gave him a *quid pro quo*—something that was equivalent thereunto. He took the cup of Christ's agony, and he put in there, suffering, misery, and anguish, such as only God can imagine or dream of, that was the exact equivalent for all the suffering, all the woe, and all the eternal tortures of every one that shall at last stand in heaven, bought with the blood of Christ. And you say, "Did Christ drink it all to its dregs?" Did he suffer it all? Yes, my brethren, he took the cup, and at one triumphant draught of love, He drank damnation dry."[16]

The question again begs to be asked, however: If Christ died "in the place of" non-elect unbelievers, how can God demand double payment from them? Did Christ "drink damnation dry" for those who receive damnation? As Wayne Grudem elaborated:

> If Christ's death actually paid for the sins of every

> person who ever lived, then there is no penalty left for anyone to pay, and it necessarily follows that all people will be saved, without exception. For God could not condemn to eternal punishment anyone whose sins are already paid for: that would be demanding double payment, and it would therefore be unjust.[17]

No, God did not drink damnation dry for the damned. "People who are eternally condemned to hell suffer the penalty for all of their own sins, and therefore their penalty could not have been fully taken by Christ."[18]

As a general redemptionist, Daniel Akin attempts to deal with the problem of how sins get punished twice if Jesus actually died for all sins and yet unbelievers go to hell for their sins. He offers the following answer: "The rejection of Jesus' propitiation brings one's sins back upon oneself."[19] He cites, however, no biblical support for this novel notion that sins already atoned for rebound from Christ to the person for whom they were atoned. It is, in fact, antithetical to the entire trajectory of Scripture. A cardinal principle of biblical Christianity is that if God punished Christ for your sins, he will never punish you. If Christ died for your sins and paid your sin debt, you are free indeed, your debt discharged by the precious blood of the Savior! This wonderful truth cannot be jettisoned to save the idea of an indefinite atonement. In addition, Akin's proposal raises troubling questions with respect to the eternal security of the believer. If it is true that any sins actually atoned for rebound to the person for whom Christ was a substitute, this makes a mockery of Paul's argument in Romans 8:31-34 that Christ's death on the cross provides a guarantee of no condemnation for believers. For these reasons, Akin's proposal is unpersuasive.

To recapitulate, logically, non-Calvinists have two unpalatable options: They can accept the view that Christ came to actually save no one but merely to make salvation possible, which Scripture refutes, or they can defend the equally unscriptural idea that Christ, in his death secured redemption and reconciliation for the non-elect; and was a propitiation, sacrifice and vicarious substitute on behalf of the non-elect. These concepts simply cannot bear the weight which non-Calvinists place on them. The New Testament makes clear that Jesus, as a vicarious substitute, actually secured these things—reconciliation, redemption, propitiation and satisfaction—for the elect on the cross (Romans 5: 10-11; Galatians 3:13; 4:4-5; Ephesians 2:16; Revelation 1:5-6, 9). We can only conclude that, when Christ died, he paid the penalty for only those whom God elected. He redeemed only those whom God elected. He propitiated God's wrath with respect to only those whom God elected. He has secured redemption for his people.

When it comes down to it, the question of "for whom did Christ die?" becomes one of Christology. Did Christ fail in his mission or did he succeed? An indefinite atonement is an atonement that fails because the Christ who made it failed at his mission. We do not believe in such a Christ. We agree with Spurgeon who said a general atonement that saves none or that fails at its purpose is an atonement to be despised and rejected, not praised:

> [Some people] believe in an atonement made for everybody...They believe that Judas was atoned for just as much as Peter; they believe that the damned in hell were as much an object of Jesus Christ's satisfaction as the saved in heaven; and though they do not say it in proper words, yet they must mean...that in the case of multitudes, Christ died in vain, for he died for them all, they say; and yet so ineffectual was his dying for them, that though he died for them they are damned afterwards. Now, such an atonement I despise—I reject it...I had rather believe a limited atonement that is efficacious for all men for whom it was intended, than an universal atonement that is not efficacious for anybody, except the will of man be joined with it....Oh! glorious doctrine! I would wish to die preaching it! What better testimony can we bear to the love and faithfulness of God than the testimony of a substitution eminently satisfactory for all them that believe on Christ?[20]

Is There a Sense In Which Christ Died For Everyone Even If It Is Not a Salvific Sense?

There is indeed a sense in which Christ did die for all men. At the Synod of Dort and thereafter, Calvinists frequently have used the slogan: Christ's death is sufficient for all but efficient only for the elect. Calvinists may not agree as to what it means to say that Christ's death was sufficient for all.[21] Nonetheless, this much can be said: The atonement had certain indirect or "spill-over" benefits to humanity in general, and Calvinists have not hesitated to proclaim this fact. Charles Hodge, for example, said Christ's death "had the effect of justifying the offer of salvation to every man; and of course was designed to have that effect."[22] Lorraine Boettner wrote of common grace and other benefits flowing to the non-elect from Christ's death:

> Calvinists admit that it arrests the penalty which would have been inflicted upon the whole race because of Adam's sin; that it forms a basis for the preaching of the Gospel and thus introduces many uplifting moral influences into the world and restrains many evil influences....Many temporal blessings are thus secured for all men, although these fall short of being sufficient to insure salvation...[23]

Yes, Christ died for all men in some sense, but not in a redemptive sense. He died only for his people in a redemptive sense. Do we know who Christ's people are before they are saved? No. Therefore, we witness to as many people as we can during the remaining time God has given us on this earth. We invite all to come to Christ in faith and repentance, and leave the results to God.

But How Should We Interpret Passages Suggesting Christ Atoned For the Sins of Both the Elect and the Non-elect?

The biblical concepts discussed above should be sufficient to determine the extent of the atonement: It is designed to cover the elect. Although there may be side benefits to the non-elect as a result of the atonement, from a salvation perspective, Christ died to redeem his people. Accordingly, it is a superficial and unacceptable exercise to simply quote a few texts from the Bible in which such words as "world" and "all" occur in connection with the death of Christ and assume that the question is settled in favor of general atonement. Two principles of sound biblical hermeneutics must be employed in dealing with these texts.

First, the context determines which meaning of "world" and "all" is intended within a range of all possible meanings. As discussed below, to quote John Owen, whose tome on this subject, *The Death of Death in the Death of Christ* has never been answered, "*in no one place* wherein it is used in this business of redemption, [the word "world"] can be taken for all and every man in the world."[24] Indeed, Owen said, "it is nowhere affirmed in Scripture that Christ died for all men or gave himself a ransom for all men, much less for all and every man."[25] Second, more difficult passages of Scripture are to be interpreted in light of more plain passages. Accordingly, these passages must be construed to comport with the plainer passages teaching particular redemption discussed above.

Finally, we should add that in discussing certain passages that non-Calvinists use to support their general atonement theories, it is not our purpose to lay down any sort of definitive interpretation. We may disagree among ourselves as to the correct interpretation of some of these passages and other Calvinists may disagree with us. It is simply our purpose to show that these passages, whatever they mean, do not support general redemption.

JOHN 3:16. This well familiar passage declares: "For God so loved the world that He gave His only begotten Son, that whoever believes in Him should not perish but have everlasting life." To properly interpret this verse, three concepts must be clearly understood.

1. "God so loved the world." The first concept is the love of God. What kind of love is John talking about here? There is no doubt, on the one hand, that God loves the non-elect. "The Lord is good to all, And His tender mercies are over all His works" (Psalm 145:9). "He makes his sun to rise upon the evil and the good, and sends rain upon just and unjust" (Matthew 5:45). "He is kind to the unthankful and to the evil" (Luke 6:35). Christians are to "love [our] enemies" and therefore to emulate the love of God toward sinful man. If we model God's love by loving our enemies, it must follow that God loves his enemies—even those who reject him and end up in hell. As John Murray has said, "our virtues are patterned after God's own perfections" and "this is surely true of the preeminent virtue, love."[26]

Yet this surely is not the love that is in view in this verse.

"God loves all mankind," Fuller says, "but the question is whether he loves them all alike."[27] Here, John speaks of a special love, a superlative love. God "so loved" the world that he "gave his only begotten Son." God "so loved" that he sent Jesus to die for sinners, to be their redemption, propitiation, reconciliation, substitute, and sacrifice. As John Gill, eminent eighteenth century Baptist theologian wrote in his commentary on John: "Not every man in the world is here meant, or all the individuals of human nature; for all are not the objects of God's special love, which is here designed."[28] As John Owen said, "the love here intimated is absolutely the most eminent and transcendent love that ever God showed...towards any miserable creature."[29] The word "so" means "to such a remarkable, astonishable height." God so loved his own that Jesus went to the cross to become a satisfaction, propitiation, expiation, substitution for his own, that he gained reconciliation and redemption for them.

2. Who is the object of God's special love? This brings us to the meaning of the term world (*cosmos*). The general redemption view assumes that this word must refer to each and every person that ever lived. But this is not the biblical meaning. In the first place, the Greek word *cosmos* has no inviolate meaning in every context. It has a wide, varied and complex range of meanings in *koine* Greek, the "street language" of the New Testament. *Cosmos* had the original meaning of "order." This was the sense in which the epic poet Homer used the term in *The Iliad* in the 8th or 9th century BC. From this meaning, the definition of *cosmos* as referring to the "cosmic order" or "ordered universe" gradually developed. The Greek philosophers frequently used the term in this sense in the 3d and 4th century BC. In this sense, the word corresponded to the Hebrew "heaven and earth," meaning the creation. As time progressed, a new range of meaning for *cosmos* emerged. The word began to be used to refer to the "earth" and its inhabitants. The "inhabited world" was thought to be coterminous with the Roman Empire, and the term became synonymous with that sense.

In the Septuagint, as in the classical literature, *cosmos* is used to refer to a wide variety of things: (1) "the heavens and the earth" (Genesis 2:1); (2) the host of heaven, the stars, the moon (Deuteronomy 4:19); (3) "ornament" or "adornment"(Exodus 33:5); (4) a generic "all things" (Psalm. 8:6).

In the New Testament, *cosmos* is no more restricted in its

meaning. Peter uses it once to refer to adornment (1 Peter 3:3). In every other reference, however, it refers to the "created world" in one sense or another. Over half the references are in John's books (78 in the gospel, 22 in 1 John, one in 2 John and three in Revelation). Paul uses it 46 times. The synoptic gospel writers use it 15 times. James uses it five times, as does Peter in his second epistle and the author of Hebrews. Peter uses it one time in his first epistle as does Luke in his Acts.[30]

A Greek-English Lexicon of the New Testament and Other Early Christian Literature defines *cosmos* as follows:

> adornment, adorning. 2. the orderly universe. 3. the sum total of all beings above the level of animals. 4. the earth, the planet upon which we live. 5. the world as mankind. 6. the world as the scene of earthly joys, possessions, cares, sufferings. 7. the world, and everything that belongs to it, appears as that which is hostile to God, i.e. lost in sin, wholly at odds with anything divine, ruined and depraved. 8. totality, sum or total.[31]

The *Theological Dictionary of the New Testament* likewise defines *cosmos* in the following ways: 1. order. 2. the sum of all created beings. 3. the theater of history, the abode of men, the earth, the inhabited world. 4. humanity, fallen creation, the theater of salvation history.[32]

We have labored long enough to show that the word *cosmos* has no inviolate meaning; its meaning among a wide range of choices in a particular passage is determined by the context. At the same time, while *cosmos* can sometimes refer to humanity in general, taken as an unspecified mass, *in no place in the New Testament does cosmos refer to every single person who has ever lived as part of a set*. Despite its wide range of possible meanings, none of those meanings involves each and every person ever born. This is an assumption smuggled into the word rather than a definition read out of the word.

What does the term "world" mean, then in John 3:16? Calvinists generally adopt one of two possibilities. Some like John Gill assert that the word "world" refers to the elect, and specifically, to the elect from among the Gentiles. He says one must remember that, in John 3:16, Jesus is speaking to Nicodemus, a preeminent Jewish scholar:

> Nothing is more common in the Jewish writings than to call the Gentiles...the world; and...the whole world; and...the nations of the world; hence the apostle Paul calls them kosmos, the world, in Romans 11:12,15. It was a controversy...among the Jewish doctors, whether when the Messiah came, the Gentiles, the world, should have any benefit by him; the majority was exceeding large on the negative of the question, and determined they should not; only some few, as old Simeon and others, knew that he should be *a light to lighten the Gentiles, as* well as *the glory of the people of Israel.* The rest concluded, that the most severe judgments and dreadful calamities would befall them; yea, that they should be cast into hell in the room of the Israelites. This notion John the Baptist, Christ, and his apostles, purposely oppose, and is the true reason of the use of this phrase in the Scriptures which speak of Christ's redemption.[33]

Other Calvinists believe this view is too restrictive. Warfield spoke for many when he opined that the Arminian view (that the "world" means each and every person) "fails to rise to the height of the conception of the love of God embodied in it" and the traditional Calvinist view adopted by Gill (that the "world" means "believers" or "the elect") "appears to do something less than full justice to the conception of the world which God is said to love." They thus offer different views. For example, John MacArthur believe that the word "world" refers to "humanity in general." It is a synonym for the human race. In a broad sense, God's love is set on the whole human race, not just the remnant of elect individuals.[34] Warfield believed that the "world" is a "synonym of all that is evil and noisome and disgusting."[35] "The world, the flesh and the devil," he said, "this is the pregnant combination in which we have learned from Scripture to express the baleful forces that war against the soul: and the three terms are thus cast together because they are essentially synonyms." Hence, when we are told that God loves the world, "it is much as if we were told that He loves the flesh and the devil. And we may, indeed, take courage from our text and say it boldly: God does love the world and the flesh and the devil. Therein indeed is the ground of all our comfort and all our hope: for we—you and I—are of the world and of the flesh and of the devil."[36]

These interpretations are consistent with the teaching elsewhere in Scripture that Christ died in a special way for the elect, to redeem them and serve as substitutionary atonement for them. No matter which interpretation is granted, in either event, John's use of the word "cosmos" does not support the general redemption view that "world" means each and every person who ever lived.

3. Finally, it should be noted that the word "whosoever" is not an indefinite phrase that can be wrenched out of context to support general redemption. The Greek word is "all" or "every" (*pas*). When used with a participle, it means simply every one who is referenced in a specified set—in this context, every one who believes. The point is that everyone who believes has eternal life. The giving of the Son guarantees that.

Yet this verse does not indicate whom the "whosoevers" are. Another passage in John does that. In John 6:37 and 44 Jesus said:

> All that the Father gives Me will come to Me, and the one who comes to Me I will by no means cast out.
>
> No one can come to Me unless the Father who sent Me draws him; and I will raise him up at the last day.

To sum up, John 3:16 is not inconsistent with particular redemption at all. It instead wholly supports the idea that God loved his own to such a degree that he gave his Son Jesus to die for them and thereby guarantee their salvation.

1 JOHN 2:2. 1 John 2:1-2 is one of the key verses cited by evangelical Arminians. It says:

> My little children, these things I write to you, so that you may not sin. And if anyone sins, we have an Advocate with the Father, Jesus Christ the righteous. And He Himself is the propitiation for our sins, and not for ours only but also for the whole world.

One Southern Baptist leader said of this verse: "I take it at face value. I believe Jesus died for every man on the face of this earth and every woman...everybody." Another Southern Baptist leader gleefully proclaimed that this verse "gives the...Calvinists fits." Is he right? Let's see.

Notice first off that Jesus "is" the propitiation for our sins (not that he merely makes propitiation possible). Did Christ accomplish propitiation for everyone who ever lived? Non-Calvinists assume that this is the meaning of "the whole world," calling their preconceived notion taking the verse at "face value." But as we have seen in our discussion of John 3:16, while the term *cosmos* has a wide range of meanings, it never refers to every single person who ever lived. And as we also saw earlier in this chapter, Christ did not accomplish propitiation for non-elect unbelievers. Hence, this little word "is" alone refutes the general redemption theory.

We believe the better interpretation of this verse is ethnological—that Jesus is the propitiation for our (Jews') sins, and not for the sins of Jews only, but also for those of Gentiles as well (the whole world). In other words, this verse, possibly like John 3:16, is talking about the expansion of the Gospel from being directed just to Jerusalem Jews to expand to cover Gentiles as well, particularly in those places where Christianity was beginning to make its way.

Why do we suggest this is the correct interpretation? In determining what *cosmos* means in this particular passage, we start with Galatians 2:9, which says Peter, James and John were apostles to the Jews, while Paul was an apostle to the Gentiles. Therefore, it is reasonable to assume that Peter's, James's and John's epistles were directed to Jewish readers. This is seen in other verses in 1 John (what we have seen with our eyes...and our hands have handled; I write...an old commandment which you had from the beginning; I write unto you fathers because you have known him from the beginning). It also is confirmed in Peter and James's letters where they make clear that their intended audience was Jewish believers of the dispersion (James 1:1; 1 Peter 1:1). It's reasonable to assume that 1 John is similarly directed. Thus, the intended readers, the "us" were Jewish believers.

It is important to recognize that the advance of the gospel from Jews to Gentiles, and thus, to the whole world, is not a strained construction imposed on this passage from without. Fuller rightly commented that "the Jews, it is well known, were at that time [that is, the time of the New Testament] very tenacious of exclusive privileges. Their prejudices taught them to expect a Messiah whose blessings should be confined to their own peculiar nation."[37] Thus, as Schreiner points out, "bringing the gospel to the Gentiles was a distinctive advance in the mission of early Christianity," one that Paul saw more clearly than did Peter, James and John, at least in the earliest days of the church.[38] Peter, James and John saw their ministry as being primarily to Jews, although they confirmed Paul's ministry to the Gentiles (see Acts 15). Whatever his earlier prejudices may have been, by the time John wrote his gospel and epistles, surely he could marvel at the fulfillment of the extension of the gospel beyond Jewish believers to the Gentile world.[39]

That the "us" is a Jewish reference and the "whole world" is a Gentile reference in 1 John 2:2 is confirmed by an explicit statement to this effect in John's gospel, John 11:51-52. There John summarizes Caiaphas' prophecy in John 11:50 as being that "Jesus would die for the nation, and not for that nation only, but also that He would gather together in one the children of God who were scattered abroad." He says in verse 51: "Now this he did not say on his own authority." In other words, the Holy Spirit put words into the mouth of the unbelieving high priest that expressed God's intention that the gospel would spread beyond the Jews to the Gentiles. This supports our view that the "us" were Jewish believers and the "whole world" referred to Gentiles scattered abroad, or spread throughout the globe.

The derivation of the word "propitiate" also supports this conclusion. John knew full well that the word had a Hebrew derivation (referring to the mercy seat in the Holy of Holies). He undoubtedly marveled at the fact that this uniquely Jewish concept was being applied to people from every tribe, kindred, nation and people group. Fuller says on this subject: "Christ is that of which the Jewish mercy-seat (or propitiatory) was a type. The Jewish mercy-seat was the medium of mercy and communion with God for all the worshippers of God of old...Christ is that in reality which this was in figure, and is not, like that, confined to a single nation. He is the medium through which all believers of all ages and nations have access to God and receive the forgiveness of their sins. All this perfectly agrees with the scope of the apostle, which was to encourage backsliding believers against despair."[40]

Finally, in 1 John 2:1-2, Jesus' propitiation is linked to his advocacy. In the risen and ascended Jesus we have an advocate with the Father when we sin. Paul says of this intercessory ministry that the Christ who died and rose again "is even at the right hand of God, who also makes intercession for us" (Romans 8:34). Hebrews 7:25 amplifies: "He is also able to save to the uttermost those who come to God through Him, since He always lives to make intercession for them." As these passages make clear, Christ's intercessory advocacy is for believers, not the lost. Hence, those for whom Jesus propitiates, as stated in 1 John 1:2 can be no different than those for whom he advocates and intercedes, as stated in 1 John 1:1.

Some non-Calvinists recoil at our interpretation of 1 John 2. Andrew Fuller didn't. His theological understanding sparked the first Baptist missionary drive to evangelize the unreached nations. The apostle John didn't. Whether he understood it earlier or not, by the end of his life, he understood the amazing truth that there is neither Jew nor Gentile in Christ. Far from recoiling, he marveled at the incredible thought that God's love extends to all races and all people groups in all ages. In Revelation 5:9-10, the apostle of love recorded:

> And they sang a new song, saying: "You are worthy to take the scroll, And to open its seals; For You were slain, And have redeemed us to God by Your blood out of every tribe and tongue and people and nation, And have made us kings and priests to our God; And we shall reign on the earth."

What an awesome thought is expressed in the praise recorded in this passage! Jesus was slain in order to redeem a chosen people out of every tribe and tongue and nation. The cross accomplished this redemption. And it did it for "us," those who will be kings and priests to our God, who will reign on the earth. He did it for believers. In sum, this passage, like John 3:16, supports a definite atonement, not a general one.

HEBREWS 2:9. Hebrews 2:9-13 states:

> But we do see Him who has been made for a little while lower than the angels, namely, Jesus, because of the suffering of death crowned with glory and honor, that by the grace of God He might taste death for everyone. For it was fitting for Him, for whom are all things, and through whom are all things, in bringing many sons to glory, to perfect the author of their salvation through sufferings. For both He who sanctifies and

> those who are sanctified are all from one Father; for which reason He is not ashamed to call them brethren, saying, "I will proclaim Thy name to My brethren, In the midst of the congregation I will sing Thy praise." And again, "I will put My trust in Him." And again, "Behold, I and the children whom God has given Me." (NASB)

Hebrews 2:9 says Christ tasted death "for everyone." The little word "for" here is a critical one. It is *huper*, meaning "on behalf of," "for the sake of," "in place of" or "in the stead of."[41] Did Christ taste death "in place of" or "in stead of" everyone? As we have already seen, the Bible elsewhere makes clear that Christ could not have died in the place of the non-elect. He was not their substitute before the Father.

Moreover, the word "everyone" (*pantos*) literally means "for the whole."[42] It is derived from *pas*. The extent and content are decided by the context. When the context is considered, who is referenced in this verse as "everyone"? It is the many sons to be brought to glory, for verse 10 says that Christ's purpose in coming to earth and dying was to bring "many sons to glory." Verse 11 says it is the sanctified. Verse 12 says it is those Christ is not ashamed to call his brethren. Verse 13 says it is "the children whom God has given" to Christ. As John Murray says, "there is not the slightest warrant in this text to extend the reference of the vicarious death of Christ beyond those who are most expressly referred to in the context."[43] The "everyone" for whom Christ tasted death as referenced in this passage is the elect.

1 TIMOTHY 2:1-6. This passage states:

> First of all, then, I urge that entreaties and prayers, petitions and thanksgivings, be made on behalf of all men, for kings and all who are in authority, in order that we may lead a tranquil and quiet life in all godliness and dignity. This is good and acceptable in the sight of God our Savior, who desires all men to be saved and to come to the knowledge of the truth. For there is one God, and one mediator also between God and men, the man Christ Jesus, who gave Himself as a ransom for all, the testimony borne at the proper time. (NASB)

This passage does not support general redemption. Verse 4 may support the idea that God desires in some sense that everyone be saved, but that is not God's greatest desire or else it would be a reality.[44]

Verse 6 says Christ "gave Himself as a ransom for all." Non-Calvinists insist that this "all" really means that Christ gave himself as a ransom for every single person who ever lived. But as we have seen from other passages, this is not possible. Verse 5 also slams the door on such an interpretation. It says there is "one mediator...the man Christ Jesus" who gave himself as a ransom for all. Is Christ a mediator for all? Hebrews 12:15 says no, he is not. He is a mediator of the new covenant by his death, that those who are called may receive the promise of the eternal inheritance. It strains credulity for non-Calvinists to insist (erroneously) that, in this passage, Christ is a ransom for unbelievers who never turn to Christ in faith and repentance but to equally hold (correctly) that he is a mediator only for those who believe.

There is another inconsistency in the non-Calvinist view of this passage. Verse 1 says prayers, petitions and thanksgivings should be made "on behalf of all men." Does "all" in verse 1 really mean every single person who ever lived, as the non-Calvinists must insist in order to hold their position with respect to verse 6? Gill points out the ludicrousness of such a position:

> The exhortation of the apostle, in verse 1, that *supplications, prayers, intercessions, and giving of thanks, be made for all men.* But surely by *all men,* is not meant every individual man, that has been, is, or shall be, in the world; millions of men are dead and gone, for whom prayer is not to he made; many in hell, to whom it would be of no service; and many in heaven, who stand in no need of it; nor should we pray for such who have sinned *the sin unto death.* (1 John 5:16.) Besides giving of thanks, as well as prayers, were to be made for all men; but surely the apostle's meaning is not that the saints should give thanks for wicked men, and persecutors, and particularly for a persecuting Nero; nor for heretics or false teachers, such as Hymeneus and Alexander, whom he had delivered to Satan.[45]

What is meant here, then? In verse 1 Paul is exhorting Timothy to pray and offer thanksgivings for all classes or kinds of men, not literally all men who ever lived.[46] This is why in verse 2 he speaks of kings and all who are in authority. The "all" in verse 6 should be construed the same way. The same meaning is in view in Titus 2:11 where Paul tells Titus of the grace of God which brings salvation to "all men."

1 TIMOTHY 4:10. In this verse, Paul wrote to his young minister friend: "For it is for this we labor and strive, because we have fixed our hope on the living God, who is the Savior of all men, especially of believers" (NASB). There are a number of ways this passage can be interpreted that do not support universal or general redemption.

Some Calvinists have suggested that the word for "savior," *soter*, means saving from serious peril, cure from an illness, preserving, protecting, keeping, benefiting. Lexically, certainly, the word can mean "savior, deliverer, or preserver."[47] Gill says of this passage in *The Cause of God and Truth*:

> The words are to be understood of providential goodness and temporal salvation; which all men have a share in, more or less; God the Father and not Christ, is here called *the living God,* who is *the Savior of all men,* that is, *the preserver of all men*; who supports them in their being, and supplies them with all the necessaries of life.[48]

He adds that there is good reason not to read the word *soter* as referring to salvation, for if it were read in that fashion, this passage would support universalism, not limited atonement. If God is the Savior of all men in a redemption sense, all men will be saved. But verses like John 3:18 tell us in no uncertain terms that Christ is *not* the savior—in a redemption sense—of those who do not believe and who stand condemned already.

Other Calvinists read *soter* as a redemptive word, at least partially. They point out that this verse suggests different respects in which God is a savior. Thomas Boston, for example, suggested that Jesus was the "official Savior" of the world of mankind indefinitely and the actual savior only of the elect. He analogized to the commissioning of a surgeon general. He is the surgeon general "of that whole society" even though many individuals never employ him but receive care from other physicians.[49] Read that way, this verse differentiates between Christ's being the savior of "all men" and his being the savior of believers. He actually accomplished salvation for the elect and his death had spill-over benefits for the non-elect.[50]

There is yet another way to read this passage that also does not support general atonement. Howard Marshall, although a proponent of general redemption, seems to acknowledge that this passage does not support that concept. He says this passage as usually translated is misleading because the word *malista* should not be translated as "especially" but as "namely." Thus, Paul "makes a statement of the character of God as the Savior of all men, and then he makes a necessary qualification: 'I mean, of those among them who believe.'" Marshall asserts: "Since this translation gives an excellent sense here, it should be adopted."[51] Read any of these three ways, this passage does not support the theory of general redemption.

2 PETER 2:1. This passage is perhaps cited most often by general redemptionists. Put in context, it reads:

> For we did not follow cleverly devised tales when we made known to you the power and coming of our Lord Jesus Christ, but we were eyewitnesses of His majesty. For when He received honor and glory from God the Father, such an utterance as this was made to Him by the Majestic Glory, "This is My beloved Son with whom I am well-pleased"—and we ourselves heard this utterance made from heaven when we were with Him on the holy mountain. And so we have the prophetic word made more sure, to which you do well to pay attention as to a lamp shining in a dark place, until the day dawns and the morning star arises in your hearts. But know this first of all, that no prophecy of Scripture is a matter of one's own interpretation, for no prophecy was ever made by an act of human will, but men moved by the Holy Spirit spoke from God. But false prophets also arose among the people, just as there will also be false teachers among you, who will secretly introduce destructive heresies, even denying the Master who bought them, bringing swift destruction upon themselves (2 Pet. 1:16-2:1).

At first glance, this verse seems to lend strong support to the unlimited atonement viewpoint. But first glances can be deceiving.

The perspicuity of Scripture demands that this obscure passage be interpreted in light of the Bible's plain teachings on the concept of redemption. Proper understanding of the Greek words is important here. In 2 Peter 2:1 two words must be carefully construed in order to correctly interpret this difficult verse. The first is the word "agorazo" which typically means "*to purchase or buy*."[52] It is used many times in LXX and NT to refer to the purchase of temporal objects such as food (e.g., John 4:8). Therefore, it does not automatically refer to redemption. In fact, Deuteronomy 32:5-6 provides support for using the term "bought" in a temporal, non-salvific sense with respect to those who "are not His children" but are "a perverse and crooked generation." There Moses bitingly said to the rebellious Israelites who had turned away from God:

> "They have corrupted themselves; They are not His children, Because of their blemish: A perverse and crooked generation. Do you thus deal with the Lord, O foolish and unwise people? Is He not your Father, who bought you? Has He not made you and established you?

Clearly, here, Christ's redemption (which had not yet occurred) is not in view. Rather, the sense is one of God's sovereignty or ownership of humanity as creator and maker. Another example of this is in Exodus 15:16: "Fear and dread will fall on them; By the greatness of Your arm They will be as still as a stone, Till Your people pass over, O Lord, Till the people pass over Whom You have purchased."

Accordingly, *agorazo* does not have to refer to salvific redemption, and in 2 Peter 2:1 it most likely does not. This is supported by the fact that *agorazo* means "redemption" in Scripture when accompanied by the technical term for a "price." Where no payment price is stated or implied, as here, *agorazo* may be better translated simply as "to acquire" or "obtain." Accordingly, Peter is not using the term "bought" in a redemptive sense. Rather, he is likely alluding to Deuteronomy 32:6. In other words, Peter is referring only to the fact that the false teachers were rebellious Jews who had denied the God to whom they rightfully belonged.[53]

The second critical Greek word is "*despotes*" or "*master*." Calvinists offer differing interpretations of this word. On the one hand, John Gill says this term does not designate Christ, but God the Father.[54] As support he states that the only places where this word is used to refer to a divine person are 2 Peter 2:1, along with Luke 2:29; Acts 4:24; 2 Timothy 2:21; Jude 1:4; and Revelation 6:10. In each of these places, Gill asserts that God the Father, not Jesus the Son, is in view. Of these verses, only Jude 4 is controverted. It states: "For certain persons have crept in unnoticed, those who were long beforehand marked out for this condemnation, ungodly persons who turn the grace of our God into licentiousness and deny our only Master [God] and Lord, Jesus Christ" (NASB). According to Gill, the word "God" is omitted in the Alexandrian and Vulgate, and hence in our English translations.

According to Gary Long, however, application of the Granville Sharp rule means Jude 4 has to refer to Jesus—but in a sovereign sense, not in a mediatorial sense.[55] This is significant because Jude 4 is a parallel passage to 2 Pet. 2:1.

Either way, the important point is that "*despotes*" is never used to refer to Christ's mediatorship. It is used of God (or Christ) as "absolute sovereign," that is, as "sovereign Lord." Gill says this word "is expressive of the power which masters have over their servants, and which God has over all mankind."[56] In sum, this verse refers to Christ as sovereign Lord, who has absolute power and authority over all his creation, including the false teachers, because he is their creator. In this regard, it is nothing more than a parallel to Romans 9:20-24:

> But indeed, O man, who are you to reply against God? Will the thing formed say to him who formed it, "Why have you made me like this?" Does not the potter have power over the clay, from the same lump to make one vessel for honor and another for dishonor? What if God, wanting to show His wrath and to make His power known, endured with much longsuffering the vessels of wrath prepared for destruction, and that He might make known the riches of His glory on the vessels of mercy, which He had prepared beforehand for glory, even us whom He called, not of the Jews only, but also of the Gentiles?

2 PETER 3:9. This verse states: "The Lord is not slow to fulfill his promise as some count slowness, but is patient toward you, not wishing that any should perish, but that all should reach repentance" (ESV). This verse, strictly speaking, does not address the issue of the extent of the atonement, but it is heavily quoted by non-Calvinists in support of their general philosophy. The "you" does not refer to everyone in general, as non-Calvinists presuppose in quoting this verse; but it refers to the specific audience to whom Peter is writing. Who is that audience? It is "those who have received a faith of the same kind as ours" (2 Peter 1:1; NASB). The "you" of verse 9 limits the "any" and "all" of the same verse. All three references refer to people who are of the elect. Peter's point in the passage is that the Second Coming of Christ will be delayed until all the elect of the earth are brought to salvation. God has purposed to bring to salvation people out of every nation group (Revelation 5:9-10), and, to the praise of his name, he is gloriously accomplishing his purpose!

The Logical Fallacies of Unlimited Atonement

The unlimited atonement view is full of additional errors in logic. In *The Death of Death in the Death of Christ*, John Owen set up the following syllogism, which is undefeatable. One of three things happened at the cross:

(1) Christ died savingly for all the sins of all men.
(2) Christ died for some of the sins of all men.
(3) Christ died savingly for all the sins of some men.

The first option is not true. If Christ did die for the sins of everyone, everyone actually would be saved. Everyone is not saved. The proponent of this option is therefore left defending the notion that Christ failed in his mission with respect to the vast majority of mankind. As Spurgeon said, "if they once believe in universal redemption, they are driven to the blasphemous inference that God's intention is frustrated, and that Christ has not received what he died to procure."[57] Christianity knows no failure at the cross! Christ's blood was not shed in vain!

Moreover, if Christ did die redemptively for the sins of everyone, it is unjust for him to punish the non-elect (i) for sins that Christ took upon himself at the cross, (ii) for sins for which Christ propitiated God's wrath, (iii) when Christ was the sacrificial substitute for them at the cross. Evangelical Arminians often respond that the lost are justly punished for the sin of unbelief. But unbelief itself is a sin which would have to have been atoned for under the Arminian scheme (John 16:9). This answer itself defeats the first option and brings us to the second.

The second option asserts that Christ died for some of the sins of all men. This also is not true. It asserts that all men would have some sins to answer for (such as unbelief). It means no one is saved.

Accordingly, the third option is the true biblical view. This view of the extent of the atonement makes the cross a place of victory, because what the Father planned, the Son purchased, and for these He prays. This is consistent with that great declaration in that messianic prophesy of His coming: "He shall see of the travail of his soul, and shall be satisfied: by his knowledge shall my righteous servant justify many; for he shall bear their iniquities" (Isa. 53:11; KJV).

Under the Arminian view, Christ could not have died for the sin of unbelief. Otherwise, if he died for the sins of every single person that has ever lived, the sin of unbelief would be forgiven and everyone would be saved. But we know that is not true. We also know that his death covered the sin of unbelief for the elect. 1 John 1:7 says that Christ's blood purified us from "all sin." Thus, it seems that Arminians, not Calvinists, are the ones with a real "limited" atonement.

Chapter 5

The Principles Behind the Points

By now, hopefully, it is clear that Calvinism is an organic system of thought. Although many have tried to take parts of it and leave other parts, their attempts have been inherently unstable, as the non-Calvinist position on the atonement demonstrates.

Calvinism is governed by one basic, fundamental principle: *the supremacy of God in all things*. We deliberately choose the term "supremacy" over the usual word "sovereignty" because supremacy denotes both sovereignty (highest in rank or authority) and superiority (highest in degree or quality). As one writer put it: "Calvinism enthrones God everywhere. It makes Him supreme everywhere. In nature and in history. He is on the throne and at the helm. He is also King of kings and Lord of lords. His authority is absolute. He does what He pleaseth in earth and in heaven. The civil powers are ordained by Him and all rulers rule under His hand."[1] Perhaps an alternative formulation would be the centrality of God in all things.[2] Either way, Romans 11:36 is the watchword for Calvinists: "For of Him and through Him and to Him are all things, to whom be glory forever. Amen."

God's supremacy over all things is proclaimed throughout Scripture. Here are only a few examples:

1. Exodus 20:3 proclaims that there is only one God. Who is like God?, the Scriptures repeatedly ask (Exodus 15:11; 2 Samuel 22:32; Psalm 18:31). The repeated refrain is: There is no one like him (Exodus 8:10; 2 Samuel 7:22; 1 Kings 8:23). As Moses sang in exultant praise after God destroyed the Egyptian army in the Red Sea after the Israelites left Egypt:

> "Who is like You, O Lord, among the gods? Who is like You, glorious in holiness, Fearful in praises, doing wonders? (Exodus 15:11).

2. Job 26 teaches that God is supreme over death (26:5-6), outer space and the earth (v. 7), the clouds (vv. 8-9), light and darkness (v. 10), things on the earth (mountains and the sea, vv. 11-12), and the sky (v. 13).

3. The theme of Psalm 93 is God's supremacy over creation and providence:

> The Lord reigns, He is clothed with majesty; The Lord is clothed, He has girded Himself with strength. Surely the world is established, so that it cannot be moved. Your throne is established from of old; You are from everlasting. The floods have lifted up, O Lord, The floods have lifted up their voice; The floods lift up their waves. The Lord on high is mightier than the noise of many waters, than the mighty waves of the sea. Your testimonies are very sure; Holiness adorns Your house, O Lord, forever.

4. God is supreme over the nations. Psalm 68:31 says nations will submit to God's lordship. Daniel told the pagan Babylonian king Nebuchadnezzar that God's kingdom will destroy all human kingdoms and live forever (Daniel 2:44). "And the Lord shall be King over all the earth. In that day it shall be 'The Lord is one,' And His name one" (Zechariah 14:9). "For the kingdom is the Lord's, And He rules over the nations" (Psalm 22:28). "All nations whom You have made shall come and worship before You, O Lord, And shall glorify Your name" (Psalm 86:9).

5. God is supreme over evil. "The Lord has made all for Himself, Yes, even the wicked for the day of doom" (Proverbs 16:4). Gill said of this passage:

> Now the sense of these words is this: that all things are appointed by God for his own glory; all things, particularly respecting man, concerning his temporal estate, the time of his birth, the place of his abode, his station and condition of life, the various vintages of it, prosperous and adverse, death itself, and all the means leading on to it; as well as all things respecting his spiritual and eternal state..., both as to the time of his coming into the world, and of his sufferings and death, with all the circumstances thereof, the conversion of a sinner, time, place, said means, all times of darkness, desertion, and comfort; yea, the final state and portion

> of all men: all these are fixed and appointed by God, and, in one way or another, make for his glory; yea, even he has appointed *the wicked for the day of evil,* which is mentioned partly to illustrate the general proposition in the text, and partly to obviate an objection, which might be taken from them against all things being made or appointed for his glory.[3]

6. The name of God the Son is superior to the angels (Hebrews 1:4). Jesus is superior to men and will be worshiped by all:

> Therefore God also has highly exalted Him and given Him the name which is above every name, that at the name of Jesus every knee should bow, of those in heaven, and of those on earth, and of those under the earth, and that every tongue should confess that Jesus Christ is Lord, to the glory of God the Father. (Philippians 2:9-11).[4]

With Scripture, Calvinism proclaims that God is supreme over all. B.B. Warfield said about this formative principle of Calvinism: "The Calvinist is the man who sees God behind all phenomena and in all that occurs recognizes the hand of God, working out his will; who makes the attitude of the soul to God in prayer its permanent attitude in all its life-activities; and who casts himself on the grace of God alone, excluding every trace of dependence on self from the whole work of his salvation."[5] Warfield asserted the Calvinist has:

> a profound apprehension of God in His majesty, with the inevitably accompanying poignant realization of the exact relation sustained to Him by the creature as such, and particularly by the sinful creature....The Calvinist is the man who has seen God and who, having seen God in His glory, is filled on the one hand with a sense of his own unworthiness to stand in God's sight as a creature, and much more as a sinner, and on the other with adoring wonder that nevertheless this God is a God Who receives sinners. He who believes in God without reserve, and is determined that God shall be God to him, in all his thinking, feeling, willing—in the entire compass of his life-activities, intellectual, moral, spiritual—throughout all his individual, social,

> religious relations—is by the force of the strictest of all logic which presides over the outworking of principles into thought and life, by the very necessity of the case, a Calvinist.[6]

Of course, the fact that the supremacy of God in all things is the foundational principle of Calvinism means that, contrary to popular belief, predestination is not. Predestination is simply the outworking or application of God's supremacy to salvation. This is underscored in John Calvin's *Institutes of the Christian Religion*. Calvin began the *Institutes*, not with a discussion of God's elective decree, but with a discourse on the knowledge of God as the source of true wisdom. In the final 1559 edition, predestination is not discussed until the end of book three; it is the conclusion of Calvin's discussion of salvation, not the starting point. It is illuminating that Calvin gave no detailed and comprehensive explanation of predestination in the early versions of the *Institutes* or in his Catechism. It was not until 1542 when Catholic theologian Pighius attacked that doctrine that Calvin felt compelled to come to the defense of the biblical view. Even then, because Pighius died in the interim, he did not respond until 1552, when continuing attacks by Jerome Bolsec necessitated a fuller treatment in *Concerning the Eternal Predestination of God*. The point is, knowing the God who is supreme over all is the foundational principle for Calvin's theology, not the doctrine of predestination.

A closely related correlate to the supremacy of God is that God's chief end is his own glory. As God declared through his prophet Isaiah: "For My own sake, for My own sake, I will do it; For how should My name be profaned? And I will not give My glory to another" (Isaiah 48:11). In *The End for Which God Created the World*, Jonathan Edwards commented on this verse: "Which is as much as to say, I will obtain my end; I will not forego my glory; another shall not take this prize from me...The words are emphatical. The emphasis and repetition constrain us to understand that what God does is ultimately for his own sake."[7]

Many derivative principles flow from the supremacy of God as a foundational principle of Calvinism. This chapter explores six key derivative principles as we seek to go beyond the five points.

Principle No. 1.

Calvinists Have a Right View of God Because They Affirm God's Specific Sovereignty Over His Creation

God's supremacy over all means that God is sovereign, or controlling, over all. God's sovereignty is virtually, but not quite, a synonym to his supremacy. "Sovereignty" refers to his power of absolute self-determination. This means that God "has the power in virtue of his ability to deliberate and make choices, as opposed to others deciding for him." It also means that "God does his own actions and that they are in accord with his choices."[8] God, in and of himself, is perfectly and absolutely free.

God's actions and his choices are in accordance with his purpose or plan. Theologians call this God's "decree." The word plan is better. Calvinists recognize that God's plan was formed in eternity, and by it he determines all things that come to pass. Indeed, the sovereignty of God over all of life is a fundamental doctrine of Calvinism. As Warburton said, "Calvinism asserts that the sovereignty of God is supreme; that He has absolute and undisputable authority over all creation, that nothing can lie outside of or be viewed as not being subject to the sovereignty of His will, that He is not only the Creator and Upholder but the Disposer of all events from the beginning of time to its close."[9]

Only a summary of the biblical data is necessary to show that God is exhaustively and meticulously sovereign over all creation.

1. God is in control of his creation. He "makes His sun rise on the evil and on the good, and sends rain on the just and on the unjust" (Matthew 5:45). He feeds the birds of the air (Matthew 6:26). He brings dew of heaven and grain and wine (Genesis 27:28). He sends pestilence to judge his people (Leviticus 26:25). He prepared a vehement east wind for Jonah (Jonah 4:8). Is it any wonder that the prophet Jeremiah exclaimed: "Ah, Lord God! Behold, You have made the heavens and the earth by Your great power and outstretched arm. There is nothing too hard for You." (Jeremiah 32:17). Given these verses, there is little wonder that Charles Spurgeon proclaimed:

> I believe that every particle of dust that dances in the sunbeam does not move an atom more or less than

> God wishes—that every particle of spray that dashes against the steamboat has its orbit, as well as the sun in the heavens—that the chaff from the hand of the winnower is steered as the stars in their courses. The creeping of an aphid over the rosebud is as much fixed as the march of the devastating pestilence—the fall of...leaves from a poplar is as fully ordained as the tumbling of an avalanche.[10]

2. God is sovereign over the actions of humans, from kings to the lowliest of men. "A man's heart plans his way, But the Lord directs his steps" (Proverbs 16:9). "Many are the plans in a man's heart, but it is the Lord's purpose that prevails" (Proverbs 19:21). "The king's heart is the hand of the Lord, Like the rivers of water; He turns it wherever He wishes" (Proverbs 21:1).

3. He is in control of even seemingly minor circumstances and situations. Not a sparrow falls to the ground apart from the Father's will (Matthew 10:29). He numbers the hairs of our heads (Matthew 10:30). "The lot is cast into the lap, But its every decision is from the Lord" (Proverbs 16:33).

4. He is even in charge of the actions of sinful men. Isaiah 10:5-12 says that Assyria, a wicked nation, is the rod of God's anger and the staff in whose hand is God's indignation. God sent the Assyrians to strike and punish the Jewish people; yet he then turned around and judged the Assyrians for their pride. John 12:40 says of Jesus that "he has blinded their eyes and hardened their hearts, lest they should see with their eyes, lest they should understand with their hearts and turn, so that I should heal them." Romans 9:18 says God hardens whom he wills. 2 Thessalonians 2:11 says God sends the wicked "strong delusion, that they should believe the lie." 1 Peter 2:8 says the wicked were disobedient "to which they also were appointed." Jude 4 says certain ungodly men "were marked out for this condemnation."

5. And of course, God was in control of the most wicked event in human history—the crucifixion of Jesus Christ. Acts 2:23 says he was "taken by lawless hands," crucified and put to death. Yet the same verse also says he was "delivered by the determined purpose and foreknowledge of God." Acts 4:27-28 says Herod, Pilate, the Gentiles, and the people of Israel had a hand in the death of Christ. Yet the same verse also makes clear that they "were gathered together to do whatever [God's] hand and

[God's] purpose determined before to be done." God controlled the entire event, down to each small detail! Thus, when the people of Jerusalem "had fulfilled all that was written concerning Him, they took Him down from the tree and laid Him in a tomb" (Acts 13:29). Gill says about the crucifixion: "Nothing was more peremptorily decreed and determined by God than the crucifixion of Christ, and yet men never acted more freely, as well as more wickedly, than the Jews did in all the parts and circumstances of that tragical scene."[11]

6. Scripture makes clear that God is sovereign over means as well as ends. Ephesians 1:4 says God "chose us in Him before the foundation of the world, that we should be holy and without blame before Him in love." 2 Thessalonians 2:13 says: "God from the beginning chose you for salvation through sanctification by the Spirit and belief in the truth." 1 Peter 1:2 says we are elect "in sanctification of the Spirit, for obedience and sprinkling of the blood of Jesus Christ."

7. In short, God is sovereign over everything. Psalm 135:6 says: "Whatever the Lord pleases He does, In heaven and in earth, In the seas and in all deep places." In Isaiah 46:10, God declares: "My counsel shall stand, And I will do all My pleasure." In Isaiah 55:11, God states: "so is my word that goes out from my mouth: It will not return to me empty, but will accomplish what I desire and achieve the purpose for which I sent it." In Job 42:1-2, after being confronted by a withering cross-examination at the hand of God regarding God's creative purposes and power, Job humbly says: "I know that you can do all things; no plan of yours can be thwarted." In Daniel 4:35 even Nebuchadnezzar, the pagan king of Babylon recognizes: "All the inhabitants of the earth are reputed as nothing; He does according to His will in the army of heaven and among the inhabitants of the earth. No one can restrain His hand or say to Him, 'What have You done?'" And as we have already seen, in Ephesians 1:11 the apostle Paul declares that God "works all things according to the counsel of His will."

Charles Mallary well summarized when he said:

> The Scriptures are explicit: 'But our God is in the heavens, he hath done whatsoever he pleased.' Ps. cxv.3. 'He doeth according to his will in the army of heaven, and among the inhabitants of the earth.' Dan. iv.35. He 'worketh all things after the counsel of his

> own will.' Eph. i:11. These passages, taken in connection, indicate that what God does is the fruit of his own counsel; in other words, that whatever God performs, he wills, counsels, purposes to do; and also that his purpose is irresistible and almighty, and cannot fail of its exact and full accomplishment.[12]

The fact that God exercises his sovereignty according to his will and pleasure means that nothing, whether big or small, is outside his plan or control. Sometimes people wonder whether they should pray for what they consider to be trivial things. The biblical answer is yes! God controls all things. It is worth repeating: He works all things "according to the counsel of his will" (Ephesians 1:11). He controls every thing from the greatest and most wicked event in human history, the crucifixion of our Lord (Acts 2:23) on down to such small and relatively unimportant events as the casting of a lot (Proverbs 16:33). God is both a God of life and death decisions and a God of parking places! As Dagg wrote:

> Some persons are unwilling to attribute to God the care and management of minute and unimportant events. They consider it beneath his dignity to be concerned about such trivial matters. they believe in a General Providence over the affairs of the world, exercised by general laws; but a Particular Providence, exercised over every particular incident of every man's life, enters not into their creed. But the Scriptures are plain on this subject. the fall of a sparrow is a very trivial event, yet it is affirmed by the teacher from heaven, to be not without our heavenly Father.[13]

Indeed, we do not know when so-called trivial events will turn out not to be so trivial after all. In human history, the very important events frequently are interconnected with and caused by small, trivial ones. Ahab, the king of Israel, died, and prophecy was fulfilled, simply because an archer "drew a bow at random" (1 Kings 22:34).

William Cowper's hymn, "God Moves in a Mysterious Way," sums up the Calvinist view of God's sovereignty:

> God moves in a mysterious way
> His wonders to perform;

He plants His footsteps in the sea,
And rides upon the storm.

Deep in unfathomable mines
Of never failing skill
He treasures up His bright designs
And works His sovereign will.

Ye fearful saints, fresh courage take;
The clouds ye so much dread
Are big with mercy, and shall break
In blessings on your head.

Blind unbelief is sure to err,
And scan His work in vain;
God is His own Interpreter,
And He will make it plain.

What do non-Calvinists do with God's sovereignty? It depends on their perspective. Evangelical Arminians generally affirm God's specific sovereignty over his creation. Herschel Hobbs, for example, wrote: "God 'keeps the reigns of government in his hands.'" He "guides the universe to his own glorious end."[14] One current Southern Baptist leader has said: "I believe in the sovereignty of God. If a man doesn't believe in the sovereignty of God, he is a sheer fool. I believe not a blade of grass moves without God's permission. I believe he knows the name of every star; he put them all there. He is almighty." But evangelical Arminians also place limitations on God's sovereignty. They believe God decided not to exercise his sovereignty in the area of human decision-making. He voluntarily withholds his sovereign control. This was Hobbs' view. He flatly declared that "the sovereignty of God is limited by God's moral and spiritual laws and by the nature of the free will of man."[15]

The evangelical Arminian view of sovereignty is inherently unstable and ultimately incoherent. What it affirms with the one hand, specific sovereignty, it denies with the other, placing a fence around human decision-making so that God's specific sovereignty cannot touch it. This makes little sense; either God is fully sovereign or he is not. And if he is not fully sovereign in the area of human decision-making, on what basis do evangelical Arminians hold that he is sovereign in other more mundane areas of life? In addition, there is a touch of hubris about this view. It affirms that God is sovereign over everything except the place where it matters the most—the area of salvation. This reflects something of what B.B. Warfield called a "not unnatural unwillingness to acknowledge ourselves to be wholly at the disposal of another."[16]

We believe the evangelical Arminian position on God's sovereignty is soundly refuted by Scripture. The Bible repeatedly insists that God's sovereignty extends to all aspects of human decision-making, including salvation. God "chose us in Him before the foundation of the world" (Ephesians 1:4). God, through Jesus Christ, "predestined us to adoption as sons...according to the good pleasure of His will" (Ephesians 1:5). We are "predestined according to the purpose of Him who works all things according to the counsel of His will" (Ephesians 1:11).

For those who question the fairness of God's self-determination of who will be saved, Paul answers for God under the inspiration of God: "I will have mercy on whomever I will have mercy, and I will have compassion on whomever I will have compassion" (Romans 9:15). As if this is not sufficiently clear, Paul reiterates: "So then it is not of him who wills, nor of him who runs, but of God who shows mercy" (Romans 9:16).

John makes the same point: "But as many as received Him, to them He gave the right to become children of God, to those who believe in His name: who were born, not of blood, nor of the will of the flesh, nor of the will of man, but of God" (John 1:12-13). So did Peter: "Blessed be the God and Father of our Lord Jesus Christ, who according to His abundant mercy has begotten us again to a living hope through the resurrection of Jesus Christ from the dead" (1 Peter 1:3). As did James: "Of His own will He brought us forth by the word of truth, that we might be a kind of first fruits of His creatures" (James 1:18).

These passages affirm God's sovereign control over all aspects of salvation, from regeneration to conversion, from justification to sanctification as well as glorification. We see, then, that evangelical Arminianism's "exception clause" when it comes to God's sovereignty over all of life has no biblical warrant.

Openness of God theologians recognize the inconsistency in the evangelical Arminian perspective. They do not agree with either Calvinists or evangelical Arminians that God is specifically sovereign over his creation. Gregory Boyd has candidly admitted: "Any view that admits that agents possess libertarian freedom has to sacrifice exhaustive divine control." No view that affirms libertarian freedom ever allows God to "always get his way."[17] Clark Pinnock said God "controls some things, but not everything." "He conducts a 'general' rather than a 'meticulous' sovereignty."[18]

Open theists believe that God, as a rule, declines to interfere with human freedom. Thus, Pinnock says, "one does not find a predestinarian decree operating behind the scenes, to ensure that God's will is always done."[19] "What God wants to happen does not always come to pass on account of human freedom. There are disasters and setbacks and God can even suffer humiliation because love makes him vulnerable....There is no blueprint that governs everything that happens." Thus, he believes God "has chosen to exercise an open and flexible sovereignty."[20] And John Sanders said: "God sovereignly decides not to control each and every event, and some things go contrary to what God intends and may not turn out completely as God desires."[21]

It is this perspective that allows Sanders to criticize a pastor preaching a funeral of a young child who told the parents "God must have had a good reason for taking her home." He calls this "a euphemism for God's killing her."[22] The strong implication is that God has no power over issues of life and death. Never mind that the Bible speaks of those who are "appointed" to die (Psalm 139:16; Hebrews 9:27), along with the fact that God did the appointing (Acts 17:26), and that God appointed man's limits which man cannot pass (Job 14:5). Job 12:10 asks the rhetorical question: "In whose hand is the life of every living thing, and the breath of all mankind?" The expected answer is, of course, God.

The fact is, open theism's general sovereignty is no sovereignty at all. The openness view is not supported by Scripture at all. As we have seen, God is a self-determined, free sovereign. He has ownership of, authority over, and control over his creation. He owns all things because he created all things. He "created all things" and "for [His] pleasure they are and were created" (Revelation 4:11; KJV). He has the absolute right to impose his will on his creation. God is the master of his universe. God's sovereignty is meticulous and exhaustive.

Does God's specific sovereignty over his creation mean, as Sanders put it, that "no event ever happens without God's specifically selecting it to happen"?[23] No it does not. God does not "specifically select" evil to occur even though, as the verses quoted above demonstrate, he is fully in control of it. As the *Baptist Confession of 1689* declares, Calvinists are careful to affirm:

> God hath decreed in Himself, from all eternity, by the most wise and holy counsel of His own will, freely and unchangeably, all things, whatsoever come to pass; yet so as thereby is God neither the author of sin nor hath fellowship with any therein; nor is violence offered to the will of the creature, nor yet is the liberty or contingency of second causes taken away, but rather established...[24]

Does God's specific sovereignty over his creation mean, as Sanders additionally charged, that "the divine will is never thwarted in any respect"?[25] Once again, no, it does not. There are different senses in which God's "will" is used. Clearly it is God's "preceptive will" that his moral law, as explained in the Ten Commandments and elsewhere, be obeyed, and yet people violate it all the time. As Mallary said, God "wills or commands men to repent, believe in the Lord Jesus Christ and live holy lives...This will, however, is resisted by multitudes; many do not repent and are not saved."[26]

God's will in terms of a "general wish" also does not come to pass in each and every instance. God wills (in the sense that he desires) that all men be saved and come to the knowledge of the truth. Yet in his decree or plan, clearly, not all men are saved.

It is God's will in terms of his decree or plan that can never be thwarted. It is this sense of God's will that must come to pass. Paul puts it plainly but emphatically in Ephesians 1:11. All things work "according to the purpose of Him who works all things according to the counsel of His will." To quote Mallary again: "God's will of sovereign purpose [his decree or plan] is not suspended upon the volitions of his creatures; the universe combined could not frustrate one jot or tittle; and in accordance with this will does he carry forward all his divine and glorious operations."[27] Puritan Thomas Manton put it all together this way:

> "Things that are most against his revealed will, fall

> under the ordination of his secret will; and, whilst men break commandments, they fulfill decrees: his revealed will showeth what should be done, his secret will what will be done."[28]

Finally, does God's specific sovereignty over his creation mean that man is not responsible for his own conduct? No! The Bible teaches both God's sovereignty and man's responsibility. In *Evangelism and the Sovereignty of God*, J.I. Packer called this an "antinomy" or apparent contradiction.[29] Both sovereignty and responsibility are true even if we, as mortal creatures, do not understand all the workings out of these concepts.

Praise God that he is in control of all things, even the evil that befalls us! If this were not so, Romans 8:28 would be a mockery. How could we legitimately say that "all things work together for good to those who love God, to those who are the called according to His purpose" if God were not in charge of all things? If God were not specifically sovereign over all things, an autonomous evil outside his control could harm us, apart from God's plan. But this will never be! God is sovereign over all things, and his sovereignty over all things is a wonderful truth!

In sum, unlike evangelical Arminians and openness theologians, Calvinists consistently apply God's sovereignty to all of life including, by necessity, the area of salvation. In this way, Calvinists submit to the truth of God's Word rather than trying to run from it. In this way, Calvinism is grounded upon an attitude of "utter dependence on God and humble trust in his mercy alone for salvation."[30] It is foursquare "the religion of dependence on God."[31]

Principle No. 2

Calvinists Have a Right View of Man In That They Adopt a Biblical View of the Will

The supremacy of God over all things also results in a right view of man. Perhaps the most common objection to Calvinism is that it runs counter to "free will." Those who assert this objection are right to consider the grace of God in connection with the will of man. They have at least an intuitive apprehension of the importance of the will in salvation. It has been said that what one believes about the will is "the watershed issue that broadly divides positions into two main camps."[32] In order to discuss the biblical view of free will, it is important to understand what various people mean by this term.

Jonathan Edwards defined the will as "that by which the mind chooses anything." He said the faculty of the will is that "power or principle of mind by which it is capable of choosing: an act of the will is the same as an act of choosing or choice." He added: "By whatever names we call the act of the will, choosing, refusing, approving, disapproving, liking, disliking, embracing, rejecting, determining, directing, commanding, forbidding, inclining, or being averse, being pleased or displeased with; all may be reduced to this of choosing."[33]

Biblically speaking, a person's "will" is closely linked to that person's desire. It may denote a desire to act or not act. Paul said in 1 Corinthians 16:12 that he had urged Apollos to come to the believers at Corinth but that Apollos was "quite unwilling to come at this time." The King James Version says "his will was not at all to come now." The New American Standard Version links the will in this sense with the underlying motive, saying "it was not at all his desire to come now." Conversely, the "will" may be linked to a desire to act that is restrained by a stronger, counteracting desire. Pilate was "willing" to release Jesus (Luke 22:20), but other considerations overruled this desire and determined his action. The choice ultimately made, however, is based on the person's prevailing desires. Pilate may have been "willing" to release Jesus but his "will" or choice was to have him crucified. Hence, Edwards says: "A man never in any instance, wills any thing contrary to his desires, or desires any thing contrary to his will." "It is that motive, which, as it stands in the view of the mind, is the strongest, that determines the will."[34]

What does it mean to say that a person has a free will?

Openness of God proponents adopt a view of freedom we have alluded to several times called "libertarian free will." Bruce Reichenbach provides a good definition:

> To say that a person is free means that, given a set of circumstances, the person...could have done otherwise than he did. He was not compelled by causes either internal to himself (genetic structure or irresistable

> drives) or external (other persons, God) to act as he did. Though certain causal conditions are present and indeed are necessary for person to choose or act, if they are free these causal conditions are not sufficient to cause them to choose or act. The individual is the sufficient condition for the course of action chosen.[35]

Pinnock likewise defines what he calls "real freedom" as "the freedom to perform an action or refrain from it."[36] He says: "Libertarian freedom recognizes the power of contrary choice. One acts freely in a situation if, an only if, one could have done otherwise. Free choices are choices that are not casually determined by conditions preceding them."[37] Thus, "we can choose between loving obedience and rebellious disobedience."[38] Pinnock believes Scripture "assumes" or "presupposes" libertarian freedom.[39] Notice he does not say that Scripture *asserts* or *presents* libertarian freedom.

Open theists are not the only ones to adopt this libertarian view of the will. Most evangelical Arminians also adopt this view, at least implicitly, though they may not work out a technical definition like Reichenback's. Herschel Hobbs was representative of many when he said: "Man is a personality with the power of choice."[40]

Non-Calvinists frequently accuse Calvinists of denying the existence of free will. They charge Calvinists with believing that God creates robots and automatons rather than free men and women. However, this accusation is based on a fundamental misapprehension of the Calvinist view of the will. Calvinists certainly believe in free will. As Dagg said: "It was God's purpose to create man a free-agent; and he did so create him."[41] Boyce also wrote: "The Scriptures recognize...the free agency, and accountability of man. Consciousness assures us of the latter."[42]

However, Calvinists do not mean by this the same thing as non-Calvinists. Calvinists reject the libertarian version of free will. As Gill wrote: "The will of man, though it is free, yet not independently and absolutely so; it is dependent on God, both in its being and acting; it is subject to his authority and command, and controllable by his power."[43] Calvinists believe in a freedom called "compatible freedom." Under this view, "genuine free human action is compatible with causal conditions that decisively incline the will without constraining it." In other words, an outside causal force moves a person to choose one option over another but the choice and resultant action are free as long as the person acts without external constraint.[44]

The "Hornet Song" expresses the essence of compatible freedom:

> When the Canaanites hardened their hearts against God,
> And grieved Him because of their sin,
> God sent along hornets to bring them to terms,
> And to help His own people to win.
>
> If a nest of live hornets were brought to this room
> And the creatures allowed to go free,
> You would not need urging to make yourself scarce,
> You'd want to get out, don't you see!
>
> They would not lay hold and by force of their strength
> Throw you out of the window, oh, no!
> They would not compel you to go against your will,
> But they would just make you willing to go.
>
> When Jonah was sent to the work of the Lord,
> The outlook was not very bright.
> He never had done such a hard thing before
> So he backed and ran off from the fight.
> Now, the Lord sent a great fish to swallow him up,
> The story I am sure you all know.
> God did not compel him to go against his will,
> But he just made him willing to go.
>
> God does not compel us to go, oh, no!
> He never compels us to go.
> God does not compel us to go against our will,
> But He just makes us willing to go.

We believe the compatible view of freedom is the Scriptural view and that libertarian freedom is profoundly unscriptural. Two theologians have addressed this issue in such impressive detail in recent works that we borrow from their conclusions. John Feinberg has an elaborate discussion of it in his monumental work *No One Like Him*. He cites Ephesians 1:11 as especially compelling. There, Paul says that in Christ, Christians have "obtained an inheritance, being predestined according to the purpose of Him who works all things according to the counsel of His will" (Ephesians 1:11). The focus of the verse is that, in Christ, Christians have obtained an inheritance. How did this happen? It happened because we were "predestined according to God's purpose." God is the one who "works all things according to the counsel of his will." Feinberg notes that God's "purpose" (*prothesin*) refers to the goal he intends to accomplish. Therefore, our election was not based on what God foresaw about how we would respond when confronted with the gospel; it means the decision was solely based on God's own desires and plan. Feinberg also notes that God's "counsel" (*boule*) indicates purpose and deliberation. Will (*thelema*) denotes choosing. Put together, the phrase "according to the counsel of his will" means that our predestination to salvation was done according to a divine pattern. Feinberg concludes:

> God deliberated about the best way to reach his goal, and from that deliberative process springs forth a plan (*boule*) that he deems best. God wills (*thelema*) that plan, and then brings it to pass (*energountos*). Nothing in this verse suggests that the purpose, the deliberating, or the choosing of the plan is based on anything other than God.[45]

What does this have to do with the correct view of freedom? Simply this. God as sovereign works all things according to the counsel of his will. He exercises his controlling power in a constant and continual display of strong sovereignty. This irrefutable biblical fact is utterly inconsistent with the idea of libertarian freedom. As Feinberg says:

> If libertarian free will contradicts this kind of sovereignty when it is exercised, then on biblical grounds, no model of providence incorporating libertarian free will should be adopted...But there is a model of providence that incorporates this strong sense of sovereignty and free will. Through this process of inferential reasoning we find that the best fit with biblical teaching about both divine sovereignty and human freedom is model of specific sovereignty that incorporates compatiblistic

> free will. Scripture does not explicitly say that humans have compatibilistic free will, but compatibilism is chosen because it is the only notion that fits a model of providence that incorporates freedom (and reflects Scripture in that respect) and a strong notion of divine sovereign control (and squares with biblical teaching in that regard).[46]

John Frame also has a lengthy discussion of the Scriptural difficulties with libertarian freedom in his *No Other God*. Like Feinberg, he agrees that the biblical data about God's sovereignty is incompatible with libertarian freedom. He adds, among other things, that (1) Scripture never grounds human responsibility in libertarian freedom or any other kind of freedom, but instead in the fact that God created us, owns us and has the right to evaluate us; (2) Scripture teaches that in heaven, the consummate state of human existence, libertarian freedom will not exist because God's people there will not be free to sin; and (3) Scripture denies that we have the independence demanded by libertarian theory; we cannot choose to act independently of our own character and desire (Matthew 7:15-20; Luke 6:43-45).[47]

Does compatiblism make the will less free? No! Everyone has genuine free will to make decisions. Those decisions are made on our own, unforced by an outside source. The will is free inasmuch as it acts according to its own nature.[48] When a woman pulls out of her driveway in her car on Sunday morning, she can decide to go left or right. But the choice that her free will makes is based on something—her heart's desires. She will go left if she desires to go to church; she will go right if she desires to go to Sunday brunch. She may have in the back of her mind a general wish to go to church because her parents taught her that was the right thing to do. But she is not a Christian, not even a particularly religious person, and her boyfriend is waiting for her at the restaurant. Her prevailing desire is to go to brunch. She turns right. This decision is unforced, but it is in accord with her nature.

When it comes to salvation, the Bible is very clear as to what an unbeliever's prevailing desire is:

> As it is written: "There is none righteous, no, not one; There is none who understands; There is none who seeks after God. They have all turned aside; They

> have together become unprofitable; There is none who does good, no, not one" (Romans 3:10-12).

As we saw in looking at the "T" in "tulip," "total depravity," every unbeliever freely chooses to run away from Christ and his demands. That is why Paul says in Romans 6:15-22:

> What then? Shall we sin because we are not under law but under grace? Certainly not! Do you not know that to whom you present yourselves slaves to obey, you are that one's slaves whom you obey, whether of sin leading to death, or of obedience leading to righteousness? But God be thanked that though you were slaves of sin, yet you obeyed from the heart that form of doctrine to which you were delivered. And having been set free from sin, you became slaves of righteousness. I speak in human terms because of the weakness of your flesh. For just as you presented your members as slaves of uncleanness, and of lawlessness leading to more lawlessness, so now present your members as slaves of righteousness for holiness. For when you were slaves of sin, you were free in regard to righteousness. What fruit did you have then in the things of which you are now ashamed? For the end of those things is death. But now having been set free from sin, and having become slaves of God, you have your fruit to holiness, and the end, everlasting life.

In other words, for all who are not saved, they have freedom to choose in accordance with their prevailing desires but the prevailing desire of their hearts is to reject God and suppress the truth about God that they know within them. Thus, they are free in a sense but their freedom is illusory. They are free but they freely (and invariably) choose to live in slavery to sin. Once again, formally, they are free, but practically speaking, they are not free at all, but slaves! This is what Martin Luther called the "bondage of the will." They lack what Frame calls "moral freedom"—the freedom to do what is good in God's eyes— because that freedom is beyond their moral ability.[49]

What does it take to give unbelievers genuine moral freedom (i.e., the true "real freedom," as opposed to Pinnock's variety)? It takes Holy Spirit regeneration. God said in Ezekiel 36:26-27: "I will give you a new heart and put a new spirit within you; I will take the heart of stone out of your flesh and give you a heart of flesh. I will put My Spirit within you and cause you to walk in My statutes, and you will keep My judgments and do them." In the process of conversion—in fact, at the beginning of that process, God gives those he has chosen new hearts and new desires. When a person is born again, he becomes a new creation in Christ and is then free to do what he was created to do in the beginning but which he was unable to do beforehand—voluntarily and freely to come to God in faith and repentance and worship.

Before we were saved, we had an illusory freedom because we were slaves to sin. Once we are saved, we have genuine freedom because we are slaves to Christ and to righteousness. In this sense, the will is not truly free until a person comes to Christ. This moral freedom is a far greater freedom than the freedom merely to choose between good and evil. This is the freedom to find satisfaction in God. It is the freedom to attempt to fulfill the purpose for which God created his people. As Feinberg said, "To be free of the ability to sin, and to be rid of its consequences in one's life, from a theological perspective, is far greater freedom than merely having the ability to do either good or evil—even better than being free to do both equally, as Adam was before the fall."[50] True freedom is the freedom to glorify God and enjoy him forever.

Principle No. 3

Calvinists Strike a Biblical Balance Between God's Transcendence Above His Creation and His Immanence In His Creation

Another way to think about God is to consider his divine transcendence and immanence. Transcendence means that God is "separate from and independent of the natural order and human beings."[51] "God unceasingly rules by His providence in pursuance of a purpose."[52] God's transcendence flows from his status as creator and our status as creatures. The great Old Testament prophet Isaiah said of God: "It is He who sits above the circle of the earth, And its inhabitants are like grasshoppers, Who stretches out the heavens like a curtain, And spreads them out like a tent to dwell in" (Is 40:22). This passage reflects what J. Gresham Machen called "the awful transcendence of God, the awful separateness between God and the world."[53]

Immanence means that God is "present to and in the natural order, human nature and history."[54] God is separate from, but active in, his creation. As Calvin put it, God "everywhere diffused, sustains all things, causes them to grow, and quickens them in heaven and in earth," who is "circumscribed by no limits" but "transfus[es] into all things his energy, and breath[es] into them essence, life, and movement."[55]

Clark Pinnock has criticized Calvinists for over-emphasizing God's transcendence over his immanence. In his book *Most Moved Mover*, Pinnock stated his concern that "God's transcendence can be emphasized at the expense of his involvement in the world, that placing too much distance between God and his creation takes away from God's glory...if it obscures the freely chosen relationships that God seeks to have with creatures."[56] In the same book, he later amplified the point: "We have too often favored God's remoteness in contrast to God's immanent presence. It is time to overcome the one-sidedness and give God's immanence its due."[57]

We do not quibble with the notion that one should eschew unbalanced "one-sidedness" in theological thinking and give God's immanence its due. However, when it comes to God's plan of salvation, we believe both the open theists and evangelical Arminians strike the wrong balance. Ironically in light of their criticism of Calvinists, both groups unduly de-emphasize God's immanence in favor of an overstated transcendence. By teaching that Christ did not actually atone for anyone when he went to the cross, but that he merely made atonement possible for those who believe, non-Calvinists conceive a God removed and remote from his creation in the act of salvation, that he chooses to stand helplessly aside and watch as most of humanity exercises its free will to make the wrong choice, to not believe, and to end up in hell. Practically speaking, this ends up being a semi-deist perspective that makes God distant and cold.[58]

Calvinists, in contrast, hold to a balanced view of God's transcendence and immanence. Calvin taught that God's sovereignty over his creation rightly emphasized both his transcendence and immanence: "Providence means not that by which God idly observes from heaven what takes place on earth, but that by which...he governs all events." He added: "Thus it pertains no less to his hands than to his eyes."[59]

Principle No. 4

Calvinism Teaches that Even Salvation Is Subsidiary to a Greater End—The Glory of God

In some Baptist circles, salvation is the beginning and ending point of theology. It is the beginning because every service contains an altar call designed to get people to walk down an aisle and give their life to Christ. It is the ending point because those that do often receive no training in Christian discipleship, or worse, never darken the door of the church building again.

Calvinism emphasizes salvation and evangelism but not as ends in themselves. Calvinists believe salvation is a means to an even greater end—the glory of God. The glory of God is the purpose for which God created humanity and for which he saves a great multitude out of humanity.

The truth of this proposition can be seen throughout Scripture. In Isaiah 43:6-7 God says: "I will say to the north, 'Give them up!' And to the south, 'Do not keep them back!' Bring My sons from afar, And My daughters from the ends of the earth—Everyone who is called by My name, Whom I have created for My glory; I have formed him, yes, I have made him." In Isaiah 60:21 God says: "Also your people shall all be righteous; They shall inherit the land forever, The branch of My planting, The work of My hands, That I may be glorified." In Isaiah 61:3 the prophet declares: "To console those who mourn in Zion, To give them beauty for ashes, The oil of joy for mourning, The garment of praise for the spirit of heaviness; That they may be called trees of righteousness, The planting of the Lord, that He may be glorified." Jonathan Edwards said of these verses: "In these places we see that the glory of God is spoken of as the end of God's saints, the end for which he makes them, i.e., either gives them being, or gives them a being as saints, or both. It is said that God has made and formed them to be his sons and daughters for his own glory, that they are trees of his planting, the work of his hands, as trees of righteousness, that he might be glorified."[60]

The New Testament also reveals that God's glory is the chief purpose of Christ's work of redemption. In John 7:18 Jesus said he did not seek his own glory in the work he came to perform but the glory of his Father who sent him. In John 12:27-28, he cried out: "Now My soul is troubled, and what shall I say? 'Father, save Me from this hour'? But for this purpose I came to this hour. Father, glorify Your name.' Then a voice came from heaven, saying, 'I have both glorified it and will glorify it again.'" In John 17:4-5 he prayed: "I have glorified You on the earth. I have finished the work which You have given Me to do. And now, O Father, glorify Me together with Yourself, with the glory which I had with You before the world was."

Indeed, Edwards observes that the glory of God is spoken of in Scripture as the goal or purpose of a number of spiritual graces: faith (Romans 4:20; Philippians 2:11); repentance (Joshua 6:19); love (2 Corinthians 8:19); thanksgiving and praise (Luke 7:18; Psalm 50:23).[61] Passages such as 1 Corinthians 10:31 ("whether you eat or drink, or whatever you do, do all to the glory of God") demonstrate that God "requires of men that they should desire and seek God's glory as their highest and last end in what they do."[62] Hence, the answer to the very first question of Spurgeon's version of the Baptist Catechism rightly states that the chief end, or purpose, of man is to glorify God and enjoy him forever.

The Calvinistic system is fundamentally based on these principles. God's primary purpose in creation and redemption is to glorify himself! How does God glorify himself in the salvation of people? He glorifies himself by doing the saving himself. In contrast, Openness and Arminian theology flow from an imperfect and deficient understanding of these things. This is best illustrated by an off-handed but revealing comment by Clark Pinnock in *Most Moved Mover*. He said that God employs his power "for the good of the partner and not self-enhancement."[63] He repeated a few pages later, "God is not a cosmic stuffed shirt, who is always thinking of himself."[64] Pinnock's understanding of God's ultimate purpose in salvation is out of line with the biblical revelation.

Principle No. 5

Calvinists Understand That a Devotional House Must Be Built Upon a Doctrinal Foundation

Many evangelical Arminians object to the Calvinistic emphasis on doctrine. Not all fit evangelical Arminians avoid doctrine, of course, but many do if their rhetoric is to be believed. Those "pragmatic Arminians" consider theological discussion to be unimportant. It "won't preach," they say. Thus, they set doctrine and evangelism over against one another and proclaim that they are "too busy saving souls" to worry about "doctrinal quibbles" such as the nature of God's saving grace. They seek to build a devotional house without a doctrinal foundation.

Most evangelical Arminians abhor theological liberalism. Yet, ironically, the mindset that sets doctrine and devotion against one another actually promotes liberalism in incipient form. For liberals too seek devotion without doctrine. They seek to undermine the Bible, theology and doctrine as the foundational basis for the Christian faith, but then they want to turn around and attempt to hold onto the Christian life. Like many evangelical Arminians, they hold that devotion to Christ is the essence of Christianity. They say that orthodox adherence to doctrines such as the virgin birth, the atonement of Christ, and the resurrection are irrelevant to devotion. These opposing factions, therefore, are aligned in proclaiming that true religion is in the area of experience.[65]

J. Gresham Machen saw the danger of this thinking a number of years ago. In his classic treatise *Christianity and Liberalism*, he responded to the assertion that "Christianity is a life, not a doctrine" by saying that this assertion has "the appearance of godliness" but "is radically false":

> The pious hearer labors under the impression that he is merely being asked to return to the simplicity of the New Testament, instead of attending to the subtleties of the theologians. Since it has never occurred to him to attend to the subtleties of the theologians, he has that comfortable feeling which always comes to the churchgoer when some one else's sins are being attacked...In point of fact, however, the attack upon doctrine is not nearly so innocent a matter as our simple churchgoer supposes; for the things objected to in the theology of the Church are also at the very heart of the New Testament. Ultimately the attack is not against the seventeenth century, but against the Bible and against Jesus Himself.[66]

Doctrine and devotion, belief and practice, should never be

separated. Paul, in Titus 2:1-8, brings them together:

> But as for you, speak the things which are proper for sound doctrine: that the older men be sober, reverent, temperate, sound in faith, in love, in patience; the older women likewise, that they be reverent in behavior, not slanderers, not given to much wine, teachers of good things—that they admonish the young women to love their husbands, to love their children, to be discreet, chaste, homemakers, good, obedient to their own husbands, that the word of God may not be blasphemed. Likewise, exhort the young men to be sober-minded, in all things showing yourself to be a pattern of good works; in doctrine showing integrity, reverence, incorruptibility, sound speech that cannot be condemned, that one who is an opponent may be ashamed, having nothing evil to say of you.

The first verse speaks of doctrine. There, Paul tells Titus, a young preacher, to "speak the things which are proper for sound doctrine." This is the foundation. In verses 7 and 8, he talks about the other side of the coin—devotion. In all things show yourself to be a pattern of good works. There, Paul talks about the house to build. He speaks of the Christian life.

Losing sight of either the foundation or the house leads to grave error. One mistake is to be sound in doctrine but sound asleep. Too many Calvinists fall into this error; they've forgotten devotion. Another mistake is to feverishly build the house, putting in windows, putting on doors, nailing on the roof, but forgetting the foundation. Too many Arminians fall into this error; they've forgotten doctrine. True Christianity is a combination of the two.

There are those who cry down doctrine and cry up experience. They proclaim: "Christ is our creed!" "The Bible is our textbook!" They sound extremely pious. But which Christ is their creed? We live in a day when there are a thousand christs on the religious market. Only the person with a doctrinal foundation can say which Christ we are talking about. In addition, all the cults in the world claim that the Bible is in some way their textbook. Somebody has to say what it means. That, of course, gets us into doctrine.

It is not enough to speak of mystical experience with God without some doctrinal knowledge. We worship God in truth, the

Bible says, as well as Spirit (John 4:23). Truth stated in words is doctrine! Any effort to be a practicing Christian without knowing doctrine will always fail.

What is Christian experience? Christian experience is the influence of sound doctrine, Biblical teaching, and applying it to the mind, the affections and the will, by the power of the Holy Spirit. J.C. Ryle said one can talk about Christian experience all he wishes, but without doctrinal roots, it will be like cut flowers stuck in the ground; it will wither and die. It is impossible, therefore, to overemphasize the first place of sound doctrine in the life of the Christian. Right thinking about spiritual matters is imperative if we would have right living.

Let the lessons of history be learned! This is not the first time evangelicalism has faced a creeping liberalism and an apathetic Arminianism. In late nineteenth century England, Baptist preacher Charles Spurgeon was a Calvinist voice crying out in the wilderness against stealth liberalism in his denomination. He lost his battle, not because the liberals won, but because non-Calvinist conservatives capitulated. This is aptly illustrated by a preface to a Victorian collection of sermons described by Michael Haykin in a recent issue of *The Banner of Truth* magazine. The book, published in 1885, contains a number of sermons by well-known nineteenth century preachers Spurgeon, Moody, Talmage and Beecher. The preface was written by an unknown editor. It began by noting the then-popular assumption that no one read sermons anymore. The editor agreed that this might be generally true but stated "there are sermons and sermons." He said, few people in his day were interested in the older style of sermons, "the dry type of doctrinal discourses that was once common in the pulpit." By his time, those sermons had been replaced by "more interesting" ones that contain "more enlivened appeals to the human heart and conscience." "The Church," he wrote, "as it has dropped dogma, has in large degree returned to its first work of evangelizing the world by the spirit and power of the Gospel; and in the true missionary spirit, it is going again into the highways and byways to reclaim the world to Christ, and to bring the prodigal back to the Father."[67]

One does not need to wonder what Spurgeon would have thought of this practice of setting doctrine against evangelism, along with its underlying assumption that too much talk of doctrine hinders the spreading of the gospel. Spurgeon was known for his rare ability to combine "rigorous theology, warm spirituality and down-to-earth practicality."[68] As Iain Murray said about Spurgeon's theology:

> "What distinguished Spurgeon from so many of his contemporaries was that all his preaching was from within a definite framework of truth, a framework massive because Biblical and yet also simple enough to be stated within a narrow compass. Spurgeon could and did state his faith in definite confessional form, and his sermons, diversified though they are, and ranging widely through Scripture, never lose touch with the system of gospel truth to which he held."[69]

Two years after this preface was published, Spurgeon was engaged in the Down-Grade Controversy.[70] That controversy began when Spurgeon's church newsletter, *The Sword and the Trowel*, published a series of articles charging that liberalism was afoot in the Baptist denomination and that the church at large was on a "downgrade" from Calvinistic conservatism to theological liberalism. In the uproar that ensued, Spurgeon withdrew his church from the Baptist Union because its leaders refused to take a doctrinal stand against liberal Christianity. Thus, in the Down-Grade Controversy, Spurgeon not only battled liberal theology in the English Baptist denomination, but also a conservative apathy to doctrine that ultimately allowed the liberals to prevail.

Hayken notes that the 1885 preface helps explain "how sectors of late Victorian Evangelicalism helped to prepare for the coming of Liberalism." The author of the preface was not a liberal, but "his easy dismissal of doctrine in favor of evangelism helps explain why some Victorian Evangelicals found themselves without any adequate response in the face of the liberal assault on Christian orthodoxy at the end of the nineteenth century and at the start of the twentieth."[71]

Today's evangelicalism parallels the conservative Christianity of Spurgeon's day in frightening ways. Among many (but again, we say, not all) non-Calvinists, there is a strong antipathy toward doctrine and a concomitant focus on doctrineless-experience. We have detailed some of that antipathy elsewhere.[72] Suffice it to say here that we agree with Spurgeon's conviction that "Arminianism has usually been the route by which [Protestants] have traveled down-ward to Socinianism." Spurgeon rightly observed that "Calvinism has in it a conservative force which helps to hold men to the vital truth."[73] Calvinists insist on both a doctrinal foundation and a devotional house.

Principle No. 6

Calvinists Accept That God Has Kept Some Things Secret From his Creation.

All humans are prone to question God when we cannot understand his ways. But Scripture counsels us to restrain this propensity. As relentless biblicists, Calvinists take seriously the teaching of Deuteronomy 29:29: "The secret things belong to the Lord our God, but those things which are revealed belong to us and to our children forever, that we may do all the words of this law." As John Dagg wrote: "We must, without taking offense, permit the Sovereign Ruler of all to have his secrets, and to make known his ways only so far as he pleases."[74]

This is the heart of where we believe non-Calvinists falter. As rationalists, they simply cannot accept what they do not understand. This is certainly true of the openness of God crowd. Gregory Boyd said in *God of the Possible*, "the mind must be thoroughly convinced if the heart is to be thoroughly transformed."[75]

In stark contrast was the simple faith of John Bunyan. He wrote: "Shall God the only wise be arraigned at the bar of thy blind reason, and there be judged and condemned for his acts done in eternity? Who hath directed the Spirit of the Lord, 'or who hath been his counselor?' Do you not know that he is far more above us, than we are above our horses or mules that is without understanding? 'Great things doeth he, which we cannot comprehend.' Great things and unsearchable, marvellous things without number."[76]

When it came to the deeper mysteries of God, a long litany of church leaders have been willing to leave them alone and let them rest in God's hands. Bunyan wrote: "God did not intend that all that ever he would do, should be known to every man, no nor yet to the wise and prudent. It is as much a duty sometimes to stay ourselves and wonder, and to confess our ignorance in many things of God, as it is to do other things that are duty without dispute."[77] He went on to add that we will understand better in eternity:

> You shall see in that day what a harmony and what a glory there will be found in all God's judgments in the overthrow of the sinner; also how clear the Lord will show himself of having any working hand in that which causeth eternal ruin...[78]

The old Scottish preacher John Dick similarly said, "Let us never forget that it is not reason, but revelation, which is our guide in religion, and that, when the latter speaks, it is the province of the former to listen and acquiesce."[79]

******

A number of other subsidiary principles flow out of Calvinism's submission to the supremacy of God in all things. To take just one, Henry Meeter says with respect to the Calvinist's perspective on culture:

> The Anabaptist withdraws from the world, condemning it as a wholly bad manifestation in which nothing but the devil operates. The Pelagian and the Roman Catholic seek to maintain that the science, art, and industry of the world are products of good that is still left in natural man. But the Calvinist sees everywhere, in the pagan world and among unbelievers, wherever science, art, and culture are brought to higher levels, the working of God's Holy Spirit, fruits which God has brought to pass in spite of the wickedness of the natural heart of man. The Calvinist thankfully accepts these fruits as products of God's grace and claims them for God's kingdom. Not to withdraw from the world, and on the other hand not to become conformed to the world but to make it his business to use these gifts of God's common grace for the glory of God and for the establishment of his kingdom—that is the duty and the glorious ideal of every good Calvinist.[80]

Cultural, political and social ramifications of the Calvinist system are beyond the scope of this work. They can be explored to great profit in such works as Meeter's *The Basic Ideas of Calvinism* or Kuyper's *Lectures on Calvinism*.[81]

Suffice it to say that J.I. Packer was absolutely right in declaring that, without Calvinism, "you cannot begin to explain modern Britain—England, Wales, Scotland, Ireland—nor modern Europe, nor modern America, nor indeed any English-speaking country anywhere."[82]

To sum up, Calvinism teaches that God is supreme over all. We conclude this chapter by noting that in this supremacy there is great hope. God has a plan for the future! He is working out his plan in minute detail! All things work for the good of those who love God and who are called according to his purpose! Even evil is working for the good of the Christian and the glory of God. Thus it is that the saints of God can sing:

> "You are worthy, O Lord, To receive glory and honor and power; For You created all things, And by Your will they exist and were created" (Revelation 4:11).

> And every creature which is in heaven and on the earth and under the earth and such as are in the sea, and all that are in them, I heard saying: "Blessing and honor and glory and power Be to Him who sits on the throne, And to the Lamb, forever and ever!" (Revelation 5:13).

GOODNESS

Chapter 6

The Goodness Of God In Calvinism

Non-Calvinists often charge those who hold to Calvinist theology with underemphasizing the goodness and love of God. For example, Clark Pinnock once called the God of Calvinism "some kind of terrorist who goes around handing out torture and disaster." He offered the opinion: "One need not wonder why people become atheists when faced with such a theology" and "a God like that has a great deal for which to answer."[1] These kind of statements, though needlessly inflammatory, reflect a genuine difficulty in understanding how God can be simultaneously good and loving, and yet pass over some for salvation. This chapter seeks to address the real concerns behind this sentiment.

God Is Good!

There is no question that God is good. All the time. All Christians, including Calvinists, affirm this. But what do we mean when we speak of God's goodness? On the one hand, we can think of God's goodness as an internal attribute. In this respect, we can consider it as equivalent to his holiness. We see this conception of God's goodness in Exodus 33:19 when the Lord tells Moses that he will make his "goodness" pass before Moses on Mount Sinai. On the other hand, we can think of God's goodness toward humanity. In this respect, God's goodness refers to his "kindness, benevolence or beneficence toward others."[2] Thus, the Bible speaks of the "richness of His goodness" that leads to repentance (Romans 2:4).

John Dagg has an extensive discussion of this aspect of God's goodness in his *Manual of Theology*. He links God's goodness to his love, grace and mercy:

> God's goodness, as exercised toward his creatures, is often expressed in the Scriptures by the term love. Love is distinguished as benevolence, beneficence, or complacence. Benevolence is love in intention or disposition; beneficence is love in action, or conferring its benefits; and complacence is the approbation of good actions or dispositions. Goodness, exercised toward the unworthy, is called grace; toward the suffering, it is called pity or mercy.[3]

God's goodness is seen in the work of his creation. Dagg says in this regard: "When we consider the innumerable living creatures that are, at this moment, receiving pleasure from the abundant and varied stores which his creating power has furnished; and when we reflect, that this stream of bounty has flowed incessantly from the creation of this world, we may well consider the fountain from which it has descended as infinite."[4]

God's goodness is seen in his common grace. He "makes His sun rise on the evil and on the good," and he "sends rain on the just and on the unjust" (Matthew 5:45). He also institutes government as a restraining force to hold back lawlessness. "The Lord is good to all, and His tender mercies are over all His works" (Psalm 145:9).

God's goodness is also seen in his salvation of the elect. In 2 Thessalonians 1:11-12 Paul prayed for the Thessalonian believers: "Therefore we also pray always for you that our God would count you worthy of this calling, and fulfill all the good pleasure of His goodness and the work of faith with power, that the name of our Lord Jesus Christ may be glorified in you, and you in Him, according to the grace of our God and the Lord Jesus Christ." Paul's main point was to inform the Thessalonians that he was praying that their salvation (justification) would be made plain by evidence of their sanctification. He put it three ways. First, he prayed that God would fulfill in them "the work of faith with power." Second, he prayed that God would count them "worthy of [their] calling," that is, the effectual calling by which God brought them from death to life, gave them new hearts and made them a new creation. Third, he prayed that the name of Jesus "may be glorified" in them. Fourth, and most significantly for our purposes, he prayed that God would fulfill "all the good pleasure of his goodness" in them. God's goodness led to their salvation. It gave him "good pleasure" to pour out his grace upon them. He exercised that goodness in the outworking of their salvation. They were saved "according to the grace" of God the Father and Jesus, God the Son.

God Is Love!

Let's go one step further. Along with being good, God also is a God of love. The Bible repeatedly asserts that love is one of God's central communicative attributes. Indeed, the apostle John twice declares that love is an essential part of God's nature. "God is love" (1 John 4:8, 16).

Calvinists enthusiastically affirm that God is love. James Boyce observed that there are five "kinds" of God's love mentioned in the Bible.[5] First, there is "the love of complacency" or "approbation." This is love given to a worthy object. It is exercised by God, most purely, in the love of the members of the Trinity toward each other. But this love cannot extend to the guilty. Sinful man cannot receive the love of complacency. Even the believer in Jesus does not receive this love until glorification in eternity.

Second, there is the love of benevolence, which corresponds to the idea of God's goodness toward his creation. This love manifests itself in common grace toward both the wicked and the righteous.

Third, there is the love of compassion. This corresponds to our idea of pity. It is a benevolent disposition toward those in distress. Boyce says we see this in God's forbearance with which he delays the punishment of the guilty. We see it in Jesus' continual offers of mercy, his yearnings after sinners' salvation, and in sending Jesus to offer eternal life to them.

Fourth, there is mercy. Mercy is undeserved compassion to the guilty. It is given only to the guilty. It consists, not only in a desire not to punish an offender, but in the pardon and cleansing of the offender. However, Boyce took pains to point out that this mercy must be exercised in accordance with the truth and justice of God.

Finally, there is affection. Affection differs from complacency because the object of affection does not need to hold intrinsic worth. It differs from benevolence because its object is not viewed in general with all others, but is one of special interest. It differs from compassion and mercy because the object need not be in distress nor sinful. Calvinists believe that it is from God's affection toward the elect that grace proceeds. By definition, grace is undeserved favor to innocent or guilty parties arising from affection.

God's Ways Are Not Our Ways

Even though Calvinists obviously affirm the goodness and love of God, non-Calvinists frequently charge Calvinists with inadequately emphasizing those facets of God's nature in salvation. Evangelical Arminian Hobbs wrote that the doctrine of unconditional election is "error" because it "magnifies some aspects of God's nature to the neglect of all others"—specifically, it "emphasizes God's will and power and minimizes his righteousness and love."[6] Pinnock puts it more bluntly: "A God who loves cannot be conceived in a deterministic way, like the power of the puppeteer."[7]

Are they right? Do Calvinists minimize God's goodness and love by accepting the Biblical revelation that God's election is according to the good pleasure of his will (Ephesians 1:5-6)? As we have seen, Calvinists, of course, affirm that God is both good and loving in his essential attributes. But are the non-Calvinists right in suggesting that we practically deny what we formally affirm?

We say no! The problem is that the non-Calvinists have a conception of God's goodness that is laden with hidden presuppositions, the most basic of which is that they cannot conceive of a good God that does not allow libertarian freedom. In their web of beliefs, God's goodness and libertarian freedom must go hand in hand. They cannot conceive of one without the other. Indeed, one is defined by the other. Thus, they assume in their theology that (1) a good God, in order to be good, must yield his sovereignty to man's libertarian freedom and (2) a loving God would not create a universe in which man did not have libertarian freedom. This means that they per force reject the notion of unconditional election because it does not fit into their concept of what a good God will do.

In so thinking, non-Calvinists err by starting their reasoning process with a conception of human goodness and love and then seeking to apply those conceptions upward to God. This is a grave mistake. It fails to account for the fact that human ideas cannot apply *univocally* to God. In other words, there is no one-to-one correspondence between the goodness of man and the goodness of God and the love of man and the love of God (or any other attribute that can be applied to both God and man). In God, goodness and love exist infinitely and perfectly. In man, goodness and love exist altogether finitely and imperfectly. The relationship between God's love and goodness and human love and goodness is analogous, not univocal.[8] God and man are not on the same level, and therefore, we cannot think of God's love in the same way as we think of our love for other humans.

This is not to say that there is no relationship between love and goodness as divine attributes, and love and goodness as human qualities. There clearly is such a relationship. Otherwise it would be meaningless to even talk of God's attributes. We understand at least something of God's nature by our own experience of these things. But our own experience is not the starting point of thinking about these things. Rather, God's revelation of who he is must be the beginning point of analysis. Therefore, when it comes to love, for example, we must start with the biblical revelation that defines and limits divine love, rather than with our conception of what God's love should be like based on our own experience or human conception of love. In short, to understand God properly, we must think God's thoughts after him.

This will still leave us with a gap in understanding. God's thoughts are not our thoughts, and his ways are not our ways. Therefore, as Dagg poignantly queried with respect to God's goodness: "If God is infinitely good, why is human life begun in pain, and closed in pain, and subject to pain throughout its whole course?"[9]

Dagg was not merely engaging in speculative theology. He knew of what he spoke. His life continually was filled with sorrow and tragedy. Among other things, his first wife died while giving birth. Dagg recalled in his Autobiography that "this was the severest blow that I had ever received; but the gracious Being who saw it needful to inflict it, sustained me under it."[10] He was forced to abandon the pastorate in the prime of his ministry because of the loss of his voice. By the time he wrote his systematic theology text, he was virtually blind. He kept up his writing ministry through the use of a "writing board" which kept the lines straight and letters at a proper distance apart when he could not see. Through adversity, Dagg never lost his joy or love for the Savior or his ability to serve others and find ways to be useful. Moreover, despite his own suffering, Dagg never turned his back on a biblical view of God's goodness and love.

He may not have fully understand the relationship between God's revelation of goodness (all things work for the good; Romans 8:28) and his own conception of goodness (the absence of pain). But he accepted that God was not only good but infinitely good. When his understanding failed him, he left room for mystery. Hence, he wrote in *A Manual of Theology* that "we comprehend but a very small part of God's way." Nonetheless, he said, "we should exercise faith in the wisdom and goodness of our heavenly Father, and believe that his ways are full of goodness, even when they are inscrutable." He pointed out, "Enough of his goodness is seen elsewhere to satisfy us of its existence when mystery hides it from view."[11] He added, "We have found every other attribute of his nature incomprehensible to us, and it ought not to surprise us that his goodness is so."[12]

God's goodness in the area of salvation is no different. Bunyan, who knew something of suffering himself, perceptively stated:

> "Whatsoever God doth, it is good because he doth it; whether it be to give grace, or to detain it; whether in choosing or refusing. The consideration of this, made the holy men of old ascribe righteousness to their Maker, even then when yet they could not see the reason of his actions. They would rather stand amazed and wonder at the heights and depths of his unsearchable judgments, than quarrel at the strange and most obscure one.[13]

In other words, when we consider the issue of why God elected some to salvation and passed over others, and whether his electing is good or not, we must cease our deliberation when we come to the words of our Lord: "Even so, Father, for it seemed good in your sight" (Matthew 11:26). To do otherwise is simply the height of folly. As the fictional pastor Martin Spenser told an inquirer in Douglas Wilson's *Easy Chairs, Hard Words*,

> "Your friends are concerned that God be seen as good. But seen as good by whom? Those who believe the Word of God will know that God is light and in Him is no darkness at all. Of course He is good—by definition. And those who do not believe the Word of God will

> persist in thinking that there is a tribunal or court somewhere in which God will one day be arraigned. On the day of judgment, their folly will be apparent to all—even to them.[14]

God's Love and Our Love

Non-Calvinists also seize upon the issue of reprobation as a point of argument, asserting that the God of Calvinism cannot be loving toward those he does not choose for eternal life. The objection frequently runs something like this: God commands us to love our neighbor, and even our enemies. Yet God himself, in the Calvinistic system (according to the accusation), fails to follow his own command and show love for those he passes over for salvation.

John Piper has answered this argument with force.[15] He points out that it is based on a fallacious assumption—that the love we are commanded to show to our neighbor, and our enemies, is the same as the love God fails to show to the non-elect. This assumption is false because we are never commanded to dispense or withhold electing love. This is a privilege that belongs to God alone. Rather, we are instructed to be kind to one another, to show dignity to one another, to call men to faith and repentance. In his common grace, God does all these things to the non-elect. Thus, when he loves the non-elect, God does exactly what he commands us to do. When he chooses not to choose the non-elect to life, he is exercising a privilege that belongs to God alone.

God's Sovereignty and Arbitrariness

A related problem non-Calvinists have with the doctrines of grace is that God's election of some to salvation and his passing over of others seems arbitrary to our human minds. Why did God choose me? Why doesn't he choose my friend who, to my mind, is a decent man who loves his wife and kids, works a steady job, and never did anything to hurt anyone? The practical answer to this last question is—perhaps he has! Pray that God will save the lost, for we are all Calvinists on our knees! No one knows who is elected and who is not until the moment of death anyway.

At the more philosophical level, moreover, it is clear that the supposition of arbitrariness in the Calvinistic scheme simply is not true. Fuller said:

> The term *arbitrary* conveys the idea of caprice; and in this connection, denotes that in predestination, according to the Calvinistic notion of it, God resolves upon the fates of men, and appoints them to this or that, without any reason for doing so. But there is no justice in this representation. There is no decree in the Divine mind that we consider as void of reason. Predestination to death is on account of sin; and as to predestination to life, though it be not on account of any works of righteousness which we have done, yet it does not follow that God has no reason whatever for what he does. The sovereignty of God is a wise, and not a capricious sovereignty.[16]

Dagg also answered this objection of arbitrariness by again pointing to God's goodness:

> Sovereignty is to be distinguished from arbitrariness. In the latter, the will of the agent directs the action, without reference to a wise or good purpose to be accomplished. When God acts, it is according to his good pleasure. His pleasure is good, because it is always directed to a good end.[17]

How all this plays out, our finite minds cannot understand. God's goodness is made known to us in many respects. But there remains mystery in the divine nature, even with respect to something as familiar to us as God's goodness. Ultimately, we must leave this mystery in God's hands. Here, as in other places, when we cannot see his hand, we simply must trust his heart.

God's Election and God's Justice

Non-Calvinists have difficulty with God's justice as well as his goodness. They do not understand how a God who elects some to salvation but not others can be just. For example, one Southern Baptist leader offered the following hypothetical situation to illustrate his complaint against the God of Calvinism. He equated God to a farmer whose farm contained a lake. He posted a sign near the lake that said "no swimming." But several boys from town trespassed onto his property, read the sign, ignored it, and went swimming in the lake anyway. Each began to drown. The farmer happened by and saw the boys struggling in the water. He had the power to save each boy but decided to go into the water and save only one boy. He selected a boy in blue trunks, and saved him, but let the rest drown. This is how non-Calvinists view the God of the Bible! We will return to this illustration in a moment. For now, let's focus on the meaning of the crucial word "justice."

After the September 11, 2001 terrorist attacks on the Pentagon in Washington and the World Trade Center in New York that resulted in the loss of several thousand lives, there has been much talk in the United States of bringing the perpetrators of these dastardly deeds "to justice." To different people this means different things. To some it means a bullet (or rocket) to the head of the leaders of the terrorist groups who committed these acts. To others, it means a quick trial before a military tribunal. To still others, it may mean a civilian jury trial in New York. The word "justice" in our common vernacular does not have a fixed meaning. Our nation found that out after the O.J. Simpson murder trial. Statistics say that many white Americans thought the jury's verdict acquitting Simpson of killing his ex-wife was a "travesty of justice." Yet many black Americans thought that, in the jury's verdict, "justice prevailed." Americans say we believe in "justice for all." We simply have trouble defining what that means.

It is obvious that different people have differing conceptions of what justice is. However, most people would agree at least that, for justice to be done, the punishment must fit the crime. However, yet again, people often have varying conceptions of the seriousness of a crime; they therefore have varying conceptions of how severe punishment must be to "do justice." Justice by human conception has no grounding.

Not so with the justice of God. Theologically speaking, justice is "that rectitude of character which leads to the treatment of others in strict accordance with their deserts."[18] Theologians distinguish between two types of justice: commutative justice and distributive justice. Commutative justice is a commercial term referring to "fair dealing in the exchange of commodities." Distributive justice rewards or punishes men according to their actions. It belongs to government. It is in this sense that God is just.

Non-Calvinists have difficulty believing God would be just in determining the salvation of some and leaving others to perish. In fact, this objection is perhaps the largest stumbling block that non-Calvinists have to accepting the doctrine of grace. Is God just in damning sinners? Is he just in acting to save some but not all? Is he righteous in bringing some people into the world who will never have a chance to be saved because God has passed them over and not bestowed his saving grace upon them? These are all good and legitimate questions. We now attempt to answer them.

The objection reflects (unconsciously, no doubt) a weak view of sin. Mallary called it "the want of a full and proper conviction that all men, in consequence of sin, deserve the wrath of God."[19] Remember what justice is: getting what one deserves. What does all humanity deserve? Death. The truth is, God would be just to not save anyone, but to pass over all humanity. The Bible says all have sinned and the wages of sin is death. Thus, Scripture squarely places the basis of a person's condemnation on the person himself, not on God. As John Bunyan, the author of *Pilgrim's Progress*, rhetorically asked in his treatise on reprobation:

> Is [God] therefore the author of your perishing, or his eternal reprobation either? Do you not know that he may refuse to elect who he will, without abusing of them.

In other words, if God saves some who are under the sentence of condemnation, he is not under any obligation to save all. There must be, then, a clear distinction between condemnation and justice, on the one hand, and reprobation and sovereignty, on the other. Reprobation is "a simple leaving of the creature out of the bounds of God's election." It is an act of God's sovereignty. Condemnation is "to bind them over to everlasting punishment."[20] It is an act of God's justice. People go to hell because they have died in their sin not because they were passed over by God in accordance with his divine sovereignty. As Bunyan put it:

> The non-elect perish by reason of sin, notwithstanding present mercy, because of eternal justice; and that the elect are preserved from the death, though they sin and are obnoxious to the strokes of present justice, by reason of eternal mercy. What shall we say then? Is there unrighteousness with God? God forbid; "He hath mercy on whom he will have mercy; and compassion on whom he will have compassion." (Rom. 9:15).[21]

Thus, the non-Calvinists' argument that it is unjust of God to create people in order to damn them is a straw man. As Dagg put it:

> The objection, originating in dislike of God's justice, wholly misrepresents the character of his righteous judgment. It leaps from the creation of man to the final doom of the wicked, and wholly overlooks the intermediate cause of that doom. It proceeds as if sin were a very inconsiderate matter, and as if it must have been so regarded by God; and therefore, it represents the punishment inflicted for it as if inflicted for its own sake. The sentence pronounced will be, in the judgment of God, for just and sufficient cause; and in all the purpose of God respecting that sentence, the cause has been contemplated.[22]

Simply put, people are damned because of their sin, not because of God's elective plan. In Mallary's words: "election harms no man—election damns no man."[23] God is not an autocratic despot, consigning his creatures to eternal misery without any consideration for their guilt. No one will stand before God at the final judgment and claim that their condemnation is not just. Every mouth will be stopped (Romans 3:19).

Indeed, we must not forget that God did not make man as he now is. God originally "made man upright" (Ecclesiastes 7:29). Adam, of his own free will, sinned and plunged the human race into its sinful condition.

What of the illustration of the farmer and the drowning boys? Evangelical Arminians may not realize it, but they are faced with the same challenge to God's justice. They too believe that people are damned because of their sin, not because of a refusal to believe Christ (since many people die without having ever heard of Christ). Let's change the illustration slightly to make the point. Suppose there are four boys drowning in the lake after having read the "no swimming" sign and ignored it. As in the prior example, the farmer has the power to save all the boys. But if the Arminian God is typified by the farmer, he will choose to actually save none. In fact, he won't get into the water at all. He will stand on the shore and throw a lifeline to each boy, standing helplessly by as the boys struggle for life. But this farmer is omniscient. When he threw the lifeline, he already knew the first boy was unable to swim and so couldn't reach the lifeline; he drowned. The farmer already knew the second boy wasn't looking his way and couldn't see the lifeline thrown to him; he also drowned. The farmer further knew in advance that the third boy would choose to ignore the lifeline and try to swim to shore on his own. He also drowned. Only the fourth boy grabbed the lifeline and was saved. Is this farmer who formulated the plan to throw lifelines, knowing in advance that only one boy would be saved by them, in any different position than the farmer who chose to get into the water and physically pull only one boy out of the lake? We say no.

For those who still object to God's electing plan, the apostle Paul has another response, one that will likely be disconcerting to those who persist. In Romans 9:19-20, he answers an objection:

> "You will say to me then, "Why does He still find fault? For who has resisted His will?"

We may think this is a good question. We even may have asked it ourselves. But Paul, writing under the inspiration of the Holy Spirit, does not think it is a good question. He thinks it to be a very impertinent one. He responds in terms that effectively close the discussion:

> But indeed, O man, who are you to reply against God? Will the thing formed say to him who formed it, "Why have you made me like this?"

Why does Paul respond this way? Is this the way to engage in polite debate? Perhaps it is not. But Paul is not engaged in polite debate. He sees in the inquiry not an intellectual difficulty but a heart problem, a refusal to submit to the will of our creator. The objector simply does not have in mind the things of God. Paul's point is that God is the creator, and he owes his creation no explanation for who he is and why he acts the way he does. He draws upon the Old Testament for an analogy:

> Does not the potter have power over the clay, from the same lump to make one vessel for honor and another for dishonor? What if God, wanting to show His wrath and to make His power known, endured with much longsuffering the vessels of wrath prepared for destruction, and that He might make known the riches

> of His glory on the vessels of mercy, which He had prepared beforehand for glory, even us whom He called, not of the Jews only, but also of the Gentiles? (Romans 9:21-24).

We are fashioned according to the will of the Potter. Because God is our creator, no created being has the right to object to his sovereign decision-making.

Two Final Thoughts

Two final thoughts are worthy of consideration when it comes to the issue of how God can be simultaneously good, loving, merciful, compassionate, and yes, just, in electing some to salvation and passing over others? One important point to remember is that none of these attributes control any other. We cannot say, as liberals do, that because God is love, he does not allow anyone to go to hell. "Consider the goodness and severity of God" (Romans 11:22). When we consider God's nature and what he can or can't do, or what he will or will not do, we must do so in the light of all his moral attributes. Some theologians put this in terms of God's simplicity. This means that God's nature is uncompounded; his attributes are united in the one being that is God. They are not capable of separation.[24] Others are less comfortable with this terminology.[25] All agree, however, that God is not composite. All his attributes are interrelated. As E.Y. Mullins cogently explained:

> God is a person. His attributes are the qualities of his being as personal. They are not attached to him from without as if they were separate from his nature. They are not independent of each other as if one could be active without the others. They are not in conflict with each other as if there could be schism in the divine nature. There are not gradations among the attributes as if there could be a hierarchy of powers within God himself...[26]

Thus, God's wisdom is good. His goodness is wise. His goodness is holy, and his holiness is good. God's justice is pure. His love is a holy love, and his holiness is a loving holiness. The practical outworking of this is that it is a profound mistake to attempt to emphasize a single one of God's attributes at the expense of all others. This is a classic mistake of non-Calvinists. They weight God's love and kindness over his justice and holiness in a fashion that overthrows the latter characteristics in the area of salvation.

The second point is that in this as in every other area of life, our responsibility is to walk the walk of faith even in the absence of understanding. As Dagg so cogently put it: "If right principles prevailed in our hearts, we would not presume to dictate to the Infinitely Wise, nor find fault with his plans, but wait with pleasure on the development of his will: and when we cannot see the wisdom and goodness of his works, we should, in the simplicity of faith, rest assured that his plan, when fully unfolded, will be found most righteous and wise."[27] We come back to the distinction between a biblicist and a rationalist. To be a biblicist means to say, "I believe in order that I may understand." This is nothing less than the Christian's calling for life.

Chapter 7

Answering Hardball Objections and Heartfelt Questions

In this chapter, we answer several commonly offered "hardball objections" and heartfelt questions put to the Calvinist doctrines of salvation. Only the Holy Spirit of God can get a person to see that the doctrines of grace, as taught in the Bible and as reflected in Calvinistic theology, are good and precious. However, we hope God will use the answers to some of these objections and questions as part of the means to that end.

Hardball Objections

Objection No. 1: The condemnation of sinners without a chance of salvation makes God a monster.

This objection decries what the objector sees as God's unfairness in creating people who are not part of the elect. This objector asks, "How can you believe in a God who creates non-elect people and then 'damns them' to hell without giving them any chance for salvation simply because they are not chosen?" One Southern Baptist leader voiced this objection when he said:

> If these people over here, the vast majority, God created them to damn them, and by the way, I have a substantive problem with that, but that is the only consistent Calvinism...that means God has chosen to damn some people. Ladies and gentlemen, there is no way that you can derive a just God out of that. If God has deliberately created people to damn them because he needed to do that in order to show himself to be a God of judgment, you can believe that if you want to...there is never a time in my life when I have

believed that or will ever believe that."

Another Southern Baptist leader voiced something similar to this objection when he said: "The idea that a child is born into this world having done nothing good or evil...that child is going to hell because that child is not one of the elect, I totally, totally reject." The implication, of course, is that such a God is a monster who deserves derision and rejection rather than worship and devotion. For some, this objection is nothing but a rhetorical device. This objector knows that it mischaracterizes Calvinist theology but uses it anyway because it prejudices people against the doctrines of grace.

For others, this objection may be a sincere emotional response. Yet sincerity does not make it valid. The Bible simply does not allow someone to say that unbelievers who die and go to hell can blame God for their fate. Scripture clearly places the responsibility for a person's eternal destiny on the person. Jesus told his enemies in John 5:40: "You are not willing to come to Me that you may have life." When he lamented over the coming destruction of Jerusalem, our Lord cried out that he "wanted to gather [his] children together" but "you were not willing." (Matthew 23:37). Paul likewise makes clear that all people are without excuse for their sin: "For since the creation of the world His invisible attributes are clearly seen, being understood by the things that are made, even His eternal power and Godhead, so that they are without excuse" (Romans 1:20). Hence, as Wayne Grudem observes, "[w]hen people rejected Jesus he always put the blame on their willful choice to reject him, not on anything decreed by God the Father."[1] Charles Spurgeon likewise exclaimed: "Election does not involve reprobation...I hold God's election, but I testify just as clearly that if any man be lost he is lost for sin; and this has been the uniform statement of Calvinist ministers. I might refer you to our standards, such as "The Westminster Assembly's Catechism," and to all our Confessions, for they all distinctly state that man is lost for sin, and that there is no punishment put on any man except that which he richly and righteously deserves."[2]

The fact is, this objection reflects a weakness of faith. Dagg was unapologetically blunt on the point: "If men will pronounce the character of God unamiable, because he is just, and dooms sinful beings to hopeless misery, they prove thereby that they do not love the God whom the Scriptures reveal, and by whom they are to be judged. Their quarrel with the doctrine of election is, in truth, a quarrel with the justice of God, from which that election has not delivered them."[3]

Objection No. 2: Predestination Makes God a Respecter of Persons

Some objectors claim that the Calvinistic view of election makes God a respecter of person. They cite Romans 2:11 which says that there is no respect of persons with God (KJV) or as more modern translations put it, there is no partiality (NASB, ESV) or favoritism (NIV) with God. There are several flaws with this objection. First, it implicitly assumes that impartiality means equality. God treats all humanity impartially, as this verse teaches, but that does not mean he is required to treat everyone equally. Impartiality means that everyone receives what is justly due him and that no one receives arbitrary and capricious unfavorable treatment. As discussed earlier, God in his justice gives unrepentant sinners exactly what they deserve in leaving them in their sins, separated from him for eternity. At the same time, he is not bound to give to everyone an equal measure of undeserved grace.

Moreover, no one who really thinks about it wants everyone to be treated with the scrupulous equality this objector claims to desire. If God treated everyone equally and gave them what they deserve, he would give everyone justice—and leave them to their condemnation. For our part, we are glad God does not treat everyone equally, but chooses a part of humanity for salvation!

Objection No. 3: Predestination Kills Evangelism

This objection runs something like this: If a person has been elected, he will be saved no matter what he does. Therefore, it doesn't matter whether Christians evangelize. As Clark Pinnock caustically put it: "If God wants to save you, he will certainly do so, and without your lifting a finger to help him."[4] One Southern Baptist leader asserted that Calvinism "will stultify evangelism and missions." He claimed that, as a class, "five pointers" are not "red hot soul winners" but are proselytizers of those who are already saved. Another put it this way:

> Now, I don't care what any Calvinist has to say about it. Calvinism, as a doctrinal commitment, has always had the effect of being a drag, to put it the best way, kindest way, a drag on missions and evangelism. All you have to do is prove me wrong, but you have to do it in some other way than citing Spurgeon because he's been cited often enough and it is not really impressive to cite Spurgeon and one or two others and say we've proved you wrong. No, look at the whole. Look at what has happened across the centuries. Wherever Calvinism takes a strong root, evangelism begins to suffer and world missions begin to suffer. And it is understandable why. Here is a man who believes that God has created this number of people over here to be saved and, because he believes in irresistible grace, they're going to get saved no matter what. So what is the necessity of my going to them?[5]

Clever rhetoric aside, the concern expressed by these sentiments is a proper one. All Christians should be concerned to protect evangelism from any theology that stifles it. Thus, if Calvinism does indeed kill evangelism, we will join the evangelical Arminians in attempting to suppress it.

However, of course, Calvinism does nothing of the sort. The fact is, this is an all-too-predictable and feeble charge. Biblically speaking, all that is necessary to refute it is to point out that God's plan embraces both the end (salvation) and the means (the preaching of the gospel). Those God elects to eternal life, he brings to life through means, specifically, through the preaching of the gospel (Romans 10:14-15). Surely those who raise this objection understand this. The point is made often enough; over 100 years ago, Mallary called this objection "a gross perversion."[6] Dr. Thomas Ascol answered it most recently in a passionate article in *The Founders Journal*.[7]

Despite its obvious biblical invalidity, however, the objection persists. This is because Calvinism does kill a certain type of evangelism. It kills unbiblical, man-centered evangelism and some of the carnal unbiblical methods employed in that evangelism. However, it will not kill God-centered evangelism where biblical methods are employed in the great work of carrying out our Lord's clear command to go into all the nations and tell. This has been historically confirmed time and time again (and we can cite not just Spurgeon but also, among many, many others, Bunyan, Whitefield, Edwards, Carey, Fuller, and Lloyd-Jones).

Indeed, far from harming God-centered evangelism, true Calvinism quickens it. It was Calvinism and its passion for God's glory that fueled the eighteenth and nineteenth century Baptist missionary movement. It is Calvinism and its devotion to God's supremacy that fuels the desire for reformation and revival in Baptist churches today, where perhaps millions of unconverted people sit in the pews, lost, deceived, and unaware of their precarious spiritual condition. Oh, that others would catch the Calvinist vision for God and his plan for the nations, to call out of every people group those he has chosen and called to adoption as sons!

What is evangelism? It is the communication of a divinely inspired message that we call the gospel. It is a message that is definable in words, but must be communicated in word and power. "For our gospel did not come to you in word only, but also in power, and in the Holy Spirit and in much assurance..." (1 Thessalonians 1:5). The gospel message begins with information and includes explanation, application and invitation.

The information conveyed in evangelism is how God, our creator and judge, in mercy, made his Son a perfect, able and willing savior of sinners. The invitation given in evangelism is God's summons to mankind to come to that savior in faith and repentance, and find forgiveness, life and peace. "And this is His commandment: that we should believe on the name of His Son Jesus Christ and love one another, as He gave us commandment" (1 John 3:23). "Jesus answered and said to them, 'This is the work of God, that you believe in Him whom he sent'" (John 6:29).

To sum up, our definition of the evangelistic task is: To present Jesus Christ to sinful men, in order that they may come to put their trust in God, through Christ, to receive him as their Savior and serve him as their King in the fellowship of his church. You will notice that this definition includes the church. Our Lord gave his Great Commission to the church.

What is God centered evangelism? In a nutshell, it is evangelism based on a doctrinal foundation that God is supreme and that salvation is of the Lord. It is evangelism that has a firm doctrinal foundation. The doctrinal foundation for biblical evangelism is as important to the work of the evangelist as the skeleton is to the human body. Doctrine gives unity and stability. It is the doctrinal foundation that produces the spiritual strength that enables the evangelist to endure the storms of opposition, hardship and persecution that so often accompanies true missions. Therefore, the church that neglects the doctrinal foundation for biblical evangelism will soon find its efforts weakened, and spurious conversions will be produced. The lack of a doctrinal foundation will work against unity and invite error and instability in evangelistic endeavors. It is impossible to exaggerate the importance of a sound biblical foundation for true God-centered evangelism!

Doctrine shapes our destiny, and we are presently reaping the fruits of unbiblical evangelism. The great apostle Paul, instructing young minister Timothy to do the work of an evangelist, told him that doctrine is the first purpose of Scripture. "All Scripture is given by the inspiration of God and is profitable for doctrine" (2 Timothy 3:16; KJV). Evangelism without a doctrinal foundation is building on the sand (cf. Matthew 7:24-26). It is like cut flowers stuck in the ground; without doctrinal roots, they will wither and die. Calvinists have a doctrinal foundation for evangelism.

The Calvinistic foundation of God-centered evangelism guarantees its success. This is because we are assured that God the Father has chosen some to salvation (John 1:18, 15:16, Ephesians 1:4, 1 Thessalonians 2:13, John 6:37, 39, 44, 64, 65).

We are assured that God the Father gave his Son, the Great Shepherd, some sheep, and the Great Shepherd made atonement for those sheep that the Father gave him. The atonement was a planned atonement—the cross was not an accident. God planned it. He was not sleeping or caught off guard at the cross. He had an unchangeable, immutable plan, and it was perfectly carried out. The apostle Peter preached this as part of his first message: "Him, being delivered by the determinate counsel and foreknowledge of God, ye have taken, and by wicked hands have crucified and slain" (Acts 2:23; KJV). Moreover, the apostles not only preached it; they prayed it. Hear their prayer in Acts 4:27-29:

> "For of a truth against thy holy child Jesus, whom thou hast anointed, both Herod, and Pontius Pilate,

> with the Gentiles, and the people of Israel, were gathered together, for to do whatsoever thy hand and thy counsel determined before to be done" (KJV).

God was the master of ceremonies at the cross.

The Calvinistic foundation of God-centered evangelism additionally guarantees its success because God the Father had an unchangeable, immutable plan and power to execute it. "For I came down from heaven, not to do minc own will, but the will of Him that sent me. And this is the Father's will which hath sent me, that of all which he hath given me, I should lose nothing, but should raise it up again at the last day" (John 6:38-39; KJV). Jesus taught: "I am the good shepherd. The good shepherd gives His life for the sheep" (John 10:11). "I know my sheep" (John 10:14). Jesus described two characteristics of His sheep: (1) "My sheep hear My voice," and (2) "they follow Me" (John 10:27). In other words, our Lord's sheep have a disposition to know his will (they hear his voice) and a disposition to do his will (they follow him).

Calvinism also answers why some do not believe. Jesus said: "But you do not believe, because you are not of My sheep" (John 10:26).

The doctrines of grace, then, comprise an important element of the message of the cross, the message of evangelism. They teach that Christ's death was not in vain, but rather, everyone for whom he savingly died, will come to faith. It is interesting to note that when the angel announced our Lord's birth to Joseph, the angel was straight on this point: "And she will bring forth a Son, and you shall call his name Jesus, for He will save His people from their sins" (Matthew 1:21). Christ came to save "his people."

God used the fact that He had some people, some sheep, to encourage the evangelizing of that wicked city of Corinth. The apostle Paul was afraid to go to Corinth, and God encouraged him by saying: "Do not be afraid, but speak, and do not keep silent; for I am with you, and no one will attack you to hurt you; for I have many people in this city." (Acts 18:9, 10).

Jesus' coming was for his people: "And she will bring forth a Son, and you shall call His name Jesus, for He will save His people from their sins" (Matthew 1:21). His purchase on the cross was for his people. As John 10:11, 14, 15: states: "I am the good shepherd; and I know My sheep, and am known by My own. As the Father knows Me, even so I know the Father; and I lay down My life for the sheep."

His prayer was for all that the Father gave Him. "As You have given Him authority over all flesh, that He should give eternal life to as many as You have given Him" (John 17:2). "I pray for them. I do not pray for the world but for those whom You have given Me, for they are Yours." (John 17:9).

Is this the message of the cross that you have heard? A Christ whose death is not in vain and will not fail to accomplish all that was intended? Or, have you heard the message of a poor, impotent, pathetic, and sometimes effeminate Jesus who died just to make salvation possible and who is standing impotently by, waiting to see what these mighty, powerful sinners are going to do with him?

This is not just a different emphasis. It is a different content of the message of evangelism. The biblical gospel is God-centered, God-honoring, and good to sinners. God-centered evangelism has a doctrinal foundation, and this foundation guarantees its success. If a reader continues to be troubled that Calvinism kills evangelism, several resources are available to assist in examining and correcting one's understanding of these issues.[8]

Objection No. 4: Predestination Is Inconsistent With Christ's Universal Invitation

Another objection is that the doctrine of predestination is inconsistent with the invitation of the gospel. These objectors wonder how God legitimately could offer salvation to those he had already excluded from salvation. As one current Southern Baptist leader argued after citing Jesus' lament that Jerusalem would not receive him as Messiah, "If they 'could not' rather than they 'would not,' this is the biggest charade in history." He later said: "If you say that only certain people are elected and only certain people therefore can be saved, you can take all the 'whosoevers' in the Bible and make them a lot of mumbo-jumbo."

Over a century ago, Dagg responded to this type of objection:

> It is highly presumptuous in us to charge God with insincerity, because we cannot reconcile the two things with each other. We ought to remember that we are worms of the dust, and that it is criminal arrogance in

> us to judge and condemn the infinite God. But in truth, there is no ground whatever for this charge of insincerity. God requires all men to believe in Christ; and this is their duty, however unwilling they may be to perform it. The fact that they are unwilling, and that God knows they will remain unwilling, unless he changes their hearts, abates nothing from the sincerity of the requirement. God proves his sincerity, by holding them to the obligation and condemning their unbelief.[9]

He later reiterated:

> It has been asked, for what purpose does God send his outward call to the non-elect, since it will be ineffectual, unless accompanied with his omnipotent grace. We might as well ask for what purpose does God give men his law, when they will not obey it; or why does he institute a moral government over them, when they will not submit to it. Instead of demanding God's reasons for what he does, it becomes every man rather to inquire, what reason he can render to God, for violating his holy law, and rejecting the call of his gospel. We may be sure that God will do right, and will be able to vindicate his ways before the intelligent universe; and we should regard our propensity to call in question the wisdom and righteousness of his procedure, as an alarming evidence of our want of submission to his will.[10]

Then, as a practical matter, Calvinists must invite the lost to come to Christ because we do not know who is elected by God and who is not. It is not our place to know whom God will draw to himself, and so we must invite all to come.

And the fact is, the Arminians have nothing on the Calvinists when it comes to giving gospel invitations. No one has pleaded with sinners to be saved more so than did John Bunyan or Jonathan Edwards or George Whitefield or Charles Spurgeon! Spurgeon cried out: "Our souls are not stony; our bowels are not withdrawn from the compassion which we ought to feel for our fellow-men; we can hold all our views firmly, and yet can weep as Christ did over a Jerusalem which was certainly to be destroyed."[11] And indeed he proved it with every sermon and every book. Who can match the fervor for the lost of the Prince of Preachers in the following plea?

> He who does not take the step of faith, and so enter upon the road to heaven, will perish. It will be an awful thing to die just outside the gate of life. Almost saved, but altogether lost! This is the most terrible of positions. A man just outside Noah's ark would have been drowned; manslayer close to the wall of the city of refuge, but yet outside of it, would slain; and the man who is within a yard of Christ, and yet has not trusted him, will be lost. Therefore I am in terrible earnest to get my hesitating friends over the threshold. Come in! Come in! is my pressing entreaty. "Wherefore standest thou without?" is my solemn inquiry. May the Holy Spirit, render my pleadings effectual with many who shall glance at these pages! May he cause his own Almighty power to create faith in the soul at once![12]

Objection No. 5: Calvinism Is No Different Than the Fatalism of Islam

Some Southern Baptist leaders have called the Calvinistic system fatalistic. Others have equated it with Islam. These objections are malicious, demonstrating an acute lack of understanding and respect for the historical Baptist position. Islam is a false religion devoid of the power to save souls. Calvinism is the Christianity of Augustine, Luther, Calvin, Edwards, Whitefield and our Baptist forefathers, not to mention the biblical theology revealed by God through our Lord Jesus Christ and the apostle Paul. Islam reduces God to a category of the will and makes him a despot who stands above humanity. As the events of September 11, 2001 demonstrate, the attribute of love is absent from Allah. By contrast, the biblical God, the God of Calvinism, is a God of grace and love. To quote Spurgeon again:

> Between the predestination of Scripture and the fate of the Koran, every sensible man must perceive a difference of the most essential character. We do not deny that the thing is so ordained that it must be, but why is it to be, but that the Father, God, whose name is love, ordained it; not because of any necessity in cir-

> cumstances that such and such a thing should take place. Though the wheels of providence revolve with rigid exactness, yet not without purpose and wisdom. The wheels are full of eyes, and everything ordained is so ordained that it shall conduce to the grandest of all ends, the glory of God and next to that the good of his creatures.[13]

Fatalism is blind, attributing future events to random acts. It has no answer to the problem of evil. The ancient Greeks were fatalists. Homer articulated a fatalistic outlook in *The Iliad* when he had Achilles tell Priam, king of Troy, after Priam came to beg for the body of his beloved son Hector, whom Achilles had just killed:

> So the immortals spun our lives that we, we wretched men live on to bear such torments—the gods live free of sorrows. There are two great jars that stand on the floor of Zeus's halls and he holds his gifts, our miseries one, the other blessings. When Zeus who loves the lightning mixes gifts for a man, now he meets with misfortune, now good times in turn. When Zeus dispenses gifts from the jar of sorrows only, he makes a man an outcast—brutal, ravenous hunger drives him down the face of the shining earth, stalking far and wide, cursed by gods and men.[14]

In contrast to this, the God of Calvinism is an intelligent, all-wise God. Calvinism shows God more mighty and almighty to bring good out of evil than not to allow evil to exist. The cross is the best example of this. It remains the most wicked deed ever committed by the hands of sinful men, and yet, praise God, the greatest good that ever came to mankind. In sum, the objection that fatalism and Calvinism may be equated is wholly spurious.

Objection No. 6: Calvinism Teaches That God Damns Babies

One of the most scandalous charges some evangelical Arminians make against Baptist Calvinists is the accusation that they believe God damns babies who die in infancy. For example, one Southern Baptist leader has said:

> Think about little babies that die. How many babies die in the world today? Think about all the little babies that are aborted every year, about a million and a half. Well, let me ask you a question. Are the little babies that die that are not part of the elect, do they go to hell? They didn't know their name. They never did any good or evil. Some of them never even got born. I have a little baby boy in heaven, I am sure he is there. But I couldn't be sure if I didn't think he might not be one of the elect. Well, you say, maybe your little boy is not in heaven. Maybe he wasn't one of the elect. I don't want to serve a God who let my little baby die and fry.

This is a dangerous charge. It is dangerous for a minister of the gospel to turn one's back on the God Who Is, rejecting him, refusing to serve him, failing to worship him, simply because one does not understand or appreciate an aspect of his character.

It is also an inflammatory charge, though not a new one. The earliest Baptists apparently faced it and felt compelled to put their response in the 1689 *Baptist Confession of Faith*: "Infants dying in infancy are regenerated and saved by Christ through the Spirit." Spurgeon also faced a similar accusation:

> Among the gross falsehoods which have been uttered against the Calvinists proper, is the wicked calumny that we hold the damnation of little infants. A baser lie was never uttered. There may have existed somewhere, in some corner of the earth, a miscreant who would dare to say that there were infants in hell, but I have never met with him, nor have I met with a man who ever saw such a person. We say, with regard to infants, Scripture saith but very little, and therefore, where Scripture is confessedly scant, it is for no man to determine dogmatically. But I think I speak for the entire body, or certainly with exceedingly few exceptions, and those unknown to me, when I say, we hold that all infants are elect of God and are therefore saved.[15]

It is next an irresponsible charge. Simply put, no Calvinist believes infants who die in infancy are damned. Charles Hodge, a venerable Presbyterian Calvinist of the nineteenth century, flatly declared, "all who die in infancy are saved."[16] Spurgeon's words, though uttered in 1861, are still true: "As for modern

Calvinists, I know of no exception, but we all hope and believe that all persons dying in infancy are elect. Dr. Gill, who has been looked upon in late times as being a very standard of Calvinism, not to say of ultra-Calvinism, himself never hints for a moment the supposition that any infant has perished, but affirms of it that it is a dark and mysterious subject, but that it is his belief, and he thinks he has Scripture to warrant it, that they who have fallen asleep in infancy have not perished, but have been numbered with the chosen of God, and so have entered into eternal rest."[17] It is true that some Calvinists prefer not to express an opinion on the subject, taking the position that they should not venture to speak where the Bible itself is for the most part silent, but no Calvinist affirms that infants who die in infancy are damned. "Shall not the Judge of all the earth do right?" (Genesis 18:25).

This is finally a deeply ironic charge, for non-Calvinists must transform themselves into "temporary Calvinists" in order to avoid a countercharge of hypocrisy. Think about it. Who is it that says salvation is solely of the Lord? It is the Calvinists! Arminians, by contrast, introduce their libertarian freedom into the salvation equation, making the salvation decision man's responsibility. But as the Baptist leader correctly pointed out in the quotation above, infants cannot make volitional decisions. They cannot make "decisions for Christ." They cannot exercise faith.

Thus, Arminians must transform into Calvinists and say salvation is solely of the Lord in order to explain the salvation of the very infants they wish to defend. They cannot fall back on their typical construction of John 3:16 and say "whosoever will may come" because babies, by their nature, cannot come because they are incapable of belief. If dying infants are saved, their salvation is solely of God's mercy and grace. Calvinists say that is not only true of infants but of everyone who actually is saved.

The view of those Calvinists who prefer not to even deal with this subject should be addressed. Scripture does say very little about the death of infants. Where Scripture is silent, we do best to withhold from dogmatic opinions. Nonetheless, there are several compelling inferences from Scripture that lead evangelical Calvinists to believe that dying infants are part of the elect of God. The first is David's statement in 2 Samuel 12:23 after the death of the infant son Bathsheba bore him. David was inconsolable while the child was ill. But after the child died, he arose, composed himself, and said, "But now he is dead; why should I fast? Can I bring him back again? I shall go to him, but he shall not return to me." R.A. Webb pointed out that this statement is especially significant because of the change that took place in David at the point of the child's death. Deep sorrow and remorse changed to comparative optimism. But the only new information David had was that the child was dead. From this Webb concludes that David recognized the child would be in heaven and he believed he would join the child there someday.[18] The second compelling inference comes from Jesus' words in Matthew 19:14 "Let the little children come to Me, and do not forbid them; for of such is the kingdom of heaven."

Indeed, most Calvinist Baptists believe that an infant's death is certain proof that the child is elected to eternal life. It is a "sheer impossibility" for infants to die in a reprobate state. This is because, for punishment to have a rightful purpose, the person being punished must be aware of the punishment and the reason for it. An infant is too immature to understand and appreciate the reason for suffering; therefore, the infant is incapable of being punished. The child's guilt is Adamic and federal; but it is guilt of which he is not aware and can only become aware by growing to greater maturity. Webb said: "Providence must delay the death of the reprobate infant until he comes to maturity, and translates his original sin into conscious actual sin, so there may be a basis, not simply in law and truth, but in consciousness and conscience and experience for penalty."[19] Deuteronomy 1:39, Isaiah 7:15-16, and Jonah 4:11 all support this view by suggesting that God chooses not to punish children who lack the cognitive capacity to appreciate the difference between right and wrong.

Answering Heartfelt Questions

We conclude this chapter by answering three common questions we often receive and which a former president of the Southern Baptist Convention recently put to one of us:

Can I go to any man I meet and tell him that God loves him and wants him saved?

Most emphatically, yes! First, God loves both those who will die saved and those who will die in their sins. With respect to the latter, Mark 10:21 says that Jesus loved the rich young ruler even though he went away unsaved. Boyce called this the "love of benevolence" or "love of compassion."[20] Yet this love to the unregenerate is not saving love.

There is another love, a deeper love, that God exhibits to the elect. Can anyone doubt that God loves his own people to a greater degree than those who will die in their sins? Paul writes "God shows his love for us in that while we were yet sinners Christ died for us" (Romans 5:8). He also spoke of "the Son of God who loved me and gave himself for me" (Galatians 2:20). This corresponds with what Boyce called "mercy" and "affection."[21]

Does God want everyone to be saved? Paul writes of God our Savior "Who desires all men to be saved and to come to the knowledge of the truth" (1 Timothy 2:4). In Ezekiel 18:32, it is written: "'For I have no pleasure in the death of one who dies,'" says the Lord God. 'Therefore turn and live!'"

The non-Calvinist believes these passages contradict the idea that God has only chosen certain people to be saved. But that is not at all what these passages are saying! Rather, they speak of God's revealed will, not his hidden will (his eternal plan for what will happen). These verses simply tell us that God invites and commands every person to repent and come to Christ for salvation, but they do not tell us anything about God's secret plan regarding who will be saved.

Moreover, no one but universalists takes these verses as saying that God saves everyone. Evangelical Arminians as well as Calvinists are faced with the prospect that God wills *something* greater than he wills to save everyone. Under the Calvinist view, God deems his own glory more important than saving everyone (Romans 9). Under the non-Calvinist view, God deems man's libertarian free will more important than saving everyone. We have already seen that libertarian free will has no scriptural support. Here the important point is that both sides must say that there is something that God deems more important than saving everyone. Therefore, these verses do not assist the non-Calvinist in getting around the problem that: (i) On the one hand, God generally wishes that all be saved. (ii) On the other hand, God has decided that not all will be saved.

Does anyone who trusts Christ as his Savior and Lord receive the forgiveness of sins and justification?

Yes! By all means! This is the unequivocal teaching of the Bible. But as discussed above, under the view that Christ's death atoned for the sins of every single person, the non-Calvinist must assert that Christ's death atones for all those who *never* turn to Him as savior and Lord. Therefore, by implication, the non-Calvinist also must assert that those who are never saved will receive forgiveness of sins and justification *and* that those *same* people will pay the penalty for their own sins in hell. We have argued at length in Chapter Four that this is nonsensical and unbiblical.

Can I tell any man that I meet that Christ died for him?

Our answer is, it depends on what you mean by this. Do you mean that Christ died and completely paid the penalty already for all the man's sins? Or do you mean that Christ died in order to offer the man forgiveness for his sins. If the former, we demonstrated in Chapters Three and Four that this is not biblically accurate unless the person has been chosen by God and until that person comes to Christ in faith and repentance. If the latter, however, why use ambiguous language? Why would you insist on telling someone that Christ died for him (that is, has paid the penalty for his sins) when you simply do not know whether that is true or not? Why not simply tell him that Christ invites (indeed, demands) him to come to him in faith and repentance? Why not use Jesus' own words: "Come to Me, all you who labor and are heavy laden, and I will give you rest. Take My yoke upon you, and learn from Me, for I am gentle and lowly in heart, and you will find rest for your souls. For my yoke is easy and My burden is light" (Matthew 11:28-30).

These answers to non-Calvinists' hardball objections and heartfelt questions should suffice to satisfy any open-minded person. But Spurgeon had it right when he suggested that the most powerful answer to the non-Calvinist is the spirit-filled life of the evangelical Calvinist: "The better way...of proving this point is for each of us who hold these truths, to be more prayerful, more watchful, more holy, more active than we have ever been before, and by so doing, we shall put to silence the gainsaying of foolish men. A living argument is an argument which tells upon every man; we cannot deny what we see and feel. Be it ours, if aspersed and calumniated, to disprove it by a blameless life, and it shall yet come to pass, that our Church and its sentiments too shall come forth 'Fair as the moon, clear as the sun, and terrible as an army with banners.'"[22]

Beauty

Chapter 8

The Closet Calvinist

Jack was the pastor of Green Valley Baptist Church for thirty years before his sudden death. The heart attack that took him to his reward was a shock to all. Jack was active in his local association and beloved by all his people. But the bigger shock was what the visiting preacher said at the funeral. He knew Jack from teaching at the local seminary extension. He said Jack was a "Calvinist!" The other pastors in the association who attended the funeral discounted the remark. They remembered Jack for his piety, but they couldn't remember him ever entering into a theological discussion. Nor did they remember him standing up to defend the few Calvinist "boys from the seminary" who had come into the valley to pastor scattered churches over the years. Most of those "boys" hadn't lasted long. They generally were run out of town when their congregations found out they "didn't believe in getting people saved" because they stopped conducting altar calls. Or they "resigned" under pressure for trying to change the worship services only months after arriving, getting rid of praise choruses and musical solos, preaching forty minutes to an hour each service. When the association stepped into these situations to negotiate settlements between the churches and their pastors, Jack would always urge the besieged pastor to leave quietly. He didn't want anyone to make any waves.

The people who attended Green Valley Baptist Church were astonished. How could they know their pastor for so long and never realize he was one of those "dipped Presbyterians," as Grandpa Rose derisively called the Calvinistic Baptists. Pastor Jack believed in election? He never preached it to us, several people thought to themselves.

Rufus Jones, the oldest deacon in the church, was simply confused. After the funeral service, he walked into the pastor's library and picked up a copy of a battered old book from Jack's bookshelf called *The Five Points of Calvinism.* As he leafed through it, his brow furrowed in puzzlement. Even though the book was underlined, highlighted and dog-eared on virtually every other page, Rufus could not remember his pastor ever talking about these things from the pulpit or mentioning them in private conversation. If Pastor Jack had believed them, why wouldn't he preach them? As he read, Rufus realized in his heart that the doctrines being taught in the book were true. Then his puzzlement turned to anger. Why hadn't his beloved pastor preached these things? Why hadn't he shared the truth with his congregation? Deacon Rufus felt robbed. The people of Green Valley had discovered that Jack was a "closet Calvinist."

What Is a Closet Calvinist?

Closet Calvinists are people who claim to believe that the doctrines of grace are true, but they do not preach and teach them. They may fail to see how they relate to life. They may fail to find in them any practical relevance. Or they may fear the consequences of being labeled "soft on evangelism." They may hold back and keep their views secret because they do not want to face the disapproval of their peers. For whatever reason, they do not preach or teach the truth that they know. They make no converts to the full-orbed biblical Christianity that they know.

One critical error of closet Calvinists is a failure to recognize that truth always has an ethical content. It always affects life. Thus, they unintentionally drive an artificial wedge between theology and life and between doctrine and devotion. Indeed, they implicitly accept the same error adopted by liberals and many evangelical Arminians—that of separating theology and life. To be sure, closet Calvinists do not reject the intellectual content of Christianity, the biblical doctrines of grace. However, they do ignore it. Closet Calvinists may believe the doctrines of grace, but they practically and effectively, if not formally, separate doctrine from devotion.

We see four basic reasons why closet Calvinists should "come out of the closet" and not only embrace, but spread the truth they know. The first is that those who know the truth must see the truth as beautiful, love and embrace it, and radiate it to others.

Forgotten Beauty

Closet Calvinists fail to see beauty in God's grace, for if they truly found it beautiful, they would not hide it abashedly. When a man is first smitten by a woman's beauty, he wants to have her on his arm as they walk in restaurants or shopping malls or parks. He is not ashamed of her; he is pleased to be seen with her and to show her off. There is nothing wrong with that. One does not hide that of which he is unashamed. The closet Calvinist may grudgingly see the truth of the doctrines of grace, but he does not find them beautiful.

There is a damnable saying prevalent in both secular culture and the evangelical subculture—that "beauty is in the eye of the beholder." This is utterly false. Beauty, like goodness, is to be found in what God calls beautiful, not in our personal tastes or predilections. In the Bible, God called Rebekah and Rachel and Moses beautiful (Genesis 24:16; 29:17; Exodus 2:2; Hebrews 11:23). Do we dare question his judgment? Beauty has objective content, God is its standard, and what God calls beautiful, we can be sure, is in fact altogether lovely and excellent.

This is because beauty exists in and emanates from God himself. Beauty does not define God; God defines beauty. It is generally agreed that three qualities inherent in beauty are (1) internal unity or integrity; (2) proportion or harmony; and (3) splendor.[1] In all his qualities, God is perfect unity, harmony and splendor. God is perfectly and supremely beautiful. Hence, David declared in Psalm 27:4:

> One thing I have desired of the Lord, That will I seek: That I may dwell in the house of the Lord All the days of my life, To behold the beauty of the Lord, And to inquire in His temple.

Of course, this means that the Trinity is beautiful. The Son is the image of the invisible God (Colossians 1:15) and the Spirit proceeds from the Father and the Son.[2] It also means that everything that God is, in terms of his attributes, is beautiful. Psalm 29:2 commands: "Give unto the Lord the glory due to His name; Worship the Lord in the beauty of holiness." But God's attribute of holiness is not alone in being beautiful. God's love is a beautiful love; his justice a beautiful justice.

God is not only beautiful in his person; he is also beautiful in his plan or purpose. Ephesians 1:11 says he works "all things according to the counsel of His will." This means, at a bare minimum, that God's plan emanates from his thoughts. Because God is beautiful in his nature, the thoughts he thinks are beautiful, and therefore, a beautiful plan emanates from a beautiful God. There is internal unity and coherence in God's plan. There is also perfect harmony in the Trinity that results in Father, Son and Spirit agreement as to the outworking of God's plan. Then, there is splendor in God's plan. As Lindsey has said:

> There is a perfect harmony between the purpose and the performance, for everything which takes place in time corresponds exactly to what God purposed in eternity. There is also a perfect harmony between the various parts of God's purpose, so that they fit together in one logical and historical continuum with no irreconcilable appendages. Yet variety is also present in that the historical unfolding of the divine purpose is realized step by step and observed by man part by part.[3]

Finally, God's redemption plan, in all its manifestations, including the doctrines of grace, is beautiful. It emanates from God; therefore, it must be so. As Jonathan Edwards recognized, "That wonderful and unparalleled grace of God which is manifested in the work of redemption, and shines forth in the face of Jesus Christ, is infinitely glorious in itself...it is a great part of the moral perfection and beauty of God's nature."[4] Even God's wrath is beautiful, according to Scripture. As terrible as it seems to us in our imperfect knowledge and understanding, even that is designed to "make known the riches of His glory" to believers (Romans 9:23).

What must man's response be to something God calls beautiful? Lindsay rightly says man's "aesthetic response would include, at the least, amazement, adoration, and joyful praise."[5] In this vein, Paul declared in Ephesians 1:6 that the proper result of understanding God's elective purpose is "the praise of the glory of his grace." In Romans 11:33-36 Paul broke out into rhapsodic doxology after discussing these things, exclaiming:

> Oh, the depth of the riches both of the wisdom and

> knowledge of God! How unsearchable are His judgments and His ways past finding out! "For who has known the mind of the Lord? Or who has become His counselor?" "Or who has first given to Him And it shall be repaid to him?" For of Him and through Him and to Him are all things, to whom be glory forever. Amen.

In sum, the right response to a vision of God's beautiful grace is to love it, embrace it, and develop a passion for it. If God is to be supreme in our lives, he must be supreme in our passions as well as our thoughts. The doctrines of grace are altogether lovely and beautiful, even if, at the same, time full of mystery and incomprehension. In the area of election and sovereignty as anywhere else, "the biblical reality, historical recognition, and theological reach of divine beauty should lead each believer to radiate the beauty of God in his life."[6] Hence, it is not just the closet Calvinist that should pray: "And let the beauty of the Lord our God be upon us, And establish the work of our hands for us." (Psalm 90:17).

Preaching the Whole Counsel of God

If appeal to beauty does not convince the closet Calvinist to passionately love and proclaim the doctrines of grace, perhaps appeal to duty might. A second reason why the doctrines of grace publicly should be preached and taught is simple yet profound: They are revealed in God's Word as truth. That alone should be sufficient to the inerrantist. After all, what good is recovering an infallible and inerrant Bible if men are afraid to say what it teaches?

As John Gill wrote:

> Some are of opinion that this doctrine of election, admitting it to be true, should not be published, neither preached from the pulpit, nor handled in schools and academies, nor treated of in the writings of men; the reasons they give, are because it is a secret, and secret things belong to God; and because it tends to fill mens' minds with doubts about their salvation, and to bring them into distress, and even into despair; and because some may make a bad use of it, to indulge themselves in a sinful course of life, and argue, that if they are elected they shall be saved, let them live as they may;

> and so it opens a door to all licentiousness: but these reasons are frivolous and groundless; the doctrine of election is no secret, it is clearly and fully revealed, and written as with a sunbeam in the sacred scriptures.[7]

John Calvin also strongly disagreed with the notion that "the doctrine of predestination is hostile to preaching and renders it useless."[8] He wondered: "Why should the men in our day, convinced about the vehemence of truth, think it right to say that, though what is said about predestination is true, it should not be popularly preached?"[9] Are we unwilling to say what Scripture allows to be said? The apostles, and the teachers of the Church who followed them, were not afraid to proclaim the Scriptures. Why should we be different? The biblical truthfulness of the doctrines of grace is the most important reason why the doctrines of grace should be a beacon shining on a hill rather than hidden under a bowl.

What do we see in the Scriptures? We see a God who is absolutely sovereign in creation, redemption and providence. Just as clearly, we see that the Bible teaches that man is one hundred percent responsible for his decisions. Sometimes, both doctrines are found in the same verse. John 6:37 says, "All that the Father gives Me will come to Me, and the one who comes to Me I will by no means cast out." The errors to be avoided are:

1. Soft peddling either of these subjects. If a preacher does this, he has a God who is something less than sovereign or a man who is something less than responsible. Because both teachings are true, a preacher must be true to the Bible and preach both as being true.

2. Either being unwilling to go as far as the Bible goes on these subjects, or using human reasoning, logic or speculation to go beyond what the Bible reveals. Deuteronomy 29:29 is a good place to camp: "The secret things belong to the Lord our God, but those things which are revealed belong to us and to our children forever, that we may do all the words of this law."

3. Trying to reconcile God's sovereignty and man's responsibility, which is humanly impossible. In one sermon, Basil Manly, Sr. told a group of ministers:

> Let us not then give up either the doctrine of human activity and responsibility, or that of the divine

> sovereignty and efficiency. Why should they be thought inconsistent? Or why should those who cling to one be disposed to doubt, or disbelieve, or explain away the other?[10]

Manly continued:

> The greatest reason...why the Christian family is divided on one or the other side rejecting one or the other of these great doctrines is that the doctrine of dependence on the Divine being, throws us constantly into the hands, and on the mercy of God. Proud man does not like it; [he] prefers to look at the other side of the subject; becomes blind, in part, by gazing at one view of the truth, alone; and forgets the Maker, in whom he lives and moves and has his being.[11]

While a belief in compatible freedom, as explained herein, may explain how divine sovereignty and man's free will are not incompatible, it does not attempt to explain (a) either the specific way in which they are compatible or (b) how God exercises his sovereignty in such a way that man is both free and responsible for his action.[12] Once again, these are subjects above and beyond us as mere creatures. They are divine mysteries that belong to God and God alone.

Living What One Believes

A third reason closet Calvinists should "come out of the closet" and embrace the truth they know is to live out in practice what they claim to believe about God's sovereignty. Many good men fail to live what they believe because they exhibit an inordinate fear of disapproval from either fellow preachers or their congregation. The fear of man is one of the chief causes of pastoral ineffectiveness in general. "The fear of man brings a snare," says Proverbs 29:25. Many pastors struggle with this temptation. Perhaps some readers see themselves in these candid words of a pastor quoted by Charles Bridges in *The Christian Ministry*:

> Here I find my own deficiency, as much or more

> than in any other respect; and often I feel an inward timidity, when about to preach upon an unpopular doctrine, or expose a foible, when some one of my congregation, whom I otherwise love and esteem, is remarkable for.[13]

But Jesus was not afraid to teach hard things. His teachings of Calvinist theology actually drove people away! In John 6, he taught: "All that the Father gives Me will come to Me, and the one who comes to Me I will by no means cast out" (John 6:37). "No one can come to Me unless the Father who sent Me draws him; and I will raise him up at the last day" (John 6:44). At these and other difficult words, many of His disciples said, "This is a hard saying; who can understand it?" But Jesus responded: "Does this offend you? What then if you should see the Son of Man ascend where He was before? It is the Spirit who gives life; the flesh profits nothing. The words that I speak to you are spirit, and *they* are life. But there are some of you who do not believe...Therefore I have said to you that no one can come to Me unless it has been granted to him by My Father" (John 6:61-65). The Gospel of John records that, from that time on, many of his followers "walked with Him no more." (John 6:66). Jesus then plaintively asked the Twelve, "Do you also want to go away?" (John 6:67). At that question, Peter answered for every true Christian: "Lord, to whom shall we go? You have the words of eternal life. Also we have come to believe and know that You are the Christ, the Son of the living God" (John 6:69). Even at this, Jesus did not back off his hard teachings about predestination. Instead, he confirmed both the positive truth of election and the negative truth of reprobation: "Jesus answered them, 'Did I not choose you, the twelve, and one of you is a devil?'" (John 6:70).

Spurgeon said about another point in Christ's ministry:

> Not even to prevent these displays of bad temper did our Lord keep back the discriminating truths of the Word. Here, when addressing the Jews, he did not hesitate to speak, even to a rude rabble, concerning that glorious doctrine. He says, "Ye believe not, because ye are not of my sheep, as I said unto you.?" He does not lower the standard of doctrine; but he holds his ground, and carries the war into the enemy's camp. The notion

> that certain truths are not fit to be preached to a general assembly, but are to be kept for the special gathering of the saints, is, I believe, horribly mischievous. Christ has not commanded us to keep a part of our teaching sub rosa; reserved from the common folk, and set aside for the priests alone. He is for openly proclaiming all truth. "What I tell you in darkness, that speak ye in light: and what ye hear in the ear, that preach ye upon the housetops." There is no truth that we need be ashamed of, and there is no truth that will do any harm.[14]

We would modify Spurgeon's statement to read that there is no truth that will cause harm when properly handled. Living out what one believes is being valiant for the truth.

The prophet Jeremiah lamented in his day that there were not enough people willing to be valiant for the truth. He was not cowardly in defending the truth. But neither did he revel in it. He faithfully reproved sin and threatened God's judgment for sin. Yet he did not rejoice in iniquity or calamity, but bitterly lamented the people's sin and coming judgment. He expressed great grief for the miseries of Judah and Jerusalem. He justified God in the greatness of the destruction brought upon them, and called on others to bewail the woeful cause of it. The great prophet showed the people the vanity of trusting in their own strength, wisdom, privileges—anything but God alone. But the people were not "valiant for the truth" (Jer. 9:3). They were adulterers; false, unfaithful to God and one another. They bent their tongues for lies, turning as naturally to it as a bow to the string. They did not defend God's truth, which was delivered to them by Jeremiah. They had no courage to stand by an honest cause which had truth on its side, when worldly greatness and power were on the other side. Truth had fallen in the land, and the people could not lend a hand to help it up.

Like Jeremiah in his day, in our own, those who will be faithful to the truth must be valiant for it, undaunted by opposition. Individuals will answer not only for their enmity in opposing truth but also for cowardice in defending it.

The antidote for the fear of man, of course, is trust in the Lord. As Proverbs 29:25 reminds us after warning that the fear of man brings a snare: "Whoever trusts in the Lord shall be safe." The Psalmist in Psalm 56:11 likewise declares: "In God I have put my trust; I will not be afraid. What can man do to me?" Hebrews 13:6 is in the same vein: "So we may boldly say: 'The Lord is my helper; I will not fear. What can man do to me?'" Isn't this the way it should be for one who asserts a belief in the comprehensive sovereignty of God over all things?

What Is At Stake?

Ultimately, the doctrines of grace should be taught and preached because the vitality of the church is at stake. All the differences between Calvinism and Arminianism boil down to one thing: Calvinism is God-centered and Arminianism is man-centered. Individual Arminians certainly may live God-centered lives (even though they inconsistently believe a man-centered theology). We know many people who hold man-centered beliefs who live godly, pious lives. But when the church *as a whole* is made up of a majority of individuals who believe in a man-centered theology, as time passes by, that theology works its way out in the church in the form of predominantly man-centered practices and man-centered lives. In time, the Arminians whose experience of God is greater than their theology become fewer and fewer. The point is that Calvinistic doctrine preserves orthodoxy. In contrast, Arminian doctrine ultimately erodes it.

Practical Benefits From Preaching the Doctrines of Grace

Far from being a hindrance to salvation and godliness, the enthusiastic preaching and teaching of the doctrines of grace results in many practical benefits for the life of the church. John Calvin saw this clearly:

> This matter is not a subtle and obscure speculation, as they falsely think, which wearies the mind without profit. It is rather a solid argument excellently fitted to the use of the godly. For it builds up faith soundly, trains us to humility, elevates us to admiration of the immense goodness of God towards us, and excites us to praise this goodness. There is no consideration more apt for the building up of faith than that we should listen to this election which the Spirit of God

> testifies in our hearts to stand in the eternal and inflexible goodwill of God, invulnerable to all storms of the world, all assaults of Satan and all vacillation of the flesh. For then indeed our salvation is assured to us, since we find its cause in the breast of God....Nor is it a negligible support when, believing in Christ, we hear that this is divinely given to us, that before the beginning of the world we were both ordained to faith and also elected to the inheritance of heavenly life. Hence arises an impregnable security.[15]

The Puritans likewise recognized the benefits of the public proclamation of the doctrines of grace with full vigor. We see an example of this in a remarkable sermon preached by David Dickson, a Scottish minister whose preaching was instrumental in spreading revival throughout Scotland between 1625 and 1630. He said:

> The doctrine of election and reprobation is a doctrine which may be safely taught and propounded unto people, albeit men say it should not be meddled with, because (say they) it makes some men despair, and others become careless what they do. I answer, let God make an answer for his own doctrine, who has commanded us to teach it...
>
> The apostle says boldly, the election obtained it, and the rest were blinded. Would Christ have propounded this doctrine if it had been dangerous? Therefore we oppose to such carnal men, secure sleepers in sin, this doctrine of Christ and his apostles, clearly set down in scripture. Let none take offense at this doctrine, for Christ's sheep will hear his voice, and if any will startle away, let him go...
>
> This doctrine is a strong attractive to draw back those who have fallen in error or vice, that they lie not in it, for this doctrine forces such men to turn to God, or else, to take on the name of reprobates...
>
> It is a doctrine meet for this age, wherein God is mocked and blasphemed by the lewd lives of those who are called Christians, to tell them, that they must either turn to God, or take home with them these black tidings, that they are vessels of dishonor, fitted for destruction. This doctrine is very needful to put men to their decisions; and yet it condemns not a man to hell

> presently, who is lying in sin; but it tells him, that there are some elect, who will come home, and some reprobate, who will not come home.[16]

How is the preaching of Calvinism useful to the Christian? From the quotations set forth above, we can see that there are several practical reasons why preaching the doctrines of grace is useful to the life of the believer.

First, the doctrines of grace teach Christians of the majesty, the power, the sovereignty, and the holiness of the God we serve. "It is surely a worthy view of God," said Mell, "to represent him as a sovereign and efficient ruler, who accomplished all his good pleasure, and is never thwarted; who is the author of everything good in his system; and who is especially entitled to all the praise of our salvation."[17]

John Owen saw a strong connection between election and holiness. He believed the denial of the sovereignty of God "and all that it involves" was a foremost cause of apostasy from the gospel in his day.[18] Indeed, the doctrines of grace point toward the greatness of our Sovereign Lord who does according to his will with respect to angelic beings who dwell in heaven and with respect to the inhabits of earth. Who can question God and say to him, "What are you doing?" The obvious answer is "no one."

Second, the doctrines of grace teach us to be humble and remind us to be thankful and grateful that God, of his own sovereign will, decided to reach down and save us. This is what Charles Spurgeon said about God's grace:

> I feel that I should have been a very king of sinners, if God had let me alone. I cannot understand the reason why I am saved, except upon the ground that God would have it so. I cannot, if I look ever so earnestly, discover any kind of reason in myself why I should be a partaker of Divine grace. If I am not at this moment without Christ, it is only because Christ Jesus would have His will with me, and that will was that I should be with him where He is, and should share His glory. I can put the crown nowhere but upon the head of Him whose mighty grace has saved me from going down to the pit.[19]

Patrick Mell similarly said: "So long as he has no doubts, that God, by his own sovereign grace, without any merits perceived or foreseen in him, regenerated him by his spirit and adopted him into his family, does he experience the depths of gratitude and ascribe praise to him for that salvation.[20]

Third, the doctrines of grace teach us to be secure in our salvation, trusting confidently that it is God who saves us and God who keeps us, not we ourselves.

Fourth, the doctrines of grace offer an illustration of the exceeding riches of God's grace.

Fifth, the doctrines of grace provide encouragement for evangelism. They comfort us that, through the means of witnessing, God is bringing to himself a people already chosen. For those appointed to eternal life, evangelistic success is guaranteed!

Sixth, they give a solemn and impressive view of God's justice and severity. As a result of predestination, God's justice appears the more awful and inflexible because it is manifested at the same time with God's love. "Behold the goodness and severity to God, his goodness to the chosen, his severity to the rest."[21]

Seventh, the faithful preaching of the doctrines of grace are often God's means for bringing revival. In God's providence, a reformation of doctrine can often be a precursor of a revival of souls. This was true with respect to the Reformation. It certainly was true in eighteenth century America, when the First Great Awakening blazed into being through the strongly Calvinistic preaching of Jonathan Edwards and George Whitefield. It was true of the Second Great Awakening, as Isaac Backus confirmed:

> The enmity which men have discovered against the sovereignty of the grace of God as revealed in Holy Scriptures hath now prevailed so far that every art is made use of to put other senses upon the words of revelation than God intended therein. He said to Moses, "I will have mercy on whom I will have mercy, and I will have compassion on whom I will have compassion. So then it is not of him that willeth, nor of him that runneth, but of God that showeth mercy." Rom. 9:15-16. This was the doctrine that God made use of in all the reformation that wrought in Germany, England and Scotland after the year 1517; and by the same doctrine he wrought all the reformation that has been in our

> day, both in Europe and America.[22]

How is the preaching of the doctrines of grace useful for the unconverted? For the unbeliever, the doctrines of grace are useful to afflict comforted souls and comfort afflicted souls. They afflict comforted souls by stripping the unbeliever of the pretension that he can at any time exercise his free will and attain salvation. As Patrick Mell once wrote:

> What is the influence of Calvinism upon the unconverted? Its tendency is to produce in them that conviction, without which they cannot be induced to take the first step toward attaining the salvation wrought out by Christ. The great difficulty in the way of their prompt movement is the lurking hope, if not belief, that their case is not a desperate one; that their sins are not so heinous but that they can be obviated, very easily. In their delusion, they suppose it is only necessary for them to will, which they can easily do at any time; and put into execution their resolution, which is also, completely in their power, and their salvation is at once secured. They consequently act upon the principle that it is running no great risk to postpone salvation to a more convenient season....Now let the doctrine that Calvinism teaches be received by the sinner, and his self-complacency is gone, and his sense of security is gone.[23]

At the same time, the doctrines of grace comfort the afflicted. They teach that God loves sinners, chooses particular sinners and makes specific provision for their salvation. They teach that, from first to last, salvation is of the Lord. And the very fact that Calvinism teaches salvation is of the Lord, not our own works, provides comfort to awakened and distressed souls. Thomas Horton said the doctrine of election "is a doctrine of comfort, as it takes all out of ourselves, and our own deservings." Elnathan Parr wrote in his commentary on Romans: "This doctrine affords comfort; the unworthiness may dismay thee, but remember that thy election depends not upon thy worthiness but upon the will of God." Thomas Goodwin proclaimed: "Oh despise not election! Therein lies all your hope that there is a remnant who shall infallibly be saved."[24] Mell similarly added: "Seeing that he is totally destitute of any good—that he is inexcusably complicated with sins of the darkest dye—that he is utterly helpless—he abhors himself, repents in dust and ashes, and cries to God for help....So, Calvinism teaches the sinner that he is utterly lost, and that God alone is his help; and urges him to look to God and to call upon him."[25]

Chapter 9

Valiant-For-Truth And His Enemies

Val was a brand new Calvinist. His prayer life was renewed because he had found a new God, a sovereign God, a God of grace, a God who had chosen *him* for salvation. The thought overwhelmed him. Val also loved to read his Bible in the quiet hours of the morning. It was a new Bible to him. Even in reading familiar passages in God's Word, he discovered fresh insights about God's nature and his love for his people that he had glossed over before.

Val also loved to tell everyone he met about the exciting truths he had newly learned. He was not subtle in his approach. A salesman by trade, Val was characteristically loud and brusque. His way of doing business was to come on strong in his sales pitch, and he viewed encounters with fellow believers who were unenlightened on the doctrines of grace as a grand sales opportunity. Enthusiastic at first, Val got frustrated easily when those around him didn't seem to accept his arguments as quickly as he thought they should. For example, when his friends voiced the opinion that God gave man a free will to choose to believe, Val told them in a condescending tone that they didn't understand the difference between moral ability and natural ability and referred them to Jonathan Edwards. When his mother asked him why he didn't believe that Christ died for the sins of the world, he confronted her with quotations from his underlined copy of John Owen's *The Death of Death in the Death of Christ*. He corrected his work assistant who was witnessing to the express mail deliverer and told him that Christ died for his sins. He badgered his pastor, who struggled with the doctrines of grace, seeking to argue fine points of theology after Sunday night sermons and sending him nightly emails of quotes by Spurgeon, Gill, Calvin and the Puritans. He told his Sunday School class members that they needed to repent because they didn't want to talk about his hobby-horse issues during discussion time. Soon Val's friends avoided him. He had burned his bridges. Like the proverbial "bull in the china shop," Val had run roughshod over things that should be treated delicately.

Just as the closet Calvinist hinders the propagation of the truth of God's grace, our fictional Val typifies another so-called "friend" of Calvinism that equally hinders its advancement. He is a "bull-in-the-china-shop" Calvinist. He has Calvinism as his hobby-horse, and he rides it every chance he gets. He has newly discovered the truth of the doctrines of grace, and he typifies the saying, "An idea newly grasped stirs the blood to aggressiveness."[1] He is obsessed with his new-found discovery of the doctrines of grace. Instead of preaching the gospel to the lost, he preaches the "Five Points." He is quick to enter into a debate with non-Calvinists, and he may get easily frustrated when his opponents do not see the truth of his position. He is aggressive and even overbearing in his defense of the five points.

This person turns people off with his arrogant, officious and wild-headed doggedness with which he defends the five points. He has no consideration for the struggles of others, and no judgment as to when to plough ahead and when to back off. He does not understand why everyone does not immediately see the truth as he sees it, and he demands that those who disagree with him repent and get right with God.

Do you know such a man? John Bunyan did. He called him Valiant-for-Truth.

Valiant-for-Truth

Valiant-for-Truth was a character in *Pilgrim's Progress*. He was born in "Darkland," and his mother and father are still there. Darkland was on the same coast as the City of Destruction from which Christian came. Valiant-for-Truth found Darkland unsuitable and unprofitable, and thus he left it. He gave the following reasons for leaving:

> We had an individual named Mr. Telltrue come into our parts, and he told about what Christian, who had left the City of Destruction, had done—namely, how he had forsaken his wife and his children and taken upon himself a Pilgrim's life.... In a word, that man told the

> story of Christian and his travels in such a way that my heart fell into a burning haste to go after him. Nor could my father or mother stop me, so I left them and have come this far on my way.[2]

Valiant. His name tells us that he was a contender for the truth. The truth was entrusted to him, and he was its custodian. He was bound to defend it. In his words, "Though an army besiege me, my heart will not fear; though war break out against me, even then will I be confident." As a result, he lived a life of controversy.

As he journeyed to the Celestial City, Valiant-for-Truth came upon three ruffians. Bunyan called these ruffians *Wild-Head, Inconsiderate* and *Pragmatic*. Through them, he warned every defender of the truth to be vigilant against the besetting temptations to be wild-headed, inconsiderate, officious, opinionated, dictatorial and arrogant.

The principal temptation of the three ruffians was to persuade Valiant-for-Truth to "become one of them." When he refused, the three ruffians attacked Valiant and fought him for three hours. It was a bloody battle. As Valiant later told it, "They've left upon me some of the marks of their valor, and they've also carried away with them some of mine." Great Heart later told him, "You've resisted to the point of shedding your blood in your struggle against sin."

In his brilliant sketches of Bunyan's characters, Alexander Whyte observed: "The bloody battle that Valiant fought, you must know, was not fought at the mouth of any dark lane in the midnight city, nor on the side of any lonely road in the moonless country. This terrible fight was fought in Valiant's own heart. For Valiant was none of your calculating and cold-blooded friends of the truth. He did not wait till he saw the truth walking in silver slippers. Let any man lay a finger on the truth, or wag a tongue against the truth, and he will have to settle it with Valiant. His love for the truth was a passion. There was a fierceness in his love for the truth that frightened ordinary men even when they were on his own side. Valiant would have died for the truth without a murmur. But Valiant had to learn a hard and cruel lesson: He had to learn that he, the best friend of truth as he thought he was, was at the same time, as a matter of fact, the greatest enemy that the truth had."[3]

We all know *Wild-Head*. He sometimes appears with his pen in hand, sometimes from behind the pulpit, sometimes in private conversation or debate. We have seen him rush at the character of some saint who was not enlightened with the truth of the doctrines of grace, whose understanding of grace was not as good as his Christian experience of it. *Wild-Head* does not remember that there are many people who are Arminian in their understanding of God but who have better Christian experience than do many Calvinists. Most, if not all, of us have also seen him in our own hearts. *Wild-Head* has not learned that truth apart from the Spirit will not develop Christian character. Grace and truth must be together. Mercy and truth must be together, as they are in Jesus.

Inconsiderate is also familiar to us. He never thinks before he speaks, and he certainly does not pray before opening his mouth. He never puts himself in another person's place. He has neither the head nor the heart to do so. He also lives in our hearts on many occasions. He does not stop to think that an Arminian to whom we are talking may never have heard a single sermon on the truths of God's grace that we hold dear. In commenting on Job 19:2, 5, Matthew Henry said: "Those who speak too much seldom think they have said enough; and when the mouth is open in passion, the ear is shut to reason."[4] *Inconsiderate* seems to forget that all truth of God must be revealed by the Spirit of God.

Pragmatic may not be as familiar to us, at least by that name. The word "pragmatic" had a different meaning in Bunyan's day than it does in our own. In that day the word meant to be active in an officious or meddlesome way; dogmatic; dictatorial. A pragmatist, then, was a meddler or busybody. When it comes to the doctrines of grace, the pragmatist is the person who always has to set everyone straight on every little point of doctrine. There is nothing he will not correct in someone else.

Truth suffers in the hands of a wild-headed, inconsiderate, meddling person, one who is never satisfied, never pleased, never thankful, always setting others right.[5] This kind of person, intending to be a friend of the truth, actually operates as an enemy of the truth. The Valiant-for-Truth who gives in to the temptations of Wildhead, Inconsiderate and Pragmatic forgets that truth "does not stand in points but in principles."[6] Truth does not dwell in the letter but in the Spirit.

Spiritual Issues Involved in Valliant's Temptations

There are three basic spiritual issues involved.

Failure To Mortify Spiritual Pride

Jonathan Edwards warns against the danger of undiscerned spiritual pride. "This is the main door by which the devil comes into the hearts of those who are zealous for the advancement of religion. It is the chief inlet of smoke from the bottomless pit to darken the mind and mislead the judgment."[7] Edwards added that the early Christians contended earnestly for the faith and defended the truth "with arguments and a holy conversation" but also "with meekness and fear." They "resisted unto blood" but "the blood that was shed in this earnest strife was their own blood, and not the blood of their enemies."[8]

Failure to Speak the Truth in Love

All true Christians are lovers of the truth. They desire to fellowship in the truth; they desire to be taught the truth and they want to be dispensers of the truth. The Bible tells us that people perish "because they did not receive the love of the truth, that they might be saved" (2 Thessalonians 2:10).

It is our hearts' desire to encourage everyone to seek diligently after truth and to defend it—to be valiant for truth and to seek to dispense it by life, lip and good, sound literature. However, the overzealous Calvinist fails to speak the truth in love (Ephesians 4:15).

In a number of passages, God makes it a point to put mercy and truth together (Psalm 85:10; Psalm 89:14; Proverbs 14:22; 16:6; 20:28). Both grace and truth came in the person of Jesus Christ (John 1:14). The safeguard against Bunyan's ruffians is to keep truth and mercy, truth and kindness, and truth and love together. What God has put together, let not man tear apart!

Failure To Understand Who Opens Eyes

The third reason an overzealous Calvinist acts the way he does is a failure to live by his own doctrines. He fails to remember who it is that opens eyes. It is God who reveals truth, not our persuasive abilities and certainly not our abrasive personalities. As Paul rhetorically queried in 1 Corinthians 4:7: "For who regards you as superior? What do you have that you did not receive? And if you did receive it, why do you boast as if you had not received it?" (NASB). This verse is a lifeline against *Inconsiderate*.

Truth must be revealed in the heart by the Holy Spirit in Christian growth, even as it was at conversion. In the eyes of non-Calvinists, we differ from them as much as they differ from us. May the Spirit help us to see with the eyes of the non-Calvinist and feel with their hearts and sympathize with their principles, and even their prejudices. We do not say compromise convictions, but sympathize and agonize a little more in prayer for the Holy Spirit to teach their hearts. Every Valiant-for-Truth must beware of that ruffian in his own heart called *Inconsiderate*. The Lord will accomplish his purposes! When we defend the sovereignty of God with our words, we must not at the same time deny that truth by our actions or attitudes in dealing with those who differ with us.

******

We want to emphasize that, in pointing out these enemies, Bunyan does not intent to discourage us in our warfare. Rather, as we face our battles for truth, his goal is to make good soldiers of Jesus Christ. The first time we encounter Valiant, he is standing at the head of a place that Bunyan calls "Deadman's Lane." He is standing there with his sword in his hand and his face covered with blood. He has won the battle but not without suffering his own wounds.

In like manner, as the apostle Paul wrote 1 Corinthians 13, the famous love chapter, it does not take much speculation to believe he moved his quill across parchment with the scars of his battles with Barnabas still on his hands. Could he have written these words without thinking of his dispute with his beloved friend:

> Though I speak with the tongues of men and of

> angels, but have not love, I have become sounding brass or a clanging cymbal. And though I have the gift of prophecy, and understand all mysteries and all knowledge, and though I have all faith, so that I could remove mountains, but have not love, I am nothing. And though I bestow all my goods to feed the poor, and though I give my body to be burned, but have not love, it profits me nothing. (1 Corinthians 13:1-3).

And could John, the apostle of love, have written these words of his first epistle, without thinking of the time when he had wanted to call down fire from heaven to devour the Samaritans?

> Beloved, let us love one another, for love is of God; and everyone who loves is born of God and knows God. He who does not love does not know God, for God is love. In this the love of God was manifested toward us, that God has sent His only begotten Son into the world, that we might live through Him. In this is love, not that we loved God, but that He loved us and sent His Son to be the propitiation for our sins. Beloved, if God so loved us, we also ought to love one another. No one has seen God at any time. If we love one another, God abides in us, and His love has been perfected in us (1 John 4:7-12).

Nor are we immune. After examining Bunyan's description of Valiant, Alexander Whyte too felt the sting of his own self-inflicted wounds: "Where do you suppose I got the true key to the veiled metaphor of Valiant-for-truth? It does not exactly hang on the door-post of his history. Where, then, could I get it but off the inside wall of my own place of repentance? Just as you understand what I am now labouring to say, not from my success in saying it, but from your own trespasses against humility and love, your unadvised speeches, and your wild and whirling words. Without shame and remorse, without self-condemnation and self-contempt, none of those great passages of Paul, or John, or Bunyan, or Law were ever written; and without a like shame, remorse, self-condemnation, and self-contempt they are not rightly read."[9]

How To Preach and Teach the Doctrines of Grace

If we are going to be "Valiants-for-Truth," we must take great care, wisdom and charity in seeking to apply the truth as we have come to see and love it. There is an appropriate time, manner and method of speaking the truth of the doctrines of grace—and an inappropriate time, manner and method.

1. As a general rule, the doctrines of grace should be preached expositionally. A minister should not make the doctrines of grace a hobby-horse to ride every time he approaches the pulpit. Attention should also be given to time and place. Although, as we've seen, John Calvin systematized the doctrines of grace, what gave them their force was Calvin's close adherence to the Bible. As Lorraine Boettner put it: "Where the Bible led, there he went; where it failed him, there he stopped short. This refusal to go beyond what was written, coupled with a ready acceptance of what the Bible did teach, gave an air of finality and positiveness to his declarations which made them offensive to his critics."[10]

2. At the same time, care should be taken that the doctrines of grace are actually taught wherever they come up in Scripture—and they come up a lot. Hence, Spurgeon once said: Good John Newton used to say of his Calvinism, that he did not preach it in masses of dry doctrine like pieces of lump sugar, but that it was stirred up in all his preaching, like sugar dissolved in our tea."[11]

3. However, in preaching the doctrines of grace, keep the emphasis on the actual text of the Bible. Be rigorously biblical. The use of theological jargon should be avoided. Theological language has its place, but that place is not the pulpit. There simply is no need to use terms such as "limited atonement" or "Calvinism." Most people in the pew do not know what they mean, anyway, and you can be certain that most of those who think they do know what these and other theological terms mean have it wrong. Let Scripture speak for itself and use its language.

4. Be wise in your literature distribution. Do not give a layperson who has heard only a general redemption perspective her whole life a copy of John Owen's *The Death of Death in the Death of Christ* the first time you meet her. It may not wise to give an uninitiated Southern Baptist Iain Murray's *The Invitation System* or our *Worship* right off the bat. There is a

proper time for these things, and a proper method for introducing people to them. Have the wisdom to know when to move forward and when to back off.

5. Be gentle, not harsh, in your expectations. Remember that it is God who opens eyes. Pastors, as you preach, pray that God would bring your hearers to repentance.

6. Finally, do not expect new Christians to have the same understanding of the doctrines of grace that you do. As Spurgeon wisely advised: "Do not examine the new-born babe about Calvinism in its different shades, to see whether he is sound after your idea of soundness; ten to one he is a long way off sound, and you will only worry the dear heart by introducing difficult questions. Speak to him about his being a sinner, and Christ a Savior, and you will in this way water him, so that his grace in the ear will become the full corn."[12]

Conclusion

Salvation is of the Lord! This has been our manifesto throughout the pages of this book. It is a truth that will stand the test of time. Our prayer is that the doctrines of grace which stem from this point will once again find a welcome home in the Southern Baptist Convention. Here is the seedbed of reformation. Here is the forge from which revival fires are lit. Here is the gospel, pure Christianity, true religion upon which a devotional house must be built. In the end, we conclude:

1. Calvinism is not anti-missionary, but gives the biblical foundation for missions. (John 6:37; 17:20, 21; 2 Timothy 2:10; Isaiah 55:11; 2 Peter 3:9, 15).

2. Calvinism does not destroy the responsibility of man. Men are responsible for whatever light they have, be it conscience (Romans 2:15), nature (Romans1:19, 20), written law (Romans 2:17—27), or the gospel (Mark 16:15, 16). Man's inability to do righteousness no more frees him from responsibility than does Satan's inability to do righteousness free him.

3. Calvinism does not make God unjust. His blessing of a great number of unworthy sinners with salvation is no injustice to the rest of the unworthy sinners. If a governor pardons one convict, it is not an injustice to the rest (1 Thessalonians 5:9).

4. Calvinism does not discourage convicted sinners, but welcomes them to Christ. "Let him that is athirst come" (Revelation 17:17; KJV). The God who convicts is the God who saves. The God who saves is the God who has elected men unto salvation. He is the same God who invites.

5. Calvinism does not discourage prayer. To the contrary, it drives us to God, for He alone can save. True prayer is at the Spirit's prompting, and thus will be in harmony with God's will.

Calvinism is authentic, historical Baptist theology. Until the twentieth century with its emphasis on pragmatism and programs (first liberal, then conservative), most Southern Baptists and their progenitors were rock-ribbed Calvinists. The present day resurgence of Calvinism is simply an effort to restore our theological past. If it was true then, it is true now.

Truth is a powerful weapon. In *Pilgrim's Progress*, Great Heart said to Valiant-for-truth: "You've behaved yourself worthily. Let me see your Sword." Upon taking it, he looked at it and exclaimed, "Ha! It's a genuine Jerusalem Blade."

"That it is," Valiant responded. "Let a man have one of these blades, with a hand to exercise it and skill to use it, and he may confront an angel with it. He need not fear holding it if he can only know how to apply it. Its edges will never dull; it will cut flesh, bones, soul, spirit, and all."[1] The Word of God cuts and divides, and the biblical truths of God's grace also cut and divide and convict.

It remains to be seen whether the prevailing influences in contemporary Southern Baptist circles will receive with joy these precious biblical truths or whether these truths will be turned away to the profound detriment of the denomination. If today's Southern Baptist leaders will not receive the truth of God's grace with joy, however, perhaps the next generation will. Or the generation after that. We do well to remember that almost our last glimpse of Valiant-for-truth is as Christiana is about to cross the river of death. As this faithful saint entrusted her children to the protection of this great warrior, she exhorted Valiant, "Have an eye to my children." May God open the eyes of Southern Baptists everywhere—whether in this generation or another—to the preciousness of his free and sovereign grace! We conclude with yet one more Spurgeon quotation that expresses our own heartbeat on the subject:

> I long that the truth which I have preached may be established in the earth. They say that Calvinism is at a great discount now: perhaps it is. Yet to me it seems that its free grace spirit is far more spread than ever, and is quietly saturating all true evangelical preaching. If it be so, that the doctrines of grace are now despised, we still hope that we shall live to see them brought to the front again, or, if not, we shall leave behind us such a testimony that in years to come the gospel of the grace of God will be read by thousands.[2]

May the supreme God of all be glorified in our churches!
Sola Deo Gloria

Endnotes

Preface

[1] Carol "Kate" Harvey. "With All the Saints," in *Why I am a Baptist* (Macon, GA.: Smyth & Helwys, 1999), 59.

Chapter One

[1] John A. Broadus, *Memoirs of J.P. Boyce* (New York, NY: A.C. Armstrong & Son, 1893), 73.

[2] Charles H. Spurgeon, "Exposition of the Doctrines of Grace," No. 385, Metropolitan Tabernacle Pulpit ("MTP"), vol 7 (electronic version published Albany, OR: Ages Software, Inc., 1998).

[3] P. H. Mell, *An Essay on Calvinism* (Cape Coral, FL, Founders Press, n.d.), 8-9.

[4] Charles Haddon Spurgeon, *A Defense of Calvinism* (Cape Coral, FL Founders Press, n.d.), 31.

[5] John Calvin, *The Institutes of the Christian Religion*, trans. Ford Lewis Battles, vol. 1 (Westminster Press, republished in electronic format, Albany, OR: Ages Software, 1998), 1:1:1-3.

[6] Ibid, 1:6:1.

[7] Ibid, 1:11:8.

[8] See John M. Frame, "In Defense of Something Close to Biblicism: Reflections on Sola Scriptura and History in Theological Method," *Westminster Theological Journal*, vol. 59 no. 2 (Fall, 1997): 272.

[9] St. Anselm, *Basic Writings*, transl. S.N. Deane (La Salle, IL: Open Court), 1962), 7.

[10] Iain Murray, *Evangelicalism Divided* (Carlisle, PA: Banner of Truth Trust, 2000), 197.

[11] Douglas J. Wilson, "The Loveliness of Orthodoxy," in *Bound Only Once: The Failure of Open Theism* (Moscow, ID: Canon Press, 2001), 18.

[12] Roger R. Nicole, "Polemic Theology or How to Deal With Those Who Differ From Us," in *The Founders Journal*, issue 33 (Summer 1998), archived at www.founders.org.

[13] Charles H. Spurgeon, "Knowledge Commended," No. 609, MTP, vol. 11.

[14] Charles D. Mallary, *The Doctrine of Election* (reprinted Louisville, KY: Kosmosdale Baptist Church, 1988), 2.

[15] Herman Witsius, *Sacred Dissertations on The Apostles' Creed* (Escondido, CA: The den Dulk Foundation, 1993), xxv-xxvi.

[16] We can't defend Calvin's view of baptism, but he does get a bum rap when it comes to the Servetus affair. Michael Servetus was a physician and theologian who had published a book denying the Trinity. He had been condemned as a heretic by Catholic authorities in France, but had escaped prison and fled to Geneva. The city council had him arrested and gave him a choice: face extradition or submit to Genevan justice. Servetus chose to stay in Geneva (knowing full well what the result would be in France). After substantial deliberation, the city council condemned him and sentenced him to execution by being burned alive. As a minister, Calvin had no role in the Genevan justice system. Indeed, as one biographer has pointed out, the city counsel was determined to keep the right to dispense justice within the hands of the Genevan magistracy and to allow a foreigner—even one of such status as Calvin—to interfere with or influence that process was not tolerated. Calvin did seek to have the mode of execution changed to the more humane beheading, but he was ignored. McGrath notes that, in Calvin's defense: (1) the sixteenth century knew nothing of the modern distaste for capital punishment, (2) the City of Geneva had no prison system and could dispense only two penalties—banishment and execution; (3) the execution of Servetus was no more notable or significant than countless other religious executions in the same era, and (4) Calvin was isolated and vulnerable during the time of the Servetus affair and likely had very little influence on the process. In short, Calvin was a man of his times. McGrath rightly concludes that for critics to single out Calvin for vilification when his involvement in the Servetus affair was oblique "raises difficult questions concerning the precommitments of his critics." Alister E. McGrath, *A Life of Calvin* (Grand Rapids, MI: Baker, 1990), 114-120.

[17] Andrew Fuller, *The Complete Works of the Rev. Andrew Fuller*, vol. 2 (reprinted Harrisonburg, VA: Sprinkle Publications, 1988), 165.

[18] Broadus called himself "assuredly" an "admirer of Calvin." A.T. Robertson, *Life and Letters of John A. Broadus* (Harrisonburg, VA: Gano Books, 1987), 276.

[19] Mell, An Essay on Calvinism, 8.

[20] Charles H. Spurgeon, "Preface," in *The Park Street Pulpit, Vol. 1* (republished in electronic format, Logos Library System, Albany, OR: Ages Software, 1998).

Chapter Two

[1] We have adapted this summary from an earlier work, Ernest C. Reisinger and D. Matthew Allen, *A Quiet Revolution* (Cape Coral, Fl.: Founders Press, 2000), 10-11 (internal citations omitted).

[2] See Philip Schaff, *The Creeds of Christendom*, vol. I (Harper & Row, 1931, reprinted Grand Rapids, MI: Baker Books, 1996), 511-512; Paul Enns, *Moody Handbook of Theology* (Chicago, IL: Moody Press, 1989), 489-90.

[3] Schaff, *The Creeds of Christendom*, vol. III, 545-549.

[4] For details on the events leading up to the Synod of Dort, see Thomas Scott, *The Synod of Dort* (Harrisonburg, VA: Sprinkle Publications, 1993), 94-240; Stephen Strehle, "The Extent of the Atonement and the Synod of Dort," *Westminster Theological Journal* 51, no. 1 (Spring, 1989): 1-8; John R. de Witt, "The Synod of Dort," *The Banner of Truth* no. 63 (Dec. 1968), 1-5.

[5] William Cunningham, *The Reformers and the Theology of the Reformation* (1862, reprinted Carlisle, PA: Banner of Truth Trust, 1989), 367.

[6] The leading medieval theologians of the Augustinian school, Gregory of Rimini and Hugolino of Orvieto, taught a doctrine of predestination. Alister McGrath suggests that Calvin may have even "actively appropriated this aspect of late medieval Augustinianism." See Alister E. McGrath, *A Life of John Calvin* (Grand Rapids, MI: Baker, 1995), 168. Timothy George goes further, calling Calvin's work on election "unoriginal" and "in all essentials identical to what we have already observed in Luther and Zwingli, and the same could be said for Bucer as well." See Timothy George, *Theology of the Reformers* (Nashville, TN: Broadman, 1988), 232. This is not to say that Calvin knew Augustine exclusively through medieval intermediaries. While he did not have first-hand knowledge of all Augustine's writings, he did have access to and relied extensively on the anti-Pelagian writings of Augustine in polemic treatises against Pighius and in the *Institutes*. See Anthony N.S. Lane, *John Calvin: Student of the Church Fathers* (Grand Rapids, MI: Baker Books, 1999).

[7] Philip Schaff, *History of the Christian Church*, vol. 3 (Charles Scribner's Sons, 1910, reprinted, Grand Rapids, MI: Eerdmans, 1994), 790.

[8] See Eugene TeSelle, "Pelagius, Pelagianism" in *Augustine Through the Ages: An Encyclapedia*, edited by Allan D. Fitzgerald (Grand Rapids, MI: Eerdmans, 1999), 633-40.

[9] Schaff, *History of the Christian Church*, vol. 3, 802-03.

[10] Ibid, 816-56. See also Geoffry W. Bromiley, "Predestination" in *International Standard Bible Encyclapedia* ("ISBE"), vol. 3 (Grand

Rapids, MI: Eerdmans, 1988, republished in electronic format, Logos Digital Library System), 947.

[11] Schaff, History of the Christian Church, vol. 3, 855.

[12] Bromiley, "Predestination," in *ISBE*, 946-47.

[13] This chart is taken from Paul Enns, *Moody Handbook of Theology* (Chicago, IL: Moody Press, 1989), 425.

[14] John A. Broadus, *Memoirs of J.P. Boyce* (New York, NY: A.C. Armstrong & Son, 1893), 73.

[15] Charles H. Spurgeon, "Election and Holiness," No. 303, MTP, vol. 6.

[16] First London Baptist Confession of Faith, art. III, quoted in Timothy George, *Baptist Confessions, Covenants and Catechisms* (Nashville, TN: Broadman & Holman, 1996), 38.

[17] Quoted in Publisher's Introduction to James P. Boyce, *Abstract of Systematic Theology* (1887, reprinted Hanford, CA: den Dulk Christian Foundation, n.d.), ix.

[18] Ibid, ix-x.

[19] Ibid, xx.

[20] Ibid, xx-xxi.

[21] P.H. Mell, Jr., *The Life of Patrick Hues Mell* (Harrisonburg, VA: Gano Books, 1991), 17

[22] Robertson, *Life and Letters of John A. Broadus*, 396-97.

[23] Spurgeon, *A Defense of Calvinism*, 38-39.

[24] Clark Pinnock, "From Augustine to Arminius: A Pilgrimage in Theology," in *The Grace of God and the Will of Man* (Minneapolis, MN: Bethany House, 1989), 25. This thesis is spelled out more fully in Clark Pinnock, et al., *The Openness of God: A Biblical Challenge to the Traditional Understanding of God* (Downers Grove, IL: InterVarsity, 1994).

[25] Pinnock, "From Augustine to Arminius," 24-25.

[26] Charles Hodge, *Systematic Theology*, vol. 1 (reprinted, Grand Rapids, MI: Eerdmans, 1995), 400.

[27] James P. Boyce, *Abstract of Systematic Theology* (1887, reprinted Hanford, CA: den Dulk Foundation, n.d.), 119-120.

[28] The 2000 Baptist Faith and Message may be found on the SBC's official web site: http://www.sbc.net.

[29] Jack Graham and Daniel L. Akin, "Contending for the Faith in the 21st Century," *Southern Seminary Magazine* (November 2000), vol. 68: 10-12, republished on the internet at www.baptist2baptist.net under "Reports, Articles and Papers."

[30] See David Neff, "Foreknowledge Debate Clouded by 'Political Agenda," *Christianity Today* (Nov. 19, 2001), republished on the internet at *Christianity Today*'s website: http://www.christianitytoday.com/ct/2001/147/13.0.html.

[31] See John M. Frame, *No Other God* (Phillipsburg, NJ: P&R Publishing Co., 2001); Bruce A. Ware, *God's Lesser Glory* (Wheaton, IL: Crossway Books, 2000); Douglas Wilson, ed., *Bound Only Once: The Failure of Open Theism* (Moscow, ID: Canon Press, 2001). Desiring God Ministries also has some helpful information on open theism at its website, www.desiringgod.org.

[32] Clark Pinnock, ed., *The Grace of God and the Will of Man* (Minneapolis, MN: Bethany House, 1989), 16-17.

[33] Ibid, 18-20.

[34] Ibid, 20-23.

[35] Ibid, 21.

[36] Clark Pinnock, *Most Moved Mover: A Theology of God's Openness* (Grand Rapids, MI: Baker Academic , 2001), xii.

[37] John Sanders, "God as Personal," in *The Grace of God and the Will of Man*, 171.

Chapter Three

[1] Charles H. Spurgeon, "Spiritual Gleaning," No. 2585, MTP, vol. 44.

[2] Quoted in Thomas R. Schreiner, *Romans*, Baker Exegetical Commentary on the New Testament (Grand Rapids, MI: Baker Books, 1998), 1.

[3] Quoted Ibid.

[4] We have decided to leave several quotations by current Southern Baptist leaders without attribution even though the identity of the speakers is known in some circles. Similarly, we have chosen not to "name names" with respect to certain non-Calvinist SBC leaders in this work. The primary reason for these decisions is that we do not want personalities to become issues in the current conversation. We would rather focus on the ideas. The authors have the original sources on file.

[5] John Calvin, *The Institutes of Christian Religion*, abridged, edited by Tony Lane and Hilary Osborne (Grand Rapids, MI: Baker Book House, 1987), 216.

[6] Ibid, 218.

[7] John Calvin, *Concerning the Eternal Predestination of God* (London: James Clarke & Co., 1961), 69.

[8] Ibid, 71.

[9] Mallary, *The Doctrine of Election*, 4.

[10] John Gill, *A Complete Body of Doctrinal and Practical Divinity* (republished in electronic format, The Baptist Standard Bearer, 1999), 381.

[11] Ibid, 386.

[12] Ibid, 391.

[13] Ibid, 397.

[14] Ibid, 413.

[15] John Gill, *The Cause of God and Truth* (republished in electronic format, Paris, AR: The Baptist Standard Bearer, 1999), 223.

[16] Ibid, 223-24.

[17] Fuller, *Works*, vol. 2, 675.

[18] John Dagg, *A Manual of Theology* (Harrisburg, VA: Gano Books, 1990), 309-315.

[19] James Arminius, *The Works of James Arminius*, republished in electronic format, The Master Christian Library, Albany, OR: Ages Software), 343.

[20] Ibid, 223.

[21] John Wesley, *The Works of John Wesley*, vol. 7 (republished in electronic format, The Master Christian Library, Albany, OR: Ages Software), 426.

[22] Ibid, 422.

[23] Ibid, 422-23.

[24] Ibid, 424.

[25] Jack W. Cottrell, "The Nature of the Divine Sovereignty," in *The Grace of God and the Will of Man*, 111.

[26] William G. Macdonald, "The Biblical Doctrine of Election," in Ibid, 226.

[27] Herschel H. Hobbs, *Fundamental of Our Faith* (Nashville, TN: Broadman Press, 1960), 89.

[28] Ibid, 90.

[29] Ibid., 92.

[30] Ibid, 93.

[31] Ibid, 94.

[32] Ibid.

[33] Herschel H. Hobbs and E.Y. Mullins, *The Axioms of Religion*,

revised edition (Nashville, TN: Broadman Press, 1978), 70-72.

34 Ibid.

35 Wayne E. Ward, "Elected by ONE Vote," *Baptist Young People*, 59 (February 16, 1958), 21, quoted in W. Wiley Richard, *Why I Am Not a Calvinist* (Gracevill, FL: Hargrave Press, 1998), 14.

36 Richard Rice, "Divine Foreknowledge and Free-Will Theism," in *The Grace of God and the Will of Man*, 122.

37 Ibid, 123.

38 Ibid, 126-27.

39 Clark Pinnock, "From Augustine to Arminius: A Pilgrimage in Theology," in *The Grace of God and the Will of Man*, 25.

40 Pinnock, *Most Moved Mover*, 49.

41 Ibid, 184.

42 Pinnock, "From Augustine to Arminius, 20. Sanders adopts this view. *The God Who Risks*, 121. William G. MacDonald also hints at it in his "The Biblical Doctrine of Election," in *The Grace of God and the Will of Man*, 207-229.

43 God's foreknowledge is taught in four other passages of Scripture as well. In Acts 26:5 Paul states: "They knew me from the first, if they were willing to testify, that according to the strictest sect of our religion I lived a Pharisee." In Romans 11:2 he said: "God did not reject his people, whom he foreknew." 1 Peter 1:2 says that God's elect "have been chosen according to the foreknowledge of God the Father, through the sanctifying work of the Spirit, for obedience to Jesus Christ and sprinkling by his blood." 2 Peter 3:17 says: "You therefore, beloved, since you know this beforehand, beware lest you also fall from your own steadfastness, being led away with the error of the wicked."

44 Walter Baur, William F. Arndt, F. Wilbur Gingrich & Frederick W. Danker, *A Greek-English Lexicon of the New Testament and Other Early Christian Literature* ("BAGD") (Chicago & London: University of Chicago Press, 1979; electronic version 1996), 703; Gerhard Kittel & Gerhard Friedrich, *Theological Dictionary of the New Testament* ("TDNT"), translated by Geoffrey W. Bromiley (Grand Rapids, MI: Eerdmans, 1964), vol. 1, 123; Douglas Moo, *The Epistle to the Romans*, New International Commentary on the New Testament (Grand Rapids, MI: Eerdmans, 1996), 532; John Murray, *Epistle to the Romans*, The New International Commentary on the New Testament, vol. 1 (Grand Rapids, MI: Eerdmans, 1959, reprinted 1979), 315.

45 See, e.g., Frederic L. Godet, *Commentary on Romans* (1883, reprinted, Grand Rapids, MI: Kregel Publications, 1977), 325.

46 See, e.g., TDNT, vol. 1, 715; BAGD, 703; Schreiner, *Romans*, 452;

Charles Hodge, *Romans* (reproduced in electronic format, The Master Christian Library, Albany, OR: Ages Software), 440; Moo, 532-33; Murray, vol. 1, 316-17.

47 J.D.G. Dunn, *Romans 1-8*, Word Biblical Commentary (reproduced in electronic format, Dallas, TX: Word, 1998), comment on Rom. 8:29.

48 Schreiner, *Romans*, 452.

49 Murray, *Epistle to the Romans*, vol. 1, 317.

50 F.F. Bruce, *Romans*, Tyndale New Testament Commentaries (Grand Rapids, MI: Eerdmans, 1985), 166 ("when God takes knowledge of people in this special way, he sets his choice on them"); Robert Haldane, *Exposition of the Epistle to the Romans* (reproduced in electronic format, The Master Christian Library, Albany, OR: Ages Software), 537.

51 Hodge, *Romans*, 441.

52 Schreiner, *Romans*, 318.

53 John Piper, *The Justification of God* (Grand Rapids, MI: Baker Books, 1993), 19.

54 Moo, 554.

55 Murray, *Epistle to the Romans*, vol. 2, 10-11; Moo, 575; Schreiner, *Romans*, 494; Ernst Kasemann, *Commentary on Romans*, translated and edited, Geoffrey W. Bromiley (Grand Rapids, MI: Eerdmans, 1980), 262; Bruce, *Romans*, 177-78.

56 Piper, *The Justification of God*, 51.

57 Schreiner, *Romans*, 501-02.

58 Moo, 587; contra Murray, *Epistle to the Romans*, vol. 2, 22-23; Kasemann, 265.

59 John Bunyan, "Reprobation Asserted," in *The Works of John Bunyan*, vol. 2 (Carlisle, PA: Banner of Truth Trust, 1991), 333.

60 Gill, *A Body of Doctrinal Divinity*, 416.

61 Moo, 578; see also Murray, *Epistle to the Romans*, vol. 2, 13; Godet, 348.

62 Moo, 580.

63 Godet, 348-49.

64 Schreiner, *Romans*, 500.

65 Murray, *Epistle to the Romans*, vol. 2, 20.

66 Ibid, vol. 2, 30.

67 John S. Feinberg, *No One Like Him* (Wheaton, IL: Crossway Books, 2001), 680-81.

68 E.g., Bruce, 182.

[69] Kasemann, 265.

[70] Moo, 585; Schreiner, *Romans*, 496.

[71] Ibid, 587-88 (citing Augustine, *Predestination of the Saints*, 17.34).

[72] John Calvin, *Calvin's Commentary on the New Testament*, 244-45.

[73] E.g., Lewis Sperry Chafer, "For Whom Did Christ Die?" in *Bibliotheca Sacra* 105, no. 417 (January, 1948): 7; Millard Erickson, *Christian Theology* (Grand Rapids, MI: Baker Books, 1983-1985), 834-835. This "four point" Calvinism is also called Amyraldianism, after a seventeenth century proponent, Moyse Amyraut. See Stephen Strehle, "Universal Grace and Amyraldianism," in *Westminster Theological Journal* 51, no. 2 (Fall, 1989).

[74] Gill, *The Cause of God and Truth*, 41.

[75] Dagg, *Manual of Theology*, 324.

[76] Fuller, "Reply to Philanthropos," in *Works*, vol. 2, 488-49.

[77] Ibid, 494. Towards the end of his life, Fuller fell into controversy as some fellow Baptists accused him of modifying his views on the atonement. Fuller defended himself by saying that, if we were to write his "Reply to Philanthropos" again, he might make some modifications, but "the leading principles themselves I do still approve." Fuller, "Letters to Dr. Ryland" (Letter IV), in *Works*, vol. 2, 709. For a scholarly analysis of the charge and Fuller's defense, see Nettles, *By His Grace and For His Glory*, 121-130. Nettles concludes that Fuller added to his particular redemption perspective a moral government theory of the atonement, but he never abandoned particular redemption. See also Phil Roberts, "Andrew Fuller," in Timothy George and David Dockery, ed., *Baptist Theologians* (Nashville, TN: Broadman & Holman, 1990, 1999), 131.

[78] Louis Berkhof, *Systematic Theology* (Grand Rapids, MI: Eerdmans, 1939), 394.

[79] Dagg, *Manual of Theology*, 324.

[80] Wayne Grudem, *Systematic Theology* (Grand Rapids, MI: Zondervan, 1994), 601.

[81] Ibid, 596.

[82] Charles Ryrie, *Basic Theology* (Wheaton, IL: Victor Books, 1986), 318.

[83] Ibid.

[84] Ibid, 320.

[85] Robert Shank, *Life in the Son* (Springfield, MO: Westcott Publishers, 1960, 2d ed. 1961), 26.

[86] Hobbs & Mullins, *The Axioms of Religion*, 85.

[87] Hobbs, *Fundamentals of Our Faith*, 99.

[88] Terry L. Miethe, "The Universal Power of the Atonement," in *The Grace of God and the Will of Man*, 78-83.

[89] Pinnock, "From Augustine to Arminius," 22-23.

[90] Schreiner, *Romans*, 260.

[91] Moo, 309.

[92] Schreiner, *Romans*, 260.

[93] Murray, *Epistle to the Romans*, vol. 1, 325.

[94] Ibid.

[95] Godet, 225.

[96] Moo, 343. Moo and Schreiner also point out that, linguistically, "all" does not always mean "every single human being" (Rom. 8:32; 12:17-18; 14:2; 16:19).

[97] Moo, p. 854; Schreiner, *Romans*, 733-737.

[98] Moo, 854.

[99] Murray, *Epistle to the Romans*, vol. 2, 192.

[100] Ibid.

[101] Hodge, *Romans*, 424.

[102] John Calvin, *The Institutes*, Tony Lane and Hilary Osborne, ed., 88.

[103] Ibid, 90.

[104] Ibid, 91.

[105] Charles Mallary, *The Doctrine of Election*, 5-6.

[106] R.C. Sproul, *Chosen by God* (Wheaton, IL: Tyndale House, 1986, electronic edition, 1996).

[107] Mallary, *The Doctrine of Election*, 5.

[108] Edwin H. Palmer, *The Five Points of Calvinism* (Grand Rapids, MI: Baker Book House, 1972, reprinted 1980), 9.

[109] Gill, *The Cause of God and Truth*, 21.

[110] Calvin, *The Institutes*, Tony Lane and Hilary Osborne, ed., 96-97.

[111] Palmer, The Five Points of Calvinism, 11.

[112] Calvin, *The Institutes*, Tony Lane and Hilary Osborne, ed., 96.

[113] Nettles, *By His Grace and For His Glory*, 129.

[114] Fuller, "The Reality and Efficacy of Divine Grace," in *Works*, vol. 2, 546.

[115] Dagg, *Manual of Theology*, 170.

[116] Mell, *An Essay on Calvinism*, 10.

[117] Mallary, *The Doctrine of Election*, 7.

[118] Ibid, 21.

[119] James Arminius, *Disputations on Some of the Principal Subjects of the Christian Religion* in *The Works of James Arminius* (reproduced in electronic format, The Master Christian Library, Albany, OR: Ages Software), 491-493.

[120] John Wesley, *John Wesley's Notes on the Whole Bible - The New Testament* (reproduced in electronic format, The Master Christian Library, Albany, OR: Ages Software), 450.

[121] Hobbs, *Fundamentals of the Faith*, 70-71.

[122] S. Lewis Johnson, Jr., "Studies in Romans - Part IX - The Universality of Sin," in *Bibliotheca Sacra* 131 no. 522 (April 1974): 163.

[123] Quoted in Sean Michael Lucas, "Charles Finney's Theology of Revival: Moral Depravity," in *Masters Seminary Journal* 6, no. 2 (Fall, 1995): 201.

[124] Quoted Ibid.

[125] Ibid.

[126] Jay E. Smith, "The Theology of Charles Finney: A System of Self-Reformation," in *Trinity Journal*, 13 no. 1 (Spring 1992): 75-77; Lucas, "Charles Finney's Theology of Revival," 202-04.

[127] Pinnock, From Augustine to Arminius," 22.

[128] Grant Osborne, "Soteriology in the Gospel of John," in *The Grace of God and the Will of Man*, 257.

[129] Hobbs, *Fundamentals of the Faith*, 71.

[130] Shank, *Life in the Son*, 339.

[131] John Murray, *Epistle to the Romans,* vol. 1, 102.

[132] John Calvin, *Commentary on the Epistle to the Romans*, 96.

[133] Ibid, 96.

[134] Murray, *Epistle to the Romans*, vol. 1, 102.

[135] Ibid.

[136] Godet, 141.

[137] Moo, 203.

[138] Murray, *Epistle to the Romans*, vol. 1, 105.

[139] See, e.g., Kasemann, 85.

[140] Moo, 202 n. 26.

[141] Ibid, 202-203; see also Schreiner, *Romans*, 167.

[142] Ibid, 168.

[143] Ibid, 168-69. See also Haldane, 162; Jonathan Edwards, *On Original Sin*, in *Works*, vol. 1, 193-95.

[144] Ibid.

[145] Murray, *Epistle to the Romans*, vol. 1, 102.

[146] Robert Murray M'Cheyne, "Letter to Rev. Dan Edwards Before His Ordination as a Missionary to Jews," June 15, 1840, *Memoirs of McCheyne* (Chicago, IL: Moody Bible Institute, 1947; republished in electronic format, Escondido, CA: E4 Group, 1999), 95.

[147] Charles H. Spurgeon, *Able to the Uttermost* (published in electronic format, *The C.H. Spurgeon Collection*, Albany, OR: Ages Software, 1996), 105.

[148] Ibid, 106.

[149] Benjamin B. Warfield, "Election," in *Selected Shorter Writings*, vol. 1 (Phillipsburg, NJ: P&R, 1970, reprinted 2001), 286.

[150] Charles H. Spurgeon, *All of Grace* (electronic version in *The C.H. Spurgeon Collection*, Albany, OR: Ages Software, 1997), 30.

[151] Dagg, *Manual of Theology*, 331-332.

[152] B.H. Carroll, *An Interpretation of the English Bible: Galatians, Romans, Philippians, Philemon*, J.B. Cranfill, ed. (Founders Press, 2001), 172.

[153] Dagg, *A Manual of Theology*, 332.

[154] Gill, *The Cause of God and Truth*, 38.

[155] Mallary, *The Doctrine of Election*, 20.

[156] Ibid, 14.

[157] Robert V. Rakestraw, "Wesley as a Theologian of Grace," in *JETS*, 27, no. 2 (June, 1984): 195.

[158] Quoted Ibid, 196.

[159] Ibid, 197.

[160] Ibid, 198-199.

[161] Ibid, 199.

[162] Fritz Guy, "The Universality of God's Love," in *The Grace of God and the Will of Man*, 40.

[163] Pinnock, "From Augustine to Arminius," 22.

[164] Wesley, Notes on the New Testament, 474.

[165] Haldane, 535.

[166] Schreiner, *Romans*, 451.

[167] Murray, *Epistle to the Romans*, vol. 1, 320.

[168] Ibid.

[169] Bruce, 166, quoting *Westminister Shorter Catechism*, Answer to Question 31.

[170] Godet, 327.

[171] Moo, 530; Hodge, *Romans*, 443-44; see also John Murray, *Redemption Accomplished and Applied* (Grand Rapids, MI: Eerdmans, 1955), 89.

[172] Murray, *Epistle to the Romans*, vol. 1, 320.

[173] See, e.g., chapters by Bruce Reichenbach and Clark Pinnock in *Predestination & Free Will*, David and Randall Basinger, ed. (Downers Grove, IL: InterVarsity Press, 1986), 99-177.

[174] Grudem, *Systematic Theology*, 693.

[175] Lewis Sperry Chafer, "The Eternal Security of the Believer - Part I," in *Bibliatheca Sacra*, 106 no. 423 (July, 1949), 260.

[176] Calvin, *The Institutes*, Tony Lane and Hilary Osborne, ed., 222.

[177] Spurgeon, *Able to the Uttermost*, 110.

[178] Charles H. Spurgeon, "The Security of Believers, or Sheep Who Shall Never Perish," No. 2120, MTP, vol. 35.

[179] Quoted in John Jefferson Davis, "The Perseverance of the Saints: A History of the Doctrine," in *JETS*, 34 no. 2 (June, 1991): 218.

[180] Dagg, *Manual of Theology*, 295-96, 299.

[181] Thomas R. Schreiner and Ardel B. Caneday, *The Race Set Before Us* (Downer's Grove, IL: IVP, 2001) 25.

[182] Grudem, *Systematic Theology*, 788.

[183] Ibid, 788-802.

[184] John Calvin, *Commentary on the Epistle to the Hebrews*, (electronic version in *The John Calvin Collection*, Albany, OR: Ages Software, 1998), 117-120; John Owen, *An Exposition of the Epistle to the Hebrews* (Carlisle, PA: Banner of Truth Trust, 1991), 5:69-91; Wayne Grudem, "Perseverance of the Saints: A Case Study of Hebrews 6:4-6 and the Other Warning Passages in Hebrews," in *Still Sovereign: Contemporary Perspectives on Election, Foreknowledge and Grace*, ed. Thomas Schreiner and Bruce Ware (Grand Rapids, MI: Baker, 2000).

[185] Schreiner and Caneday, *The Race Set Before Us*, 38.

[186] Ibid, 40.

[187] See also Chafer, "The Eternal Security of the Believer - Part I," 265; Davis, "The Perseverance of the Saints," 221.

188 Ibid, 224.

189 Ibid. For a refutation of the Arminian view of these verses, see Grudem, *Systematic Theology*, 794-803 (adopting test of genuineness view) or Schreiner and Caneday, *The Race Set Before Us*, 193-204 (adopting means of perseverance view).

190 Davis, 226.

191 Shank, *Life in the Son*, 34.

192 Ibid, 46.

193 Ibid, 54.

194 Schreiner, *Romans*, 454.

195 Moo, 536.

196 Hodge, *Romans*, 444.

197 Carroll, *An Interpretation of the English Bible: Galatians, Romans, Philippians, Philemon*, 175.

198 Ibid.

200 See, e.g., Godet, 333 ("What Paul means is that nothing will tear us from the arms of Christ against our will, and so long as we shall not refuse to abide in them ourselves."); Wesley, *Notes on the New Testament*, 474 (Paul "does not deny that a believer may fall away and be cut off between his special calling and his glorification").

201 Schreiner, *Romans*, 466.

202 Ibid; see also Moo, 589.

203 Hodge, *Romans*, 455.

204 Benjamin B. Warfield, "What is Calvinism," in *Selected Shorter Writings*, vol. 1 (Phillipsburg, NJ: P&R, 1970, reprinted 2001), 392.

205 Grudem, *Systematic Theology*, 389.

Chapter Four

1 See Benjamin B. Warfield, "Atonement" in *The Works of Benjamin B. Warfield*, vol. IX, Studies in Theology, p. 261-62.

2 These needs are derived from Grudem, *Systematic Theology*, 580.

3 John Stott, *Romans* (Downers Grove, IL: Intervarsity Press, 1994), 113; Murray, *Redemption Accomplished and Applied*, 30.

4 It is interesting that a general redemption proponent such as Charles Ryrie holds that Christ bore the wrath of God on the cross with respect to unbelievers, apparently accepting a form of double wrath—that Jesus bore their wrath and that they too will face a second wrath of God in the form of eternal punishment. At the same time, Ryrie incongruously holds that the church will not go through the Great

Tribulation because Christ took their wrath on the cross and accordingly will deliver them from the wrath to come. See Ryrie, *Basic Theology*, 484-85.

5 John Murray, *Redemption Accomplished and Applied*, 42. Leon Morris makes the same point in his *The Apostolic Preaching of the Cross* (Grand Rapids, MI: Eerdmans, 1965, reprinted 1994), 11.

6 Stott, *Romans*, 113.

7 Morris, 13.

8 Murray, *Redemption Accomplished and Applied*, 42-50.

9 Stott, 113.

10 For an example of this view, see Daniel L. Akin, *1, 2, 3 John*, New American Commentary (Nashville, TN: Broadman & Holman, 2001), 86 n.171: "The provision made on one's behalf still requires appropriation to enjoy the application. Jesus made asaving deposit on behalf of every person. A personal withdrawal is the means whereby that deposit becomes one's own."

11 Murray, *Redemption Accomplished and Applied*, 63.

12 A.A. Hodge, *Commentary on the Westminster Confession* (1869, reprinted, Carlisle, PA: Banner of Truth, 1958, republished in electronic format, Escondido, CA: The Ephesians 4 Group, 1998), 151.

13 Morris, 220.

14 Ibid, 225.

15 A.T. Robertson, *Word Pictures in the New Testament* (Nashville, TN: Broadman Press, 1932), vol. V, comment on Heb. 2:9; *BAGD*, 838; Henry C. Thiessen, *Lectures in Systematic Theology*, revised by Vernon D. Doerksen (Grand Rapids, MI: Eerdmans, 1979), 236; Paul Enns, *Moody Handbook of Theology* (Chicago, IL: Moody Press, 1989), 323.

16 Charles H. Spurgeon, "The Death of Christ," No. 173, MTP, vol. 4.

17 Wayne Grudem, *Systematic Theology*, p. 594-95.

18 Ibid, 597.

19 Akin, *1, 2, 3 John*, 86 n.171.

20 Spurgeon, "The Death of Christ," No. 173, MTP, vol. 4.

21 Fuller's view was that the death of Christ, in itself considered, irrespective of God's design as to its application, was sufficient for all mankind, that if the whole world would believe in Christ, none need be sent away for lack of a sufficient atonement. *Works*, vol. 2, 710. For a discussion of some ambiguity in Boyce's position on the extent of the atonement, see Nettles, *By His Grace and For His Glory*, 201-02.

22 Charles Hodge, *Systematic Theology*, vol. 2 (1872, republished in electronic format, Oak Harbor, WA: Logos Research Systems, Inc.,

1997), 560.

[23] Lorraine Boettner, *The Reformed Doctrine of Predestination* (Phillipsburg, NJ: Presbyterian and Reformed Publishing Co., 1932), 160-61.

[24] John Owen, *The Death of Death in the Death of Christ* (Edinburgh, Scotland, Banner of Truth Trust, 1959, reprinted 1995), 193.

[25] Ibid, 195.

[26] John Murray, *Collected Writings*, vol. 1 (Carlisle, PA, Banner of Truth Trust, 1976, reprinted 1989), 67.

[27] Fuller, "Reply to Philanthropos," in *Works*, vol. 2, 494.

[28] John Gill, *Expositions of the Old and New Testaments-John* (electronic format, Paris, AR: Baptist Standard Bearer, 1999), 96.

[29] Owen, *The Death of Death*, 211.

[30] TDNT, vol. 3, 883.

[31] BAGD, 446-447. The authors of this lexicon construe "cosmos" in John 3:16 as referencing "all mankind, but especially of believers, as the objects of God's love." This, however, is a theological interpretation.

[32] TDNT, vol. 3, 883-895. The authors of this dictionary interpret "cosmos" even more broadly, asserting that in passages where John speaks of Jesus coming or being sent, the term refers to "the whole cosmos and not merely to the world of men." For more discussion of this range, see James Swanson, *Dictionary of Biblical Languages with Semantic Domains : Greek (New Testament)* (published in electronic format, Oak Harbor: Logos Research Systems, Inc., 1997, 2d ed. 2001), gloss on "cosmos."

[33] Gill, *The Cause of God and Truth*, 211.

[34] John MacArthur, *The Love of God* (Dallas, TX: Word Publishing, 1996), 86.

[35] B. B. Warfield, *The Savior of the World* (1916, reprinted Carlisle, PA: Banner of Truth Trust, 1991), 118.

[36] Ibid, 118-19.

[37] Fuller, "Reply to Philanthropos," in *Works*, vol. 2, 497.

[38] Thomas Schreiner, *Paul, Apostle of God's Glory in Christ* (Downer's Grove, IL: InterVarsity Press, 2001), 47-51.

[39] See the discussion of John's emphasis on the spread of the gospel from Jews to Gentiles in Joel Green and Scott McKnight, *Dictionary of Jesus and the Gospels* (Downer's Grove, IL: IVP, 1992), 263-64. Most scholars believe John wrote his gospel and his letters a number of years after Paul's death. E.g., Donald Guthrie, *New Testament Introduction* (Downer's Grove, IL: Intervarsity Press, 4th ed. 1990), 296-302, 879.

[40] Fuller, "Reply to Philanthropos," in *Works*, vol. 2, 499.

[41] See, e.g., *WPNT*, comment on Heb. 2:9; *BAGD*, 838; Theissen, *Lectures in Systematic Theology*, 236; Paul Enns, *Moody Handbook of Theology* (Chicago, IL: Moody Press, 1989), 323.

[42] Gill, *The Cause of God and Truth*, 179.

[43] Murray, *Redemption Accomplished and Applied*, 61.

[44] See Gill, *The Cause of God and Truth*, 167.

[45] Ibid, 168.

[46] This was the view of both John Gill and Andrew Fuller, among others. See Gill, *The Cause of God and Truth*, 168; Fuller, "The Reality and Efficacy of Divine Grace," in *Works*, vol. 2, 552.

[47] *Strong's Enhanced Lexicon*, gloss on "soter"; BAGD, 800.

[48] Gill, *The Cause of God and Truth*, 172.

[49] Thomas Boston, A sermon preached at Ettrick, Scotland, June 7, 1724, appended to MacArthur, *The Love of God*, 203-04.

[50] In *The Love of God*, MacArthur has an extended discussion of how Christ can be the "savior" of those who are not of the elect without being their redeemer. See Ibid, 112-116.

[51] I. Howard Marshall, "Universal Grace and Atonement in the Pastoral Epistles," in *The Grace of God and the Will of Man*, 55.

[52] TDNT, vol. 1, 125; BAGD, 12; Gill, *The Cause of God and Truth*, 198-99.

[53] Grudem, *Systematic Theology*, 600; see also John Owen, *The Death of Death in the Death of Christ*, 250-52.

[54] Gill, *The Cause of God and Truth*, 197-99.

[55] Gary D. Long, *Substitutionary Atonement: A Doctrinal Study of Three Key Problem Passages on the Extent of the Atonement* (Sterling, VA: Grace Abounding Ministries, 1977), 44-67; see also WPNT, comment on 2 Pet. 1:1; Paul Enns, *Moody Handbook of Theology* (Chicago, IL: Moody Press, 1989), 130.

[56] John Gill, "2 Peter" in *Exposition on the Old and New Testaments* (published in electronic format, The Baptist Standard Bearer, 1999), 32.

[57] Spurgeon, "Plenteous Redemption," No. 351, MTP, vol. 7.

Chapter Five

[1] Ben A. Warburton, *Calvinism: Its History and Basic Princinples, Its Fruits and Its Future, and Its Practical Application to Life* (Grand Rapids, MI: Eerdmans, 1955), 243.

[2] This was the phrase used by R.A. Finlayson to describe the principium of Calvin's theology. See R.A. Finlayson, "John Calvin's Doctrine of God," in *Puritan Papers Volume Three 1963-1964*, J.I. Packer, ed. (Phillipsburg, N.J., P&R, 2001), 121.

[3] Gill, *The Cause of God and Truth*, 226.

[4] That the supremacy of God is the foundational element of Calvinism should come as no surprise. Thomas Schreiner has said that "the priority of God in Christ emerge again and again as that which dominates his thinking." Thomas R. Schreiner, *Paul, Apostle of God's Glory in Christ* (Downer's Grove, ILL: IVP, 2001), 22.

[5] B. B. Warfield, *Calvin as a Theologian and Calvinism Today* (Philadelphia, Presbyterian Board of Publication, 1909), 23-24, quoted in H. Henry Meeter, *The Basic Ideas of Calvinism*, rev. 6th ed., Paul A. Marshall (Grand Rapids, MI: Baker, 1990), 19.

[6] Ibid, 22-23, quoted in Meeter, 20-21.

[7] Jonathan Edwards, *The End for Which God Created the World*, republished as part of John Piper, *God's Passion for His Glory* (Wheaton, IL: Crossway Books, 1998), 191. Edwards explored the theme of the supremacy of God, as applied to salvation, to great effect in his 1731 sermon, "God Glorified in Man's Dependence," published in *The Works of Jonathan Edwards*, vol. 2, 2-7. For an extremely accessible analysis of this sermon, see Stephen J. Nichols, *Jonathan Edwards: A Guided Tour of his Life and Thought* (Phillipsburg, N.J.: P&R, 2001), 71-85.

[8] Feinberg, *No One Like Him*, 294.

[9] Warburton, *Calvinism*, 64.

[10] Spurgeon, "God's Providence," No. 3114, MTP, vol. 54.

[11] Gill, *The Cause of God and Truth*, 51.

[12] Mallary, *The Doctrine of Election*, 5.

[13] Dagg, *Manual of Theology*, p. 118.

[14] Hobbs, *Fundamentals of Our Faith*, 92.

[15] Ibid, 93.

[16] Warfield, "Some Thoughts on Predestination," in *Selected Shorter Writings*, vol. 1, 103.

[17] Gregory A. Boyd, "Neo-Molinism and the Infinite Intelligence of God," paper submitted to the Evangelical Theological Society, Nov. 14-16, 2001, copy available from:
http://www.zondervanchurchsource.com/convention/schedule.htm.

[18] Pinnock, *Most Moved Mover*, 53.

[19] Ibid, 41.

[20] Ibid, 45.

[21] John Sanders, *The God Who Risks* (Downers Grove, IL: IVP, 1998), 11.

[22] Ibid, 10.

[23] Ibid.

[24] Baptist Confession of 1689, Chapter 3, section 1.

[25] Sanders, *The God Who Risks*, 10.

[26] Mallary, *The Doctrine of Election*, 5.

[27] Ibid.

[28] Thomas Manton, *On Jude*, 176, quoted in Gill, *The Cause of God and Truth*, 232.

[29] J.I. Packer, *Evangelism and the Sovereignty of God* (Downer's Grove, IL: IVP, 1961), 18-21.

[30] Warfield, "What is Calvinism," in *Selected Shorter Writings*, vol. 1, 390.

[31] Ibid, 391.

[32] Feinberg, *No One Like Him*, 626.

[33] Jonathan Edwards, *A Careful and Strict Inquiry into the Modern Prevailing Notions of that Freedom of Will*, in *The Works of Jonathan Edwards*, vol. 1, 4-5.

[34] Ibid, 5.

[35] Bruce Reichenbach, "God Limits His Power" in *Predestination and Free Will*, 102.

[36] Pinnock, *Most Moved Mover*, 41.

[37] Ibid, 127.

[38] Ibid, 31.

[39] Ibid, 41, 45, 115.

[40] Hobbs, *Fundamental of the Faith*, 93.

[41] Dagg, *Manual of Theology*, 104.

[42] Boyce, *Abstract of Systematic Theology*, 118.

[43] Gill, *The Cause of God and Truth*, 49.

[44] Feinberg, *No One Like Him*, 617.

[45] Ibid, 680-81.

[46] Ibid, 682.

[47] Frame, *No Other God*, 122-130.

[48] Jonathan Edwards, *A Careful and Strict Inquiry into the Modern Prevailing Notions of that Freedom of Will*, in *The Works of Jonathan*

Edwards, vol. 1, 5, 26-27.

[49] Frame, *No Other God*, 131.

[50] Feinberg, *No One Like Him*, 640.

[51] Ibid, 60.

[52] R.A. Finlayson, "John Calvin's Doctrine of God," in *Puritan Papers Volume Three 1963-1964*, 135.

[53] J. Gresham Machen, *God Transcendent* (Eerdmans, 1949, reprinted Carlisle, PA: Banner of Truth Trust, 1982), 17.

[54] Feinberg, *No One Like Him*, 59.

[55] Calvin, *The Institutes*, trans. Ford Lewis Battles, 1:13:14.

[56] Pinnock, *Most Moved Mover*, xii.

[57] Ibid, 35.

[58] Deism teaches that God does not interact with the world, but created the universe and withdrew from it to let it run on its own, as a person winds a clock and leaves it to run. See Feinberg, *No One Like Him*, 61.

[59] Calvin, *The Institutes*, trans. Ford Lewis Battles, 1:16:3.

[60] Edwards, *The End for Which God Created the World*, 192-93.

[61] Ibid, 197.

[62] Ibid, 198.

[63]Pinnock, *Most Moved Mover*, 35.

[64] Ibid, 41.

[65] See Iain Murray, *Evangelicalism Divided*, 6-13.

[66] J. Gresham Machen, *Christianity & Liberalism* (Grand Rapids, MI: Eerdmans, 1923), 19, 45-46.

[67] Michael Haykin, "A Lesson From a Victorian 'Preface,'" in *The Banner of Truth*, issue 457 (October 2001): 23.

[68] Mark Hopkins, "What Did Spurgeon Believe" *Christian History*, issue 29 (republished in electronic format on Christian History CD-ROM).

[69] Iain Murray, *The Forgotten Spurgeon*, (Banner of Truth Trust, 1966), 4.

[70] For more detail on the Down-Grade Controversy, see Appendix I: "Spurgeon and the Down-Grade Controversy" in John MacArthur, *Ashamed of the Gospel* (Crossway Books, 1993), 197-225; Susannah Spurgeon and Joseph Harrald, *C.H. Spurgeon Autobiography Volume 2: The Full Harvest 1860*-1892 (Edinburgh: The Banner of Truth Trust, 1987), 469-479; Iain Murray, *The Forgotten Spurgeon*, (Banner of

Truth Trust, 1966. Finally, the Down-Grade articles themselves are available as an appendix to Lewis Drummond, *Spurgeon: Prince of Preachers* (Kregel, 1992).

71 Haykin, "A Lesson From a Victorian 'Preface,'" 24.

72 See Reisinger and Allen, *A Quiet Revolution*, 19-24.

73 Charles H. Spurgeon, *Sword and Trowel* (April, 1887), 195.

74 Dagg, *Manual of Theology*, 132.

75 Gregory Boyd, *God of the Possible* (Grand Rapids, MI: Baker, 2000), 90.

76 Bunyan, "Reprobation Asserted," in *The Works of John Bunyan*, vol. 2, 345.

77 Ibid, 346.

78 Ibid," 341.

79 John Dick, *Lectures on Theology* (Philadelphia, PA: J. Whetham & Son, 1841, reprinted Edmonton, AB: Stillwater Revival Books, n.d.), 367.

80 Meeter, *The Basic Ideas of Calvinism*, 56.

81 Ibid; Abraham Kuyper, *Lectures on Calvinism* (Grand Rapids, MI: Eerdmans, 1931, reprinted 1994).

82 J.I. Packer, "John Calvin: A Servant of the Word," in *The Puritan Papers Volume Three 1963-1964*, 165.

Chapter Six

1 Clark Pinnock, "Response" to John Feinberg, in David Basinger & Randall Basinger, eds., *Predestination and Free Will* (Grand Rapids, MI: IVP, 1986), 58.

2 James P. Boyce, *Abstract of Systematic Theology*, 93.

3 John Dagg, *Manual of Theology*, 76.

4 Ibid.

5 Boyce, *Abstract*, 93-98.

6 Hobbs, *Fundamentals of the Faith*, 90.

7 Pinnock, *Most Moved Mover*, 94.

8 See Thomas Aquinas, *Summa Theologica* (1911, republished in electronic format, Albany, OR: Ages Digital Library, 1997), 157-59; also Cornelius Van Til, *A Survey of Christian Epistemology. In Defense of the Faith, Vol. II* (Escondido, CA: Den Dulk Christian Foundation, 1969), 203.

9 Dagg, *Manual of Theology*, 78.

10 "Autobiography of John Dagg" in Ibid, 6

11 Ibid, 79.

12 Ibid.

13 Bunyan, "Reprobation Asserted,"in *The Works of John Bunyan*, vol. 2, 346.

14 Douglas Wilson, *Easy Chairs Hard Words* (Moscow ID: Canon Press, 1991), 37.

15 John Piper, "How Does a Sovereign God Love." This excellent article, from which we draw heavily, is located on the Desiring God website, www.desiringgod.org.

16 Fuller, *The Calvinistic and Socinian Systems Examined and Compared as to Their Moral Tendency*, in *Works*, vol. 2, 113.

17 Dagg, *Manual of Theology*, 305.

18 Boyce, *Abstract*, 99.

19 Mallary, *The Doctrine of Election*, 21.

20 Bunyan, "Reprobation Asserted, 344-45.

21 Ibid, 358.

22 Dagg, *Manual of Theology*, 109.

23 Mallary, *The Doctrine of Election*, 21.

24 James P. Boyce, *Abstract of Systematic Theology*, 67; Louis Berkhof, *Systematic Theology*, 62.

25 See Feinberg, *No One Like Him*, 325-337; Robert L. Dabney, *Systematic Theology* (1871, republished in electronic format, Escondido, CA: Ephesians 4 Group, 1998), 43.

26 E. Y. Mullins, *The Christian Religion In Its Doctrinal Expression* (Valley Forge, PA: Judson Press, 1917, reprinted 1974), 243.

27 Dagg, *Manual of Theology*, 110.

Chapter Seven

1 Wayne Grudem, *Systematic Theology* (Grand Rapids, MI: Zondervan, 1994), 681.

2 Spurgeon, *Exposition of the Doctrines of Grace*, No. 385, MTP, vol. 7. Chapter Three, paragraph 7 of the Westminster Confession of Faith, as well as the answer to Question 13 of the Westminster Larger Catechism, declare that those passed over suffer God's wrath "for their sin." The Second London Baptist Confession does not contain a counterpart to Chapter Three, paragraph 7 of the Westminster Confession. Samuel Waldron suggests that this is to guard against the impression that the decrees of election and reprobation are parallel. See Samuel

Waldron, *Exposition of the 1689 Confession* (Durham, England: Evangelical Press, 1989, second ed. 1995). Of course, they are not. As we have been discussing, the decree of election is active and the decree of reprobation is passive. The Westminster Confession makes that distinction, as a careful reading of Chapter Three shows.

[3] Dagg, *Manual of Theology*, 520-21.

[4] Pinnock's Response to John Feinberg's essay, "God Ordains All Things," in *Predestination & Free Will*, 59.

[5] Quoted in Thomas K. Ascol, "Calvinism, Evangelism & Founders Ministries," *The Founders Journal* (Summer, 2001). This article is available on the internet at www.founders.org.

[6] Mallary, *The Doctrine of Election*, 23.

[7] Thomas K. Ascol, "Calvinism, Evangelism & Founders Ministries," *The Founders Journal* (Summer, 2001).

[8] Packer, *Evangelism and the Sovereignty of God*; Walter Chantry, *Today's Gospel* (Carlisle, PA: Banner of Truth Trust, 1970, reprinted 1997); Ernest C. Reisinger, *Today's Evangelism, Its Message and Methods* (Phillipsburg, N.J., Craig Press, 1982).

[9] Dagg, *Manual of Theology*, 319.

[10] Ibid, 334.

[11] Spurgeon, *Exposition of the Doctrines of Grace*, No. 385, MTP, vol. 7.

[12] Charles Spurgeon, *Around the Wicket Gate* (republished in electronic format, *The C.H. Spurgeon Collection*, Albany, OR: Ages Software, 1998), 3.

[13] Spurgeon, *Exposition of the Doctrines of Grace*, No. 385, MTP, vol. 7.

[14] Homer, *The Iliad*, transl. Bernard Fagles (New York, NY: Penguin Books, 1990), 605 [24:610-620].

[15] Spurgeon, *Exposition of the Doctrines of Grace*, No. 385, MTP, vol. 7; see also Spurgeon, "Infant Salvation," No. 411, MTP, vol. 7 ("we have never imagined that infants dying as infants have perished, but we have believed that they enter into the paradise of God").

[16] Charles Hodge, *Systematic Theology*, vol. 1 (reprinted, Grand Rapids, MI: Eerdmans, 1995), 26.

[17] Spurgeon, "Infant Salvation," No. 411, MTP, vol. 7.

[18] R.A. Webb, *The Theology of Infant Salvation* (Harrisonburg, VA: Sprinkle, 1981), 11, quoted in Millard Erickson, *How Shall They Be Saved? The Destiny of Those Who Do Not Hear of Jesus* (Grand Rapids, MI: Baker, 1996), 236-37.

[19] Ibid, 281-91, cited in Erickson, *How Shall They Be Saved?*, 246-47.

[20] Boyce, *Abstract of Systematic Theology*, 95.

21 Ibid, 96-98.

22 Spurgeon, *Exposition of the Doctrines of Grace*, No. 385, MTP, vol. 7.

Chapter Eight

1 See F. Duane Lindsay, "Essays Toward a Theology of Beauty—Part I: God is Beautiful," *Bib. Sac.*, vol. 131, no. 522 (April, 1974): 121.

2 The beauty of Jesus when he was on physically earth was not a physical beauty (Is. 53:2), but an internal excellence (cf. Luke 2:52).

3 Lindsay, "Essays Toward a Theology of Beauty," 134.

4 Jonathan Edwards, *On Religious Affections*, in *Works*, vol. 1, 277.

5 Lindsay, 136.

6 Ibid.

7 Gill, *A Body of Doctrinal Divinity*, 384.

8 John Calvin, *Eternal Predestination of God* (London, James Clarke & Co. Ltd., 1961), 137.

9 Ibid, 137.

10 "Notes on a Sermon Delivered by Rev. Basil Manly, D.D. at Pleasant Grove Church, Fayette Co., Ala.," in *Southern Baptist Sermons on Sovereignty and Responsibility* (Gano Books, Harrisonburg, VA: 1984), 12-13.

11 Ibid, 17.

12 John Piper believes compatible freedom explains how God can control man's actions and man can simultaneously be a free moral agent, citing Jonathan Edwards' *On the Freedom of the Will*. See John Piper, "A Response to J.I. Packer On the So-Called Antinomy Between The Sovereignty of God and Human Responsibility" (March, 1976), which is available on the Desiring God website, www.desiringgod.org. We respectfully disagree. We read Edwards as possibly pushing the antinomy back a step or two, but by no means erasing it. Specifically, how God so disposes all things (Eph. 1:11) so that in accordance with moral necessity all men make only those choices ordained by God from all eternity, remains a secret thing that belongs to God.

13 Charles Bridges, *The Christian Ministry With An Inquiry Into the Causes of Its Inefficiency* (1830, reprinted Carlisle, PA: Banner of Truth Trust, 1997), 122.

14 Charles H. Spurgeon, "The Security of Believers, or Sheep Who Shall Never Perish," No. 2120, MTP, vol. 35.

15 Calvin, *Eternal Predestination of God*, 56-57.

[16] David Dickson, *Selected Practical Writings of David Dickson*, vol. 1 (1845), 95-96, quoted in Iain Murray, "The Puritans and the Doctrine of Election," *Puritan Papers: Volume One (1956-1959),* edited by D. Martyn Lloyd-Jones (Phillipsburg, N.J.: P&R, 2000), 13.

[17] Mell, *An Essay on Calvinism*, 22.

[18] Dickson, *Selected Practical Writings*, quoted in Murray, "The Puritans and the Doctrine of Election," *Puritan Papers: Volume One*, 15-16.

[19] Spurgeon, "A Defense of Calvinism," in *A Baptist Look at Calvinism*, 26.

[20] Mell, *An Essay on Calvinism*, 20.

[21] John Dick, *Lectures on Theology*, vol. 1 (Philadelphia, J. Whetham & Son, 1841, reprinted Stillwater Revival Books), 371.

[22] Alvah Hovey, *A Memoir of the Life and Times of Isaac Backus* (1858; Harrisburg, VA: Gano Books, 1991), 356.

[23] Mell, *An Essay on Calvinism*, 19.

[24] Quotations from Ian Murray, "The Puritans and the Doctrine of Election," *Puritan Papers: Volume One*, 14.

[25] Mell, *An Essay on Calvinism*, 19.

Chapter Nine

[1] Jacques Barzun, *From Dawn to Decadence: 1500 to the Present* (New York: Perennial, 2001), 14.

[2] John Bunyan, *The Pilgrim's Progress In Modern English*, edited by Edward Hazelbaker (North Brunswick, NJ: Bridge Logos, 1998), 383.

[3] Alexander Whyte, *Bunyan's Characters, Second Series* (London: Oliphant Anderson and Ferrier, 1894), 201-208.

[4] Matthew Henry, *Commentary on the Whole Bible* (Hendrickson, 1994, New Modern Edition Database republished by Logos Digital Library), comment on Job 19:1-7.

[5] Whyte, *Bunyan's Characters*, 204-207.

[6] Ibid.

[7] Jonathan Edwards, *Some Thoughts Concerning the Present Revival of Religion in New England*, in *Works*, vol. 1, 398-99.

[8] Ibid, 402.

[9] Whyte, *Bunyan's Characters*, 209.

[10] Boettner, *The Reformed Doctrine of Predestination*, 5.

[11] Charles H. Spurgeon, "The Sieve," No. 1158, MTP, vol. 20.

[12] Charles H. Spurgeon, "What the Farm Laborers Can Do and What They Cannot Do," No. 1603, MTP, vol. 27.

Conclusion

[1] Bunyan, *The Pilgrim's Progress In Modern English*, 384.

[2] Charles H. Spurgeon, "Gladness for Sadness," No. 1701, MTP, vol. 29.

Scripture Index

Psalms

Proverbs

Ecclesiastes

Isaiah

Jeremiah

Matthew

Mark

Luke

John

John

Acts

Acts

Romans

Romans

Romans

1 Corinthians

2 Corinthians

Galatians

Ephesians

Philippians

Colossians

Colossians

1 Thessalonians

2 Thessalonians

1 Timothy

2 Timothy

Titus

Titus

Hebrews

James

1 Peter

1 Peter

2 Peter

1 John

Jude

Revelation

Subject & Person Index

Major subjects in bold type